FOR SCOTLAND

Anthology

Compiled by Margaret Stillie

This selection © Margaret Stillie 1999

Illustrations © STP 1999.

The acknowledgements on page 285 constitute an extension of this copyright page.

All rights reserved. No part of this publication may be reproduced or transmitted in any form or by any means, electronic or mechanical, including photocopy, recording or any information storage and retrieval system, without permission in writing from the publisher or under licence from the Copyright Licensing Agency Limited. Further details of such licences (for reprographic reproduction) may be obtained from the Copyright Licensing Agency Limited of 90 Tottenham Court Road, London W1P OLP.

First published by

Stanley Thornes Publishers Ltd
Ellenborough House
Wellington Street
Cheltenham
GL50 1YW

99 00 01 02 \ 10 9 8 7 6 5 4 3 2 1

A catalogue record for this book is available from the British Library.

ISBN 0-7487-4852-0

Design by Oxprint Design / STP.
Page make up by Aetos Ltd, Bathampton, Bath.
Printed and bound in Spain by Cayfosa, Barcelona

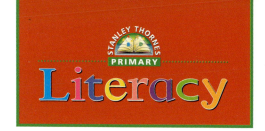

Contents

Term 1

Unit 1	The Haunted Lighthouse *by Anthony Masters*	**6**
Unit 2	Here Comes Charlie Moon *by Shirley Hughes*	**8**
Unit 3	Be Safe Outdoors *by Pete Saunders*	**22**
Unit 4	"Down at the very bottom" *by Jackie Kay*	**27**
	"Waves" *by Jackie Kay*	**27**
	"Duncan Gets Expelled" *by Jackie Kay*	**28**
Unit 5	Sabre-tooth Sandwich *by Leon Garfield*	**29**
Unit 6	Wood *by Robin Place*	**36**
Unit 7	Bill's New Frock *by Anne Fines*	**40**
Unit 8	The Dead Letter Box *by Jan Mark*	**52**
Unit 9	"Daddy Fell into the Pond" *by Alfred Noyes*	**62**
	"Clumsy" *by Max Fatchen*	**63**
	"Snake Glides" *by Keith Bosley*	**63**
	"The Blackbird" *by Humbert Wolfe*	**64**
	"Geraldine Giraffe" *by Colin West*	**64**
	"Somebody said that it Couldn't be Done" *Anon*	**65**
	"The Evening Star" *by Guillaume Apollinaire*	**65**
	"Bird Whistle" *by Guillaume Apollinaire*	**65**
	"The Cathedral" *by Guillaume Apollinaire*	**65**
	"Clock Spring" *by Simon*	**66**
	"A Boa-Constrictor" *by Lesley*	**66**
	"Excited" *by Mark Powell*	**67**
	"Haircuts" *by Cam Phung Te*	**67**
Unit 10	Nelson Mandela *by Richard Killeen*	**68**
Unit 11	Blitz *by Robert Westall*	**73**
Unit 12	The Iron Woman *by Ted Hughes*	**80**

Term 2

Unit 1	Scheherezade *by Stephen Corrin*	**88**
	Bedd Gelert *by Stephen Corrin*	**92**
Unit 2	Odysseus and Circe *by Stephen Corrin*	**95**
	Theseus and the Minotaur *by Jacqueline Morley*	**100**
	alternative ending *by Nathaniel Hawthorne*	**103**
Unit 3	Classic Italian *by Valentina Harris*	**104**
	The Food of Italy *by Claudia Roden*	**108**
Unit 4	Grimm's Fairy Tales *from Penguin Popular Classics*	**110**
	Red Riding Hood *by the Brothers Grimm*	**111**
Unit 5	Landmarks from the Past *by Gillian Clegg*	**120**
	Homes, Villages and Towns *by Gillian Clegg*	**122**
	Places of Defence *by Gillian Clegg*	**126**

Unit 6	"The Dare" *by Judith Nicholls*	**133**
	"Muffin - my Dog" *by Hayley Morris*	**134**
	"A Poem for the Rainforest" *by Judith Nicholls*	
	"Amazonian Timbers, Inc."	**135**
	"Song of the Xingu Indian"	**135**
	"Dusk"	**136**
	"The Coming of the Night"	**136**
	"Song of the Forest"	**137**
	"Tiger"	**137**
	"Shadows"	**137**
	"Wolf"	**137**
	"I love me mudder" *by Benjamin Zephaniah*	**138**
	"My Uncle Paul of Pimlico" *by Mervyn Peake*	**139**
	"Spring" *by Gerard Manley Hopkins*	**139**
	"Something told the Wild Geese" *by Rachel Field*	**140**
	"The Experiment" *by Judith Nicholls*	**141**
	"Partners" *by Judith Nicholls*	**141**
Unit 7	"The Good Fortunes Gang" *by Margaret Mahy*	**142**
Unit 8	A Fight between Lizards at the Centre of the Earth	**151**
	by Jules Verne	
	Homecoming *by Stephen David*	**157**
Unit 9	"The Rime of the Ancient Mariner"	**163**
	by Samuel Taylor Coleridge	
	"The Jumblies" *by Edward Lear*	**165**
	"The Black Pebble" *by James Reeves*	**168**
Unit 10	Seasons of Splendour *by Madhur Jaffrey*	**169**
Unit 11	Bible Stories	
	Sentence of Death *by Pat Alexander*	**184**
	The Body that Wasn't There! *by Pat Alexander*	**186**
	Easter *by Jan Pienkowski*	**188**
Unit 12	Tornadoes and Hurricanes *by Suzanne Pert*	**191**
	High Winds	**194**
	The Wizard of Oz *by L Frank Baum*	**195**

Term 3

Unit 1	The Midnight Fox *by Betsy Byars*	**197**
Unit 2	Grandpa Chatterji *by Jamila Gavin*	**209**
Unit 3	The Love Letter of Ragie Patel *by Lee Hall*	**220**
Unit 4	Bottersnikes and Gumbles *by S.A. Wakefield*	**230**
Unit 5	Look Forward to a Better Future *Friends of the Earth*	**236**
Unit 6	"My stamp album" *by John Agard*	**240**
	"Gramma's biscuit tin" *by John Agard*	**240**
	"My ball" *by John Agard*	**241**
	"Nine-o'Clock Bell!" *by Eleanor Farjeon*	**241**
Unit 7	Moonfleet *by J. Meade Falkner*	**242**
Unit 8	Tom's Midnight Garden *by Phillipa Pearce*	**250**
Unit 9	Naturally Wight *Isle of Wight Tourist Information*	**257**
Unit 10	The Silver Sword *by Ian Serraillier*	**265**
	Little House in the Big Woods *by Laura Ingalls Wilder*	**270**
Unit 11	Let's Kick Racism out of Football *Kick It Out Project*	**276**
Unit 12	"The Prelude" *by William Wordsworth*	**280**
	"Stopping by Woods on a Snowy Evening" *by Robert Frost*	**282**

Literacy

Anthology extracts

Term 1 | Unit 1

The Haunted Lighthouse

by Anthony Masters

Chapter One

The seals crowded the rock below Seal Rock Lighthouse. They gazed up at Philip who stared back in amazement. He had never seen so many, their dark skins glistening, their eyes watching him closely.

A winter storm was brewing. The sky was black and the waves were getting bigger, pounding on the reef that stretched out to sea like a row of sharp teeth.

He was standing in the top chamber where the light used to revolve, warning ships off the rocks with its bright white beam. But now that the big lamp had been shut down, the lighthouse had become a museum.

Philip and his father had moved there a month ago when his father had become curator. Philip's grandfather had been the last of the lighthouse keepers, but he had drowned whilst out fishing in his boat years before Philip was born. Philip often thought about him, wondering what his life must have been like.

Philip didn't like living at the lighthouse. He was lonely without his friends and felt uneasy being so close to the sea. It was spooky.

The biggest seal was on the very top of the rock now. His eyes seemed to be boring straight into Philip's. Philip felt uncomfortable and wondered why. Then he remembered how local people believed that inside the seals were the souls of the drowned.

Philip told himself the legend was just a made-up story. But the idea wouldn't go away and his uneasiness increased.

Lightning split the sky in a series of jagged flashes, and then a growl of thunder came from far out to sea. In the eerie silence that followed, Philip heard the sound of his father's footsteps ringing out on the spiral staircase that led to the top chamber.

Gasping for breath, Philip's father reached the top chamber, but when he caught sight of the seals he looked as scared as Philip. "I've never seen so many before."

"Neither have I," said Philip. "What are they all doing there?"

"It's just like your grandad used to say …" His father hesitated.

"What did he say, Dad?" Philip asked irritably, wondering why his father hadn't finished what he was saying.

"When the seals gather on Seal Rock, there'll be a shipwreck," he replied reluctantly and then added, "It's just an old story, of course."

They both gazed down at the rock that crouched under the lighthouse. The thunder growled again and the lightning lit the sky, making the seals look white and ghostly.

Term 1 | Unit 2

Here Comes Charlie Moon

by Shirley Hughes

Charlie Moon's Auntie Jean runs a joke shop at the seaside. Charlie loves to go and stay there and try out the comic hats, masks, rubber spiders, fake flowers that squirt water, and cushions that squeak when you sit on them... even when his clever cousin Ariadne is staying, too.

"...as breezy as a promenade, as daft as candyfloss ... this is a book that has moments of pure knickerbocker glory!"

Junior Education

Part One
Chapter One

Charlie Moon's Auntie runs a joke shop at the seaside. It sells things like comic hats, masks, rubber spiders, fake flowers that squirt water at you unexpectedly, and cushions that squeak when you sit down on them. The narrow shop front faces the sea. "JOKES AND CARNIVAL NOVELTIES" it says, and underneath, "Jean Llanechan Jones", which is Charlie's Auntie's name. It's easier to say the middle bit properly if you are Welsh, as she is. You have to spit it out rather than say it.

Charlie himself lives in a big city with his Mum, who is in the hairdressing business. There are no jokes in her shop, only a row of lady customers sitting wired up to domed space-helmet drying machines, cooking slowly to lobster red as they flick through their magazines. Charlie tends to trip over their feet whilst skateboarding through the shop from the back room to the street. They don't like it. It puts them off coming. By the end of the first week of the summer holidays Mum's patience has snapped, and Charlie is off to his Auntie Jean's at Penwyn Bay. He can't take his skateboard because it weighs down the suitcase too much. It's too full already, as Charlie is a smart dresser. He wants to pack four changes of trousers, his T-shirt with Superman on the front, and his red-and-white cap with the big peak. Also his snorkel and mask in case he wants to do some underwater swimming.

"What do you want to pack all that for?" asks Mum, forcing down the suitcase lid by sitting down on it with all her weight. "You can't see anything under water at Penwyn Bay – it's too muddy."

"I might. There might be a big fish or a seal. One of those got washed up on the beach once. I saw a picture of it in the *Penwyn Bay News*."

Term 1 | Unit 2

"You don't need a mask and a snorkel to look at seals," Mum tells him, but they get packed all the same. "You're to help Auntie Jean with the washing-up, and in the shop if she asks you to," Mum goes on. "And don't forget to make your bed properly instead of just dragging the covers up as you do here. Ariadne's going to be there," she adds.

This is not good news for Charlie. Ariadne is his cousin. She is only two years older than he is but it seems more like five because she is so clever. Not stuck up exactly, but her Dad is a very important man who writes things in the newspapers and she reads a lot of books. Charlie likes a good book too, of course, but his mind often seems somehow to slide off the page and he finds himself doing something else. He once read a book about a cave-man which was great. He'll read that again all right when he's got time. Ariadne being at Auntie Jean's means that she will be sleeping in the best room at the top of the house which looks out to sea, and will be sitting about reading all the time, or saying things that make people feel uncomfortable. She has two favourite words, one is "pathetic" and the other "typical". (Pretty pathetic and typical to go round with a name like Ariadne, come to that, thinks Charlie privately.)

Still, it isn't bad at Auntie Jean's.

Part Two

The jokes and carnival novelties are all over the place as usual. Rows of rubbery masks are hanging up behind the counter – not the underwater kind, but funny ones of red-nosed clowns, Frankensteins, gorillas and suchlike. In the passage behind the shop are piles and piles of boxes full of crackers, indoor fireworks, magic sets and squeakers that you blow out at people to make them feel jolly. Not even Auntie Jean knows what is inside some of these boxes. In fact, she has a lot of trouble finding things. She often runs out of things to eat, too. This happens on the first afternoon of Charlie's visit.

10

"I'll just be popping out for a loaf and some fish fingers for tea," she sings out, climbing into her red coat. "And I might just be dropping in at Mrs Goronwy Lewis's on the way back, just for ten minutes, see. Look after the shop, won't you? Everything's priced, and all you've got to remember is to give the right change out of the till and to be ever so polite to the customers."

"I don't suppose there'll be any," says Ariadne, after Auntie's footsteps have tittupped away up the prom. "There hardly ever are. This shop's going bankrupt, if you ask me."

She stretches out on the old sofa in the back room, with a book and Einstein, the old ginger tom cat, on her stomach. From here, with her head propped up, she can see through the open door along the passage to the shop. Charlie has disappeared. All is very still. The afternoon sun lies quietly on the dusty shop floor, and outside the sea washes gently on the stones. Suddenly a strange moaning is heard. It rises to a louder moan, then to a throaty roar. A shuffling creature on all fours advances down the passage, and a monstrous face covered in green hair appears round the arm of the sofa.

Einstein merely twitches one ear.

"You are *pathetic*," says Ariadne, calmly turning over a page.

Charlie takes off the monster mask which he has borrowed from the shop, and gets up off his hands and knees. He hadn't really hoped that Ariadne would think he was a proper monster, but at least she could have pretended for a bit. It would be more fun than just lying about with a book and not talking to people. He's just about to tell her so, too, when the shop door opens with a loud clang, and in come two boys. They are sandy-haired, piggy-eyed and look as though they might be brothers. Both of them are wearing striped jerseys, hooped like barrels around their wide middles.

"Can I help you?" asks Charlie in his best shop-assistant

11

Term 1 | Unit 2

manner, hands spread out on the counter. Ariadne, still reading, wanders out from the back room.

One of the boys starts to finger some false noses and other small items in the show-case by the shop door. The bigger one asks rudely to see some trick card games like the ones in the window. These are kept on the very top shelf behind the counter, so Charlie fetches the little step-ladder and climbs up to get the box. As soon as he has come down the boy says he has changed his mind and wants to try on a Frankenstein mask. This is even higher up behind the counter, but after Charlie has had some trouble reaching it the boy decides that it's much too expensive and wants to buy some invisible ink instead. Charlie, sighing deeply and trying hard to remember what Auntie Jean said about being polite to the customers, dives under the counter to find the box of invisible inks. It's dark under there, and a lot of boxes fall out on top of him. Some scuffling and sniggering is going on at the other side of the counter.

"Hey, stop it! Put that back!" shouts Ariadne suddenly.

Charlie pops up his head to receive a jet of water in one eye from a water pistol. As he's shaking the water out of his face, he sees both the boys helping themselves from the show-case. Ariadne is round the counter in a flash, trying to stop them. The show-case starts to wobble, false noses and moustaches fall on the floor and confetti flies about all over the shop. As she leaps forward to steady the case the two boys are off out of the shop door and away up the prom, stuffing stolen packets of stink-bombs into their pockets. Ariadne rushes out after them on to the pavement, white with rage.

"Thieves! Robbers!" she shouts, and, under her breath, *"Typical!"*

"I'll get them!" cries Charlie. "I'm the fastest runner in the world! You stay here and mind the shop, Ariadne, while I go after them!"

And he starts off after the boys, legging it like a stag. He can see their striped back-views bobbing up and down in the distance. They're weaving in and out of the shelters, looking back over their shoulders now and again. They know by now that they are being followed. Under the railings, slithering down the sea-wall on to the beach, round the back of the beach-huts, up the steps, back on to the prom again they run. Charlie comes behind, his hair flopping about all over his scarlet face. He really is a good runner, very light and quick. The two boys are not. They are a lot bigger and heavier than Charlie, and they're already getting puffed.

As he runs Charlie starts to wonder what he'll do if he catches them up. He hadn't thought of this before. Now he remembers that there are two of them and only one of him; he's already a long way from the shop. He wishes he had somebody with him. Even Ariadne would be better than nothing. If only he could see a policeman somewhere...but they all seem to have gone home for tea.

Now the boys have dodged completely out of sight. Charlie, cautious and puzzled, pants on. Suddenly, both of them pop out from behind a shelter, grinning right in his path. Charlie stops short. They all face one another. Then...crack! crack! crack! Three stink-bombs explode on the ground. Charlie reels back, holding his nose, as the boys disappear up a side road, whistling and jeering. He is left standing there helplessly as the evil-smelling cloud rises about him. At this moment two ladies, one large and the other small, appear as though by magic from the other end of the shelter. They both have handkerchiefs pressed to their noses.

"Whatever's that awful...?" begins one, but the small one starts on Charlie at once.

"You ought to be ashamed! I don't know why boys like you can't find anything better to do than to go about ruining other people's pleasure."

"Oh, come on, Mona, it's getting worse."

"One can't even admire a lovely view in peace these days. For two pins I'd take you along to the nearest police station and give you in charge for vandalism."

"It's putting me off my tea."

"You've got no sense of decency any of you. Letting off a thing like that in a public place. I don't know what they teach you in school these days but it certainly isn't reasonable behaviour. At your age I wouldn't have dared…" and so on and so on.

Charlie says nothing. It doesn't seem worth it. Angry ladies never want to have things explained to them anyway. Luckily the smell is being borne away by a brisk sea breeze. At last they hurry away up the prom, the small lady still glaring angrily back at him over her handkerchief.

There's nothing left for Charlie to do but begin the weary trudge home. Rather to his surprise, Ariadne is at the shop door, anxiously looking out for him.

"You O.K., Charlie?"

Charlie tells her the story. He's too tired to make it a good one, but he can't resist adding:

"I caught those boys up, anyway, didn't I? I told you I could run."

"I hope they don't come back," is all Ariadne answers.

• • •

Part Three
Chapter Four

"Lovely bit of material, that is," says Auntie Jean, holding up a gentleman's tailcoat, one of the many items of costume that she keeps in her back sitting-room. "Bit of moth under

the arm here, but good as new otherwise."

She blows the dust off the shoulders of the coat, and it rises in a great cloud.

"What's that purple dress, Auntie, with the black lace on it?" asks Ariadne. She and Charlie are sitting side by side on the sofa, eating sticky buns.

"Oooooh, that's a dream, that is. It's an old-fashioned costume, once worn by the leading lady in a musical play at the Royalty. A real picture she was in it, too."

"It's just like the sort of dress the ladies in my book are wearing. I'd love to sweep about with that train thing behind."

"What's that shaggy brown one over there?" Charlie wants to know.

"Some sort of animal suit, I think, Charlie. It was for the pantomime one year, if I remember right. Looks as though it needs a bit of a patch in it when I get a moment. Lovely on, though."

Auntie Jean is in good spirits. She loves going through the old costumes and reminding herself of happy times in the theatre. It is the day after Charlie's adventure in the lift, and it has been a successful one in the shop. A party of trippers strayed in during a shower and all bought false noses to cheer themselves up on the way home.

"I've got some lovely pork chops for tea," she tells them. "And chocolate ice-cream to follow – a treat, see. Why don't you

Term 1   Unit 2

slip along and ask Mr Cornetto if he wants to come round and join us? He looks as though he could do with a good meal. I don't believe he cooks anything proper, there on his own."

Charlie and Ariadne stroll up the prom, still chewing the remains of their buns. The sun has come out, warming the damp pavement under their feet, and catching the sails of two little boats, dipping along optimistically in the bay. The tide has gone out, leaving behind it a glittering expanse of rich, salty mud, garlanded with dark seaweed. In the middle distance, the children from St Ethelred's Holiday Home are straggling along the water-line, with melted ice-lollies dribbling down to their elbows. They stop now again to poke about amongst the driftwood, or push one another into the pools. The student in charge, his trousers rolled up to the knee, moves up and down his flock like a sheep-dog, herding them home to bed. Their voices echo across the bay as in an enormous bathroom.

Charlie and Ariadne arrive at Carlo's Crazy Castle to find Lordy in charge of the pay-box, his fore-paws on the till. He greets them with loud barks, which bring Mr Cornetto hurrying to the entrance. He winds up the portcullis to let them in.

"Well, there's kind of you, I'm sure!" he exclaims, when they deliver Auntie Jean's invitation. "I'm just closing up here. I'd a few people round earlier, but it's pretty quiet on the whole. Want to see round for free, while you're here, do you?"

He heads the way into an entrance hall, strangely decorated in a style half way between a medieval castle and tea-bar. There are suits of armour, a life-sized bear carved out of wood, some plastic-topped tables and chairs, and rows of old-fashioned slot-machines ranged about the walls. There is also a gilt mirror or two, some shields and helmets, and a piano with pictures of storks and flowers painted upon it. At one end of the room is an archway, covered with a heavy velvet curtain, marked "HALL OF WAXWORKS". Another archway at the other end has a curtain of beads with a notice saying "GYPSY QUEEN ROSITA, FORTUNE-TELLER AND CLAIRVOYANT". But over this is pasted another notice with the words "Temporarily Closed".

Mr Cornetto ushers them proudly into the Hall of Waxworks. Two rows of shabby lurching figures are arranged along low platforms, behind looped silk cords. Ariadne, who is fond of History, knows who most of them are without having to read the labels – Napoleon, Queen Elizabeth the First, Sir Francis Drake, Nelson, Christopher Columbus. There are other, more sinister characters, too – Dick Turpin, the highwayman, with a cocked hat and levelled pistols, and, at the far end of the room, a tableau of Mary Queen of Scots with a masked Executioner, who looks as though he is getting ready to chop off her head.

"That one's great," says Charlie. "He's really scary!"

"I like her dress – all those pearls," agrees Ariadne.

The waxworks return their gaze with glassy eyes.

"And now, the Hall of Mirrors," says Mr Cornetto, throwing open another door. They pass through it into a maze of their own reflections. In one mirror Charlie is as round and fat as Humpty Dumpty. In the next he is as tall and thin as if he had been pulled out like chewing-gum, and his eyes seem to meet in the middle of his head. Standing together, a little further on, he and Ariadne appear as two giants, their feet miles away, their bodies ballooning out round the middle, and the giggling faces flattened out like saucers.

"Bet you look like that when you're grown up," says Charlie. "You could get a job on the telly as one of those monsters from outer space."

But Ariadne doesn't bother to answer back. She has already moved on to see, reflected over and over again, an endless

Term 1 | Unit 2

vista of herself, in which every small movement turns her into a forest of arms or an army of legs.

"Like being a centipede," she murmurs. "But where do I – or rather, where does *it* – end?"

But Mr Cornetto is already leading the way through the mirror maze into another smaller room with more slot-machines in it and a huge weighing-machine which says "I SPEAK YOUR WEIGHT", past a small door marked "Private", which leads upstairs to the little flat where he and Lordy have their living arrangements, then back to the entrance hall.

"Now, I've just got to lock up and give Lordy his supper," says Mr Cornetto, when they have admired everything. "I won't be long. You two go ahead and tell your Auntie I'll be along about a quarter to seven, if that suits. Lordy can stay here and look after things while I'm out."

The evening sunlight on the airy prom seems very reassuring after the dusty fantasies of Carlo's Crazy Castle.

"Those slot-machines are a bit pathetic," says Ariadne on the way back, "sort of old-fashioned. I've seen *much* better ones in the Amusement Arcade over at Penwyn. They have lots of flashing lights and things, and you can win a whole pile of money on them – well, sometimes you can. I liked the Hall of Mirrors, though."

"And the waxworks," Charlie adds, "specially that one with Queen Elizabeth having her head chopped off."

"Mary Queen of Scots, Charlie. Don't you know *any* History?"

"Course I do. But we haven't done that bit. At our school it's all projects – Roman walls and roads and that. Not many battles. We did some good stuff once about the Barbarian Hordes sweeping across Europe, but then we had a new teacher and went back to roads again. Do you think

18

Mr Cornetto gets many customers?"

"Doesn't seem like it. As bad as Auntie Jean's – absolutely typically pathetic, in fact," says Ariadne, greatly cheered, as always, by being able to use both her favourite words at once.

Part Four

The shop door is already closed, with the blind pulled down, so they go round the back, to be met by the delicious smell of frying pork chops and onions. Auntie Jean is in her little kitchen, darting about in a cloud of smoke and steam, with Einstein weaving excitedly round her legs. Hungry as hunters, Charlie and Ariadne start to lay the table in the sitting-room, putting on a clean checked table-cloth. There is a loud, insistent knocking at the shop door.

"That'll be Mr Cornetto, I expect," calls out Auntie Jean. "He's early. Just let him in, will you, Charlie, dear?"

But the shadow Charlie sees on the blind at the end of the passage is far too big to be Mr Cornetto's. When he unlocks the door and opens it there, as large as life, is Mrs Cadwallader, beaming and looking very grand in pink and pearls. She sweeps right past him into the shop.

"I'm *so* glad I got your address right, dear," she says. "I felt I just had to thank you personally for returning both my rings to me yesterday. It really was silly of me to leave them lying about like that. Mona was furious, of course. I'm always doing it, you see. The things I've lost! You wouldn't believe it! Valuable, too. The trouble is, I can never remember what I've put on in the morning when I take it off at night. And then, of course, when I find I've lost something, it's too late to look for it. Little Scatterbrain, my poor late husband used to call me. But you saved me this time, and no mistake. I wanted to give you this, as a little token of my appreciation."

She presses a pound into Charlie's hand, and airily waves away his thanks.

"So this is your Auntie's shop," she continues, looking about her at the masks and false noses. "I like a joke myself – always have done. Poor Mona's got no sense of humour, I'm afraid, and that's a fact. Only the other day…Good heavens above!" Her flow of chatter stops abruptly, as though she has seen a ghost. Over the top of Charlie's head she has caught sight of Auntie Jean, standing in the doorway in her big flowered apron.

"I don't believe it!" gasps Mrs Cadwallader, clutching her pearls.

"It can't be…!" cries Auntie Jean.

"Well, I never did!"

"Connie!"

"Jean Jones!"

"Indeed to goodness me, where on earth did you spring from after all these years?"

Charlie, open-mouthed, just manages to step neatly out of the way as the two ladies come together in the middle of the shop in a hearty embrace.

"Come right inside, Connie, dear," says Auntie Jean, ushering Mrs Cadwallader through into the back room and sitting her down in the best armchair. "You children, lay another place at the table. We've another guest for tea!"

As the two ladies fall to chattering and laughing and exclaiming both at once, like a pair of noisy parakeets, Charlie and Ariadne, goggling with astonishment, try to piece together the explanation for this surprising reunion. Bit by bit, they find out that Mrs Cadwallader, in her days on the stage, once played a summer season at the Royalty Theatre. Auntie Jean was working there then as a dresser, and the two became firm friends. But after Mrs Cadwallader married her rich husband they somehow drifted apart, and haven't laid eyes on one another again until this very moment.

"Well, fancy your being the lady that saved this young scamp nephew of mine from being stuck in the lift yesterday," says Auntie Jean. "What a small world it is, indeed! And you one of those posh folk staying up at the Hydro!"

"I'm staying there with my sister-in-law, Mona. But they're an unfriendly lot up there. Nobody talks to anybody. Things aren't a bit like they used to be. Even the old Royalty's closed, I see."

"Yes, sad isn't it? The dear old Royalty. The times we had there, Connie! All that rush and excitement before the curtain went up, and you such a picture in those white tights and all those sparkling sequins!"

"Oh, it's such years ago now. But seeing you here makes it seem like yesterday," says Mrs Cadwallader happily. "Do you remember, Jean, that roll of drums from the orchestra pit, then *smash* went the cymbals, and up I went into the air, as light as a feather!"

"And I was always that frightened in case you fell off! There you were on that pyramid of strong men, all standing on top of one another's shoulders, with you at the very top! I never knew how you had the nerve, Connie, really I don't."

Term 1 | Unit 3

Be Safe Outdoors

by Pete Saunders

Introduction

There are many places to explore outdoors – playgrounds, streets, parks and the countryside are just a few of them. Some are safer than others. But even when you play in safe places, there may be risks. You have to learn about safety so you know how to look after yourself. The ideas in this book will help to keep you from harm, whenever you are outdoors.

Take a close look at the picture on this page. Some of the children are in dangerous situations. How many of these can you spot? You will find some of the answers on page 24.

Safety game

After many accidents, people often say that they didn't mean them to happen. This is probably true. It's just that they forgot to think, or they haven't learned any better yet.

Try to think of fun ways in which you can help others to think about keeping safe outdoors. You might make up a safety song or draw some cartoon pictures. Or you could make your own safety board game.

Project

You might want to try out the game on the next page. To make it you will need some card, something to draw and colour with, some scissors and a ruler. You will need to draw out your board. On the one shown here, the players go from the town to the park and then the countryside. You can write in your own rules, for example, go back to the start if you play near a railway line. Instead of using flat counters, you can make little people. Make sure they are the right size to fit the squares of your board.

draw up board

draw figure and colour

fold tab

leave tab on feet

glue on to base

Term 1 | Unit 3

Can you think of more hazards?

Answers to page 22

Here are some of the things the children shouldn't be doing: running on the street, climbing a tree, climbing over a fence, running on the station platform, playing on the track, running in the road, playing in the rubbish dump, playing in the roadworks, going camping wearing only a t-shirt. Can you spot any more?

First Aid

First aid is giving care and help to someone who is hurt. You need to have lessons to be good at first aid. The ideas here are to help you to know what to do if you hurt yourself or if you come across somebody who needs some help. Reading this section does not make you into an expert.

Taking a pulse

Taking someone's pulse will tell you how fast the heart is beating. The speed varies according to a person's age and what he or she has been doing. The rate for a 10-year-old child is about 90 beats a minute. For an adult who has been running it would be 140 beats a minute. A normal pulse is regular and strong. Anything else indicates a problem. The best place to take a pulse is the wrist. Place two fingers on the inside of the wrist and press gently. Count the beats for a minute.

A nosebleed

A nosebleed can happen for many reasons. People with nosebleeds should loosen anything that is tight around the neck and chest. He should sit with his head slightly forward to stop the blood going into the throat.

The nostrils should be pinched for 10 minutes. If this doesn't work, you should do the same thing for another 10 minutes. If the bleeding stops, the nose should not be blown for at least four hours.

If a nosebleed won't stop, it's best to get a doctor. Remember that seeing a lot of blood is frightening to some people.

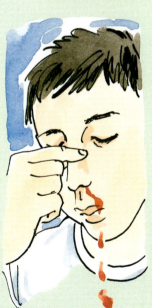

Cuts

If someone has a cut that won't stop bleeding, pressing on it will stop the flow of blood. Make sure dirt doesn't get into the cut and cover it with a clean piece of material.

Sprains

If someone has a sprained ankle, it's best to take off the shoe, and raise the foot. Take an ice pack or a cloth that has been put under a cold water tap and squeezed out. Wrap it around the sprained area and keep it in place for at least 30 minutes to stop the swelling. Afterwards, the sprain should be bandaged firmly.

As with all first aid, getting adult help is essential. This is important with sprains, as it can be hard to tell the difference between a sprain and a fracture.

Frostbite

Frostbite happens when the ears, nose, chin, hands and feet are in the cold for too long. It can cause prickling pain and numbness.

If someone has frostbite, find shelter for her. Take off any clothing from the affected area. You should warm the frostbite gradually by skin to skin contact. Use your hands or armpits. Then wrap the area in cloth and cover it with a blanket.

Emergency

Keep a clear head and don't panic.

Don't put yourself in danger.

Think of a way of getting help at once.

If it is necessary, dial 999. The call is free.

Know what kind of help you want – the police, the ambulance or the fire brigade.

Be ready to give the phone number you are using, and to explain where you are.

You will need to explain how the accident happened.

Don't put the telephone down until the person that you are talking to has finished.

When you are outdoors try to remember where the nearest phone box is.

Down at the very bottom *by Jackie Kay*

You can't see my castle. She can't either.
Nor can my big brother who is busy burying
his feet.

My castle is underneath the sand, down
at the very bottom of the sea, where
the other Carla is having her tea.

There are no big things at the side going boom.
And inside there's lots and lots of room.
So we don't get on top of each other.

Also, there are secret passages that lead to
terrapins, sea urchins, sea dragons and snakes
and if you turn right at the very bottom,

you can even go back in time; you might run into
a Tyrannosaurus rex or some kid in period dress.
The sleeping room is turquoise at first, then

all of a sudden, it goes dark green. But the best
thing is that nobody says, "if you don't ... then you
        can't ..."
Nobody talks like that in my castle under the sand.

Waves *by Jackie Kay*

There are waves to chase and waves that crash,
There are waves to jump like skipping ropes,
Waves to run away to sand, waves to leap and bound.
Waves that are turquoise, waves that are brown,
Waves full of seaweed, waves that drown.
Waves clear and calm, waves angry and wronged,
Waves that whisper, waves that roar like thunder,
Waves you'd never swim under, pounding rocks and
    shore.

Duncan Gets Expelled
by Jackie Kay

There are three big boys from primary seven
who wait at the main school gate with stones
in their teeth and names in their pockets.
Every day the three big boys are waiting.
"There she is. Into her boys. Hey Sambo."

I dread the bell ringing, and the walk home.
My best friend is scared of them and runs off.
Some days they shove a mud pie into my mouth.
"That's what you should eat," and make me eat it.
Then they all look in my mouth, prodding a stick.

I'm always hoping we get detention.
I'd love to write "I will be better" 400 times.
The things I do? I pull Agnes MacNamara's hair.
Or put a ruler under Rhona's bum and ping it back
till she screams; or I make myself sick in the toilet.

Until the day the headmaster pulls me out,
asking all about the three big boys.
I'm scared to open my mouth.
But he says, "you can tell me, is it true?"
So out it comes, making me eat the mud pies.

Two of them got lines for the whole of May.
But he got expelled, that Duncan MacKay.

Sabre-tooth Sandwich

by Leon Garfield

Chapter One

The sun went down as red and angry as my father's face; and still no sign of my uncle.

"If anything's happened to him," my mother told my father, with tears in her eyes (for my uncle is her only brother and she loves him dearly), "I'll never forgive you!" And she picked up the old mammoth tusk she thumps meat with, to make it tender.

Not that we've had any meat for the past four days, only roots and stinking fish. But before I tell you why, I ought to explain that we are a family of cave-dwellers: my father, my mother, my five sisters, my uncle, and me.

We live, says my uncle, at the dawn of history, and are really quite primitive; which drives my father mad. "Speak for yourself!" he shouts, and reaches for his club.

"Don't you dare lay a finger on him!" cries my mother, and my father mutters under his breath that he had something more substantial than a finger in mind; and he scowls like a thunder-sky as my uncle warms himself at the fire he's never fed, and stuffs himself from the pot he's never filled.

My uncle is a neat little man, with silverish hair, a fine brow, a big nose, a tremendous voice; and, says my father, two left feet. There, and even my mother has to admit it, my father has a point. My uncle has never been a great success in life. The truth of the matter is, he is more of a thinker than a doer; he likes to sit by the fire, just thinking.

My father says he is a lazy, no-good layabout, and if he wasn't my mother's brother, he'd be out of our cave faster than smoke.

But whatever might be said against him, nobody can deny that my uncle is always very well turned-out. Just because we live at the dawn of history, he says, there's no need to go about looking as if we've just got out of bed. Which is all very well, says my father angrily, but clean toe-nails and a bearskin hat won't feed nine hungry mouths!

Chapter Three

The last of the red had gone, and black dragons were sprawling across the sky. The forest was dark and quiet, like a huge ragged hole in the night, full of sharp death and, somewhere, my uncle.

We went down to the edge of the trees, and called, and shouted; but he never came, he never answered.

My mother blamed my father. My uncle must have taken my father's words too much to heart and had exposed himself to some terrible danger rather than come home without our dinner. "If anything's happened to him," wept my mother, "I'll never forgive you!"

Then, even as she spoke, there came a loud cry from outside. A moment later, a frantic creature staggered into our cave, gave another cry, and collapsed by the fire like a heap of leaves. It was my uncle.

He was a pitiable sight. His hair was wild, his clothing filthy, and his face and arms and legs all smeared with blood. But he was alive!

"Where's my club?" demanded my father, while my mother wiped my uncle's brow and picked the twigs from his hair.

My uncle stared at him as if he could scarcely believe it possible that my father should be so hard-hearted as to be more worried about his club than about my uncle's health. "Tiger," he murmured faintly. "Sabre-toothed tiger."

My father lost his temper. "I may be primitive," he shouted, "but I'm not stupid! There hasn't been a sabre-toothed tiger in these parts since your grandfather's day!" and he went on to tell my mother that, even though he was only a Stone Age man living at the dawn of history, he wasn't going to have his intelligence insulted by that idle parasite (he meant my uncle) painting himself all over with blackberry juice and saying he'd met a sabre-toothed tiger.

"If only," said my father, "he'd made a real effort to *make* me believe him, I'd have had a little more respect for him!"

My uncle sat up sharply. Once again, my father had said something that had got under my uncle's skin. He stood up and, waving aside my mother's efforts to stop him, he began to do some very strange things.

He stared round our cave. He frowned. He went to the back and cleared away some skins my sisters had been working on. He told me and my sisters to move the hollow tree-trunk to an exact spot he pointed out, while he arranged the skins in a snaky line across one corner.

This done, he stepped back and studied the effect from every part of the cave. "Yes," he murmured, "I think that will do." Then he picked up an axe handle and swung it vigorously two or three times in the air.

"Yes," he murmured again, "I think this will do."

Now he came to each of us in turn and, very quietly, told us what he wanted; and, although it was strangeness piled on top of strangeness, not even my father questioned him. Maybe it was because we were light-headed from hunger, or because we'd seen something in my uncle we'd never seen before – a lightness of step, an easiness, an air of authority – that his words filled us with a feeling of tremendous adventure.

31

Term 1 | Unit 5

Chapter Four

Everything was ready. My uncle capped his hands. "Beginners, please!" At once, we moved to our appointed places, and my uncle went outside.

As we waited, watching the entrance of our cave, I began to feel afraid that I would do something wrong. I think we all must have felt the same. I could see my sisters trembling; and my father and mother were looking pale. Then my uncle came into the cave.

He came in very stealthily, half-crouching, and grasping our axe handle as if it was my father's club. He paused at every step, and peered cautiously about him. Once, his gaze fell on me; but he didn't see me. He was no longer in our cave; he was alone in the forest, and I was a bush. I didn't dare to move.

It was truly amazing. The walls of our cave had vanished, and there was my uncle, creeping among huge, shadowy trees, fighting his way through tangled branches, and running swiftly across the open glades.

Even the snaky line of skins had disappeared. In its place, most mysteriously, was a wandering forest stream. You could tell, because my uncle knelt down and drank from it.

He rose, wiped his lips, and, with a quick glance about him, crept on, deeper and deeper into the forest.

Suddenly he stopped. He was most marvellously balanced on one foot, with the other just raised behind him, and with one hand outstretched. It was almost as if he was going to fly. He was absolutely still, save for his eyes. They turned, and glittered sharply. He had seen our dinner!

A deer was drinking from the stream; a beautiful creature with enormous brown eyes, just like my mother's.

Slowly, slowly, my uncle began to advance, with club uplifted. You could see his lips moving: "Dinner for nine!"

But my uncle was not the only hunter in the forest. Deep among the trees, glaring with horrible eyes, was a monstrous sabre-toothed tiger! Silently, and limping a little from a broken toe, it crept forward and crouched down behind a bush. I could hear its low growl and feel its hot breath on the back of my neck.

I've never been so frightened in all my life! I longed to shout out to my uncle, "Look behind you!" but I was only a bush. All I could do was to shake and shiver as if a gale was blowing through my leaves.

The deer looked up from the stream. I don't know if the shaking bush had disturbed her, or if she'd caught a whiff of sabre-toothed scent; but she was plainly uneasy. She saw my uncle; then she saw the tiger. Her beautiful eyes grew round with terror.

At once my uncle guessed, from her pitiful expression, that there was some terrible danger behind him. He turned. He saw the tiger making ready to spring. He looked back. He saw the deer's despair; and instead of flying for his life and leaving the helpless deer to be torn into pieces, he did the bravest thing I've ever seen. He rushed straight at the monster with nothing but his bare hands and our axe handle!

Of course, the sabre-toothed could have smashed my uncle with one blow of its paw; but it was distracted by the whirling club.

It snarled and snapped and at last seized hold of it in its jaws.

Then the great beast howled in fury! The club was firmly wedged in between its enormous teeth! Frantically it rushed about, shaking its head, until the club struck against a hollow tree-trunk, with a loud thwack.

At once there was a furious buzzing. The tiger had dislodged a swarm of large bees! Enraged, they flew at the disturber of their peace. In an instant, the deer and my uncle were forgotten as the sabre-toothed tried to shake off the fiercely attacking bees.

"Quick, quick!" cried the deer, too excited to hold her tongue. "Onto my back and away!" And while the maddened tiger raged and roared, my uncle jumped onto my mother's back and the pair of them galloped tremendously away!

Chapter Five

We all burst out cheering! We couldn't help it. We were all so happy that my uncle and the deer had got away.

"But why," my father asked my mother when my uncle had got off her back, "didn't he bring the deer back for the pot?"

My mother looked at him as if he was the most primitive cave-dweller she'd ever laid eyes on. "Just because you are a Stone Age man," she told him, "you don't have to have a heart of stone as well! The deer saved his life."

My father scratched his head. He turned to my uncle. "And did it really happen like that?"

My uncle looked him straight in the eye. "You saw for yourself, didn't you?" he said.

But that wasn't the end of it; the best was still to come. It turned out that some of our neighbours had been watching, from the entrance to our cave. They were amazed. They couldn't believe what they'd seen. They said it was the best thing since apples.

They came into our cave and stared round, as if wondering where all the trees had gone. They asked if we could do it all again, in their cave, as it would be a shame if their children missed it. "And we'd take it as a great favour," they said, "if you'd take dinner with us."

The second time went even better than the first, although my father saw fit to reprimand one of my sisters. "When did you ever," he said, "see a bee picking its nose? It ruins my performance."

But it was only my father who noticed. Everyone else sat open-mouthed; and when we finished, the cheers and clapping almost brought the cave down.

When we got home, my uncle, who is usually the last person to gloat over his triumphs, couldn't resist saying to my father, "Well! It looks as if clean toe-nails and a bearskin hat, so to speak, really can feed nine hungry mouths!"

He was right. Since that wonderful night, the whole world's been our hunter and our cook. We've performed up and down the land, and always to full caves. Next summer we are to go up north, on tour.

Although we live at the dawn of history, my uncle says, we've been first out of bed to ring up the curtain!

35

Term 1 | Unit 6

Wood

by Robin Place

On many excavations, nothing made of wood is found, because wood rots away in dry ground. But in wet ground, wooden structures and objects survive.

Large wooden structures that have survived include houses, trackways, well-linings and waterfronts. Archaeologists have also found weapons such as bows, arrows and spears as well as scabbards, tool-handles, household objects such as bowls and cups, pattens (medieval overshoes worn to keep feet dry on muddy roads), Roman letters written in ink on thin pieces of wood, and even Viking pan-pipes.

How old?

Finds of wood are important for another reason. They can be used to date structures and things found close to them. Wood can be dated by the radiocarbon method, counting radioactive carbon atoms that were absorbed by the living tree, and slowly lost after it was felled.

Another dating method, dendrochronology, involves measuring the yearly growth rings on oak timbers. These vary in width according to the rainfall in each year. Measurements have been collected from oak trees covering hundreds of years up to the present day. Using computers archaeologists can compare this record with the ring pattern in an ancient block of wood. The best match shows the date when the tree from which the block came was growing.

▲ Part of a neolithic arrow found near Aberdeen. It has a wooden shaft and flint head.

◀ Boxwood pan-pipes played by Vikings in York 1,000 years ago. They can still be played – the notes are A to E.

In Britain, archaeologists have found trunks of oak trees that grew at different periods of history. The oldest trees were preserved in ancient peat bogs and lake beds. Palaeobotanists (people who study ancient plants) have recorded on computer sequences of tree rings, from modern times back to very ancient times. They have linked trees of different ages by matching groups of very distinctive rings. This diagram shows matched rings (the overlapping sections) at about 1890–1900 and 1870–80.

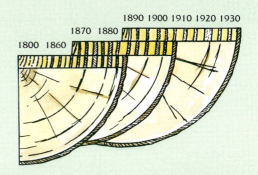

◀ Wooden pattens were overshoes worn in the Middle Ages to keep shoes above the mud in the streets. They were kept on by a leather strap.

▲ Dove-tail, half-lap and saddle joints were used for the well timbers. Braces strengthened the corners.

Clues from the Past

The skill of Roman carpenters

The wooden lining of a Roman well 1.2 m square was excavated in Skeldergate, York. The oak timbers were so well preserved that archaeologists could see exactly how the carpenters had joined the timbers together. All the joints were made by sawing, and an iron nail held each one together. In some joints, small wooden wedges had been hammered in, to give a tight fit.

Waterfronts

In Roman, Saxon and medieval times, the people of riverside towns like London and York built massive timber waterfronts, so that ships could tie up at a landing stage instead of having to unload into flat-bottomed barges. Waterfront excavations have provided clues to the size of ancient trees. In London, the Roman waterfront was built of huge oaks 200–300 years old. But so many of these big trees were felled that by the Middle Ages there were none left near London, and medieval waterfronts were built of much smaller trees only 40–80 years old.

▲ Looking down the Skeldergate well. The timbers were built inside a big pit. The space between the timber lining and the pit wall was filled in with soil.

37

Term 1 | Unit 6

▼ Timbers removed from the well show how the corners were fastened and how braces were jointed in place.

Timber must have been in short supply, as old doors and timbers from dismantled ships were built into waterfronts. The old ships' timbers also gave useful clues as to how medieval ships were built. This is important, as very few ships have been excavated.

Iron Age chariots

Archaeologists have found graves where a man, or a woman, was buried with a chariot. The chariots were mostly made of wood, which has rotted away, but we have some clues from the metal parts which have been preserved in the graves.

The iron tyre, a band around the outside of the wheel, shows the size of the wheel. The nave bands, bronze rings around the central wheel hub, show how big this was. Sometimes the whole chariot was buried in a large grave, with the person lying inside it. The distance between the wheels shows how wide the chariot was.

Other metal objects that have been found give further clues about what the chariot looked like. Rein rings and a pair of bridle bits show that two ponies drew the chariot. The archaeologist Sir Cyril Fox showed that two oddly shaped brooches, which are kept in the British Museum, London, could have been used to fasten a cloth over a pony's back. The Iron Age Celts wove brightly coloured cloth, so the chief in the chariot would have been a fine sight, with the bright cloths over the ponies and the bronze fittings gleaming in the sun.

◀ Building a waterfront in Roman London. Work was done at low tide. The space behind the new timber wall was filled with rubbish to make solid ground for warehouses. Pottery and coins found in the rubbish tell us the date when this was done.

38

Metals

An extra clue

In the grave at Wetwang Slack, Yorkshire, the wheels had been taken off the chariot and laid in the bottom of the grave pit. The wheel on the right shows how archaeologists can work out the size of the tyre and the central nave bands, as described above. But as the wood of the wheel on the left decayed, it happened to leave cavities in the ground. The diggers spotted the holes and pumped foam plastic into them. This revealed the size of the spokes and the felloe, the wooden wheel rim to which the tyre was fixed.

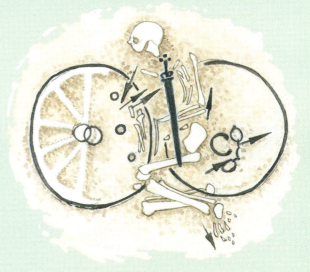

▲ A man buried with parts of a chariot at Wetwang Slack. His body may have been stabbed with spears, so his ghost would not "walk".

1 Iron tyre
2 Bronze nave bands
3 Spoke
4 Felloe
5 Skull
6 Horse bits
7 Iron sword in bronzed iron scabbard
8 Spearheads
9 Rein rings
10 Feet of skeleton

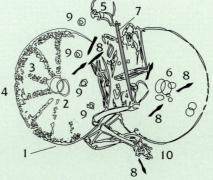

▲ A Celtic chariot, reconstructed from traces found in chariot burials. The diagram identifies the finds in the chariot burial shown above.

39

Term 1 | Unit 7

Bill's New Frock

by Anne Fines

Scene 1: Bill's bedroom

(BILL, MUM, DAD, and BELLA the cat)

(An alarm clock rings.)

BILL   When I woke up that morning, something really strange had happened. Oh, my room looked exactly the same. And all the stuff in it looked exactly the same. Even the mirror looked exactly the same. But when I looked into the mirror, *I* didn't look exactly the same at all. I'd turned into a girl!

I don't believe this! Is it a *dream*? Is it a *nightmare*? What is going on?

MUM   *(calling)* Bill! Bill! Hurry up! Time to get dressed for school!

BILL   This can't be true. This can't be happening. I must still be asleep.

MUM   *(coming in)* Oh, good. You're awake.

BILL   That's that, then. I'm not asleep.

MUM   Up you get. Time to get dressed. Why don't you wear this pretty pink frock?

BILL   I never wear frocks!

MUM   I know. It's such a pity!

BILL   Don't drop that frock over my head! Mum, don't! Stop it! I can't breathe. *(gurgle, gurgle)* Mu-um!

MUM	There. Now it's on. I'll leave you to do up all the pretty little shell buttons. I'm late for work.
BILL	This can't be true. This simply cannot be true. Where's Dad? He'll sort me out. Dad! Dad!
DAD	Well, hello, poppet! You look very sweet today. It's not often we see you in a frock, is it?
BILL	Dad –
DAD	Take care now. I'm late for work.
BELLA	Miaowwwww. Miaowwwww.
BILL	Hello, Bella. At least you don't notice any difference in me, do you? I look the same to you. Oh, Bella! Is this a dream? Or a nightmare? Do I have to go to school like this?
BELLA	Miaowwwww.
BILL	Yes. I suppose I do...

Scene 3: Inside the classroom

	(BILL, MRS COLLINS, HEADMASTER, ASTRID, FLORA, KIRSTY, ALL THE GIRLS, ROHAN, PHILIP, MARTIN, ARIF and the WHOLE CLASS)
MRS COLLINS	Good morning, everybody.
WHOLE CLASS	Good-mor-ning-Mis-sus-Col-lins.
MRS COLLINS	And here's the Headteacher to speak to you.
HEADMASTER	Good morning, 4C.
WHOLE CLASS	Good-mor-ning-Mis-ter-Phil-lips.

41

HEADMASTER	Now I want four strong volunteers to carry tables over to the playground for me.
ASTRID	Me, Sir!
BILL	Me, Sir!
KIRSTY	Me, Sir!
ROHAN	Me, Sir!
WHOLE CLASS	Me, Sir! I'm strong!
HEADMASTER	Right. This boy.
ROHAN	Yes, Sir.
HEADMASTER	And that boy.
MARTIN	Yes, Sir.
HEADMASTER	And that boy.
PHILIP	Yes, Sir.
HEADMASTER	And this boy.
ARIF	Yes, Sir.
HEADMASTER	Right. Off we go.
	(Four boys and Headmaster troop out.)
ASTRID	It's not fair, Mrs Collins.
FLORA	He always picks the boys to carry things.
MRS COLLINS	Perhaps the tables are heavy.
KIRSTY	None of the tables in this school are heavy.
ASTRID	And I know for a fact that I am stronger than at least three of the boys he picked.
BILL	It's true. Whenever we have a tug of war, everyone wants Astrid on their team.
MRS COLLINS	Oh, well. It doesn't matter. No need to make such a fuss. It's only a silly old table.

ALL THE GIRLS	But it does matter. To us.
MRS COLLINS	That's enough! Now everyone open your workbooks.
WHOLE CLASS	...mutter...mutter...mutter...
MRS COLLINS	And get on with your work. I'll come round and look at everyone's books in turn. You're first. What page are you doing?
BILL	This one.
MRS COLLINS	This is very messy. Look at this dirty smudge. And this one. And the edge of your book looks as if it's been chewed.
BILL	But I'm doing my best. And it's a lot better than what I did yesterday. Or the day before. In fact, it's a really good page – for me.
MRS COLLINS	Well it's not good enough for me. Now what about yours, Philip?
PHILIP	I'm doing this page.
MRS COLLINS	Not bad at all, Philip. Keep up the good work.
BILL	Let me see that, Philip.
PHILIP	Here you are.
BILL	But that's awful. That's disgusting. It's much, much worse than mine!
FLORA	Philip's letters are all wobbly.
TALILAH	They're straggling all over the page like camels lost in the desert.
BILL	It's much, much worse than mine. And she didn't say anything nice to me.
TALILAH	Or me.

43

FLORA	Or me.
PHILIP	Well, girls are *supposed* to be neater, aren't they?
ALL THE GIRLS	Why?
PHILIP	I don't know. They just *are*.

Scene 4: In the classroom (continued)

	(BILL, MRS COLLINS, NICK, TALILAH, FLORA, PHILIP, KIRSTY and the WHOLE CLASS)
MRS COLLINS	It's time for group reading. What page are we on?
WHOLE CLASS	Page-for-ty-se-ven-Mis-sus-Col-lins.
MRS COLLINS	Page forty-seven. Ah, yes. The story of *Rapunzel*. What a nice old fairy tale that is. And it's table five's turn to take the main parts today. So you be the farmer, Nick.
NICK	Yes, Mrs Collins.
MRS COLLINS	You be the farmer's wife, Talilah.
TALILAH	Goody!
MRS COLLINS	You be the witch, Flora.
FLORA	Oh, great!
MRS COLLINS	You be the handsome prince, Philip.
PHILIP	Yes, well, I am rather handsome.
WHOLE CLASS	...groan...bleh...groan...bleh...
MRS COLLINS	Kirsty, you be the narrator. And who does that leave?
BILL	Me.

44

MRS COLLINS	Right then, dear. You get to be The Lovely Rapunzel.
BILL	*Me*?
MRS COLLINS	Why not? It's almost as if you're dressed for the part.
BILL	I don't believe this. I do not believe this!
MRS COLLINS	Right. Everyone happy?
KIRSTY	I am. I get to say the most.
FLORA	I get to say quite a bit.
TALILAH	I do, too.
NICK	So do I.
PHILIP	And me.
BILL	I hardly get to say *anything*.
KIRSTY	You get stolen by the witch.
TALILAH	And you get hidden at the top of a tower.
NICK	And you stay there for fifteen years.
PHILIP	And your hair grows very long.
FLORA	Very long indeed.
BILL	But I don't *do* anything. I just say "Ooooooooh."
KIRSTY	That's a very good part.
WHOLE CLASS	"Ooooooooh."
BILL	No it isn't. Mrs Collins, why doesn't Rapunzel have a better part?
MRS COLLINS	What do you mean?
BILL	Well, what I mean is, it's her story, isn't it? It's called *Rapunzel*. So how come she doesn't actually do anything?
MRS COLLINS	I don't know what you mean.

45

BILL	I mean, she didn't have to just sit there quietly growing her hair, did she? And nobody forced her to just sit on her bottom for fifteen years, waiting for a prince to come along and rescue her.
KIRSTY	That's right. She could have shown a bit of spirit.
TALILAH	Planned her own escape.
PHILIP	Cut off her lovely long hair herself.
NICK	Braided it into a rope.
FLORA	Slid down it all by herself.
KIRSTY	And run home.
NICK	And she'd have been a lot more worth rescuing.
PHILIP	In fact, I don't think a handsome prince like myself would want to marry a big wimp like her.
MRS COLLINS	I don't know what's going on today. I really don't. One of you gets in a funny mood, and suddenly the whole lot of you are in a funny mood. Shall we read *Polly the Ace Pilot* instead?
WHOLE CLASS	Yes! Let's read that instead!

Scene 5: The Art Class

	(MRS BANDA, BILL, LEILA, MELISSA, PAUL, WAYNE and the WHOLE CLASS)
MRS BANDA	Time for the art lesson. What's left in the cupboard?
LEILA	Not much.
MRS BANDA	Any coloured chalks?

PAUL	No. They're all gone.
MRS BANDA	Pastels, then?
LEILA	They're still damp from the roof leak.
MRS BANDA	Any clay?
PAUL	It's all dried up.
MRS BANDA	There *must* be crayons.
LEILA	The infants came and borrowed them last week, and they haven't brought them back yet.
MRS BANDA	So it's paints again, as usual. What colours do we have left in the tubs?
WAYNE	Pink.
MRS BANDA	And what's in that one?
MELISSA	Pink.
MRS BANDA	And in that one?
WAYNE	More pink.
MRS BANDA	And that one?
MELISSA	Pink again.
WAYNE	There's more pink here.
MRS BANDA	I've found some blue – no, I haven't. It's all gone.
MELISSA	Here's another pink.
WAYNE	This is pink, too.
MRS BANDA	Pink, pink! Nothing but pink!
WAYNE	What can you do with pink?
WHOLE CLASS	Nothing.
WAYNE	You can't paint pink dogs.
MELISSA	Or pink space vehicles.

47

Term 1 Unit 7

WAYNE	Or pink trees.
MELISSA	Or pink battlefields.
MRS BANDA	There must be *something* that's all pink.
	(*First one person's eye falls on Bill. Then another's. Then another's. The silence grows. In the end, everyone is looking at Bill.*)
BILL	Oh, no. Oh, no, no, no. Oh, no, no, no, no, no. Not me. Absolutely not. You can't. Oh, no, no, no, no, no.
MRS BANDA	Yes. Pink frock. Pink freckles. And now, pink, pink cheeks. Yes, you'll do beautifully. You're all pink. Now sit down in the middle where everyone can see you.
BILL	There's a curse on me today. A pink curse!
MRS BANDA	And don't *scowl*, dear, or you'll ruin their paintings.
BILL	Grrrrrrrrr...

Scene 9: Going home

(BILL, MRS COLLINS, MUM, MALCOLM and the WHOLE CLASS)

(*The bell rings.*)

MRS COLLINS	Right. Off you go.
WHOLE CLASS	Hooray!
MRS COLLINS	(*to Bill*) Not you, dear. I'd like a little word with you before you rush off home.
BILL	What have I done?
MRS COLLINS	Nothing. Nothing. It's just – oh, I don't

	know. There's something different about you today. I can't think what, but there's something really strange about you. You're not quite *yourself*, you know.
BILL	Oh, I know. I know.
MRS COLLINS	Well. Off you go. I just hope that you're your old self again tomorrow.
BILL	Oh, so do I! So do I!
MRS COLLINS	Goodbye, then.
BILL	Bye. She's right. I'm not myself today. But how can a silly pink frock with fancy shell buttons have made such a difference – to every single thing that happened? All day long! Well, never mind. At least the day's nearly over. I'm going home now. I've had quite enough. In fact, if one more thing happens to me today ... One more thing ... Well, people had better watch out, that's all I can say.
MALCOLM	(*wolf-whistling*) Wheeeeet-whoooooo!
BILL	What was that?
MALCOLM	(*wolf-whistling*) Wheeeet-whooooo!
BILL	Who are you whistling at? Are you whistling at me?
MALCOLM	Nice pretty frock...
BILL	Because what I'm wearing is none of your business.
MALCOLM	Can't you even take a joke?
BILL	No. No, I can't take a joke. I've had enough. And I won't be whistled at, either. Whistling is for dogs. And I am not a dog. I am – I am –

Term 1 | Unit 7

BILL	What am I?
	I am a *person*, that is what I am.
	So take that! And that!
MALCOLM	Watch out! You'll have me over in the dustbins!
BILL	I don't care.
MALCOLM	Careful! I'm falling!
BILL	Good!
MALCOLM	Stop thumping me! Help! Help!
BILL	And one for luck! There!
MALCOLM	Look at me! I'm covered in carrot peelings and tea leaves!
BILL	Well, that'll teach you a lesson, won't it? In future, whistle at dogs, not at people!
MUM	Good heavens!
BILL	Mum!
MUM	I don't believe this! What *do* you look like?
BILL	I don't know. What do I look like?
MUM	You look *disgusting*. Look at this pretty pink frock. It's *ruined*.
BILL	What's wrong with it?
MUM	What's wrong with it? I'll tell you what's wrong with it. It looks as if you've been trying to play football in it.
BILL	Well, I have.
MUM	And it looks as if people have been painting with pink poster paints all around you.
BILL	Well, they have.

50

MUM	And it looks as if you've been carrying little bottles of ink close to your chest.
BILL	Well, I have.
MUM	And it looks as if you've been in a fight in it.
BILL	Well, I have.
MUM	And it looks as if you've been running races in it.
BILL	Well, I have.
MUM	And it looks as if you've been putting your grubby fingers all over the hem, to try and keep it down.
BILL	Well, I have.
MUM	And it looks as if you've been on top of the dustbins in it.
BILL	Well, I have.
MUM	Well, you can just take it off!
BILL	Can I? Can I?
MUM	Come on. Take it off at once.
BILL	I'll take the frock off, but it won't end the nightmare ... Wait a minute! I'm wrong! The nightmare has ended. Am I sure?
	(Bill turns his back discreetly.)
	Yes, I'm sure!
	(He turns round to face the world again.)
	I am a boy again! Hooray! I am a boy again!

The Dead Letter Box

by Jan Mark

The idea came to Louie while she was lying in bed thinking about an old film that she had seen on the telly at Gran's. It showed how spies didn't send their letters through the post but left them in secret places, to be picked up later by their friends.

A dead letter box was just what Louie needed to keep in touch with her friend, Glenda, who had moved away to a new house. And she knew the perfect place for it: an old book in the library.

The story of how Louie leaves her secret letters in the library, with unexpected results, makes for an unusual, funny book.

Jan Mark has twice won the Carnegie Medal – for *Thunder and Lightnings* and *Handles*. She was born in Hertfordshire and grew up in Kent. After studying at Canterbury College of Art she taught art in Gravesend. She now lives in Oxford.

Part One
Chapter One: *Louie and Glenda*

For five months now there had been a FOR SALE sign outside Glenda's house. Louie hardly noticed it any more; it had become part of the garden, like the concrete goblins, the bird-bath, and the green lamp post which grew up through the hedge; a tall tin plant with an orange flower on top that bloomed only at night.

Louie had forgotten that there was ever a time when the sign had not stood there, and she had begun to forget what it meant, so she was surprised one morning when she stopped on her way to school to wait for Glenda, and saw that the sign had changed. It no longer said FOR SALE. It said SOLD.

"You've sold your house," Louie said, when Glenda came out through the gateway.

"Last week," said Glenda. "They only changed the sign yesterday."

"You never told me."

"I forgot."

Louie remembered then what it was that *she* had forgotten: when Glenda's house was sold, Glenda would move away and Louie might never see her again, even though Glenda had been living at her end of the street as long as Louie had lived at the other. She had worked hard to forget it.

"If it was *me* I wouldn't have forgotten to tell *you*," Louie complained, as they walked round the corner into Manor Drive.

"But you're not moving," Glenda said.

"I might move one day. If I moved I'd tell you right away."

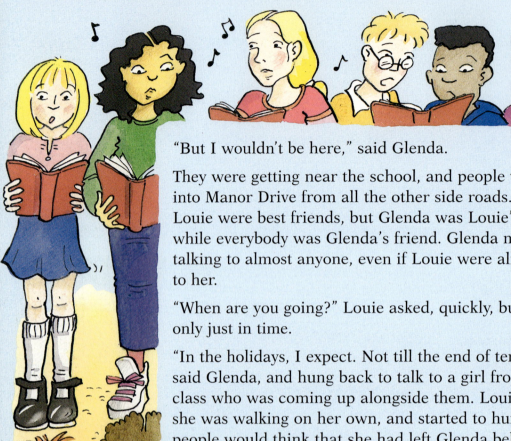

"But I wouldn't be here," said Glenda.

They were getting near the school, and people were turning into Manor Drive from all the other side roads. Glenda and Louie were best friends, but Glenda was Louie's only friend, while everybody was Glenda's friend. Glenda might start talking to almost anyone, even if Louie were already talking to her.

"When are you going?" Louie asked, quickly, but she was only just in time.

"In the holidays, I expect. Not till the end of term, anyway," said Glenda, and hung back to talk to a girl from the top class who was coming up alongside them. Louie found that she was walking on her own, and started to hurry, so that people would think that she had left Glenda behind, and not that Glenda had left her in front.

Part Two

Louie stood next to Glenda in Assembly, but there was no chance to talk because they were in the choir and everyone could see them, up at the front. There was no chance to ask questions in class, because Glenda was on the other side of the room. Once they had sat at the same table, but Miss Ward said they talked too much, so now Louie had to share with Wayne Hodges, who wore his snorkel jacket indoors and sat with the hood zipped up, so that he looked like a ship's ventilator. Glenda was over by the window with Sarah and Helen Tate who were twins and talked only to each other, and Joanne Smith who sucked her pigtails and never talked at all.

Louie sat staring at the two shifty eyes that were Wayne,

deep, deep inside his ventilator, and wondered what it would be like next term in Mrs Thomas's class, without Glenda. She would have to make another friend. She looked round the room to see who might do, but everybody had friends already. You could not go round saying to people, "Will you be my friend?" They would giggle and say "Why?" She looked at Wayne again. Being friends with Wayne would be like having a pet tortoise, and she had a pet tortoise. Half the time it wouldn't come out.

Miss Ward moved between the tables, looking at people's work.

"Now, Michael, that's not very clever, is it? Stop writing on your leg, Sarah. Wayne, take your coat off – how many more times? Yes, Glenda?"

"I've finished my card, Miss. Can I go down the lib'ry, Miss?"

"Library, not liberry," said Miss Ward. "Say it properly."

"Can I go down the *library*?" Glenda said, already half out of her seat. She always finished first, and she always ended the morning in the library, looking for a book to read, although she never seemed to find one. Louie watched her leave the room. In fifteen minutes the bell would ring. Glenda would rush home for lunch and not come back until it was time for afternoon lessons. Louie ate at school because her Mum was at work. At this rate she would never manage to speak to Glenda before home time, and then Glenda would be staying late for

Term 1　Unit 8

gymnastics, after school.

Louie had an idea, and hurried to finish her own work card.

"Can I go down the lib'ry, please, Miss?"

"Down *where*?"

"The lib'ry."

"*Library*," said Miss Ward. "How many more times? Library, not liberry. It's not a fruit. It does not grow on a liberry bush. Li-bra-ree."

"Can I?"

"All right. Off you go." Louie went. Miss Ward was still at it as she left. "Wayne, take your coat off. How many more times?"

"Here we go round the liberry bush, the liberry bush, the liberry bush," sang Louie, under her breath, as she went down the corridor.

Glenda, looking very learned, was sitting on the carpet in the library area, with books piled all round her. She was reading a comic. Louie took a book from the nearest shelf and sat down beside her.

"You got finished quickly," Glenda said, surprised. Louie usually finished everything last, because she sat and thought about things instead of writing.

"I wanted to talk to you," Louie said. "When are you moving? Have you got a new house, yet?"

"I told you. In the holidays. We're going to live at Tokesby."

"Near the sea?"

"That's right. My auntie lives there. We're going to have a bungalow. It won't cost as much as the house, so there'll be some money left over." Glenda always seemed to know how much things cost. If she didn't, she asked. "I might be able to have a pony."

Glenda had wanted a pony for years. Louie also wanted a

pony. She had once asked Mum about it.

"Where would we keep it?" said Mum. "Under the stairs?" Louie didn't ask again.

"Can I come and see your pony?" she said. "Sometimes?"

"I expect so," said Glenda.

"I'll come and see *you*, anyway," Louie said.

"I'll ask Mummy."

"I'll ask my Mum if you can come and stay," Louie said.

"My Mummy won't let me stay with people," Glenda said. "Not since I got the mumps off Julie Hodges after her party."

"We can write to each other."

"You write first," said Glenda.

"I'll write the same day you move," said Louie.

"Yes, well ... I haven't gone yet," Glenda said.

Chapter Three: *Going, going...*
Part Three

Glenda's house was full of tea chests on Sunday morning, and Glenda's mother made Louie and Glenda go and talk in the back garden while she ran about filling the tea chests with clothes and crockery, in padded sandwiches, making lists, and then taking everything out again and putting it somewhere else.

"You'd better be quick," said Glenda. "I ought to be helping."

"I had this idea," said Louie. "I saw this film yesterday, on telly."

"So did I," Glenda said. "Mummy says I can choose my own curtains in the new bungalow. And a lampshade to match. It won't half be funny, sleeping downstairs."

"Not if you haven't got an upstairs," Louie pointed out. "I meant the film about the spies. Is that the one you saw?"

"Yes, only it was dead boring, so I switched over to the racing."

"*Motor* racing?"

"No, horses, of course."

"Did you see that bit about leaving letters in a hollow tree on Hampstead Heath?"

"No, look" – Glenda sounded just like her mother, – "I can't stand around here all day, talking about old films." Louie moved quickly so that she stood between Glenda and the back door.

"There was this spy, see, and he knew people were opening his letters and that, so he stopped posting them and hid them in this tree, and then this other spy took his dog for a walk and got the letters out again, and nobody knew. I thought we could do that."

"We haven't got a dog," said Glenda. "Anyway, I'm moving on Thursday."

"I know you are. But you said you'd be coming into town on Saturdays, for shopping."

"I shan't see you," Glenda said, firmly. "We're coming in the afternoons."

"*I know*. You said. But we could have a dead letter box, too, like they did in the film. I could leave a message for you in the morning, and you could collect it in the afternoon and leave one for me."

Glenda began to look faintly interested. "Where'd you leave it?"

"In the library," Louie said.

"I don't belong to the library," said Glenda.

"You could join."

"I don't want to join."

"Well, you needn't, not if it's only to collect letters. You can just go in. Anyone can go in. It's free."

"It's on the rates," said Glenda, knowingly. "Mummy said. Look, where would you leave this letter, then?"

"I don't know. In a secret place," Louie said, wondering where she would find a secret place in the County Library, always full of people.

"But you only go to the library on Saturdays," said Glenda. "I'll be gone by next Saturday. I won't know where you've left it."

"I'll go in tomorrow, then," Louie said, recklessly, not at all sure that Mum would let her go into the city alone, "and I'll find a dead letter box and tell you about it before you go. Then you'll know where to look. All right?"

"All right," Glenda said. "But I might forget."

Part Four

The County Library stood between the Theatre Royal and City Hall, opposite the car park. At the bottom of the steps that led up to the entrance was a little shrubby tree growing inside a collar of brown cobble stones. This, thought Louie, could be the liberry bush. In spring there were clusters of pink flowers hanging from the branches but, unfortunately, no berries in winter; nothing you could make into liberry jam.

Louie had to go downstairs to reach the children's library, in the basement. The adult library was on ground level and

59

where the stairs went down there was a kind of balcony and a railing along the side where you could lean over and watch the people down below in the children's section. When she had finished choosing her books, Louie like to go back upstairs and lean over the railings, pretending that she was on the verandah of a house built onto a mountainside in wild foreign parts, or on the bridge of a star ship, gazing out over the universe, or in a skyscraper, in New York, or just enjoying the thought that, if she wanted to, she could spit on someone's head; but this morning there was no time for that. Mum had not been very pleased about her going to the city alone, and she had to be home by twelve o'clock. Also she had had to use most of that week's pocket money on the bus fare, as Mum would not let her walk so far by herself. She went straight down the stairs and began to look for somewhere to use as a dead letter box.

The children's library was disguised as a big living room, with pictures on the walls, and a carpet, and canvas bean bags, big enough to sit on, in case people got frightened by seeing so many books, and went away again without reading anything. No one could say you were rude if you sat reading in this living room, and it was not like a book shop where people grew suspicious if you stood around just looking, and didn't buy anything.

Louie stood around just looking. The first place she thought of was the card index, with all its little drawers, so long and narrow, that slid out silently when she pulled the handles. The cards, on their brass spindles, did not go all the way to the backs of the drawers. There was quite a big gap in some of them, where a letter would fit nicely and never be found except by someone who was looking for it. But as she watched, one of the librarians took out the A-L drawer and unscrewed the spindle. All she wanted to do was put some more cards in, but in so doing she found an old sweet wrapper that someone had hidden there, and crossly took it out. That might easily happen to a letter. Louie moved away.

She wondered if it would be possible to hide a letter behind one of the shelves, against the wall, but Glenda might forget where she was supposed to look, or get tired of searching. Someone might mistake it for rubbish and throw it away.

While she was examining the shelves Louie noticed that one very thin book had slipped behind the others. She took it out and looked at the author's name, so that she could put it back in the right place. It was called *The Windmill Children*, by Penelope Saltash. Louie had never heard of Penelope Saltash, so she looked inside. It did not seem to be a very popular book. There were no fingerprints in it, or dog-eared pages, but when she leafed through it, an old bus ticket fell out. She picked it up and looked at it to see if the numbers added up to seven, which was lucky. They came to twenty-three, which was neither here nor there. She looked at the date: 7 May, the day that she had date-stamped her arm. Perhaps that was lucky too. Then she looked at the last date on the front slip at the front of the book: 7 MAY 1977. All those sevens had to be lucky, but it was more than four years ago. No one had borrowed the book for four years. Perhaps no one would ever borrow it again. It was the perfect place to leave a dead letter – in the little pocket at the front, where the ticket went.

Even if someone picked it up and looked at it, they would never find a letter hidden there. It was the perfect dead letter box. Better than that, it was a dead letter book.

Daddy Fell into the Pond

Everyone grumbled. The sky was grey.
We had nothing to do and nothing to say.
We were nearing the end of a dismal day.
And there seemed to be nothing beyond,
    Then
        Daddy fell into the pond!

And everyone's face grew merry and bright,
And Timothy danced for sheer delight.
"Give me the camera, quick, oh quick!
He's crawling out of the duckweed!" Click!

Then the gardener suddenly slapped his knee,
And doubled up, shaking silently,
And the ducks all quacked as if they were daft,
And it sounded as if the old drake laughed.
Oh, there wasn't a thing that didn't respond
    When
        Daddy fell into the pond!

Alfred Noyes

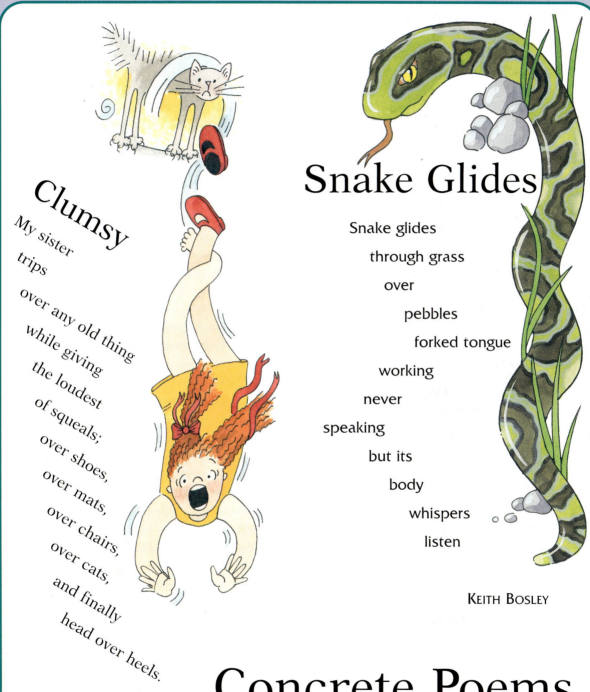

Clumsy

My sister
trips
over any old thing
while giving
the loudest
of squeals;
over shoes,
over mats,
over chairs,
over cats,
and finally
head over heels.

Max Fatchen

Snake Glides

Snake glides
through grass
over
pebbles
forked tongue
working
never
speaking
but its
body
whispers
listen

KEITH BOSLEY

Concrete Poems

The Blackbird

In the far corner,
Close by the swings,
Every morning
A blackbird sings.

His bill's so yellow,
His coat's so black,
That he makes a fellow
Whistle back.

Ann, my daughter,
Thinks that he
Sings for us two
Especially.

          Humbert Wolfe

Geraldine Giraffe

The
longest
ever
woolly
scarf
was
worn
by
Geraldine
Giraffe.
Around
her
neck
the
scarf
she
wound,
but
still
it
trailed
upon
the
ground.

          Colin West

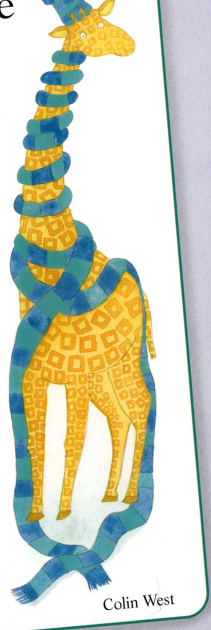

Somebody said that it Couldn't be Done

Somebody said that it couldn't be done –

But he, with a grin, replied

He'd not be the one to say it couldn't be done –

Leastways, not 'til he'd tried.

So he buckled right in, with a trace of a grin;

By golly, he went right to it.

He tackled The Thing That Couldn't Be Done

And he couldn't do it.

ANON

The evening gem shines like a rajah's punctual diamond astrap

I hear the whistle of the beautiful bird of prey the bird

I see far away the cathedral

Guillaume Apollinaire

65

Term 1 | Unit 9

Wordscapes

A boa-constrictor goes
gliding
all quietly
zig-
zag
zig-
zag
through the rough grass then
he sees
a young antelope...
He opens his great big jaws and swallows it
gallupps
it down
it goes
smaller and smaller till there's
left nothing

Lesley, aged 11

I go round and round.
I am the clock's
spring as they wind
me up tighter till
every last scrap's all
taken up turn the key
and there'll always
be enough to keep
you going...

Simon, aged 10

66

Excited

I
s
l
i
d
e
d
o
w
n
t
h
e
b
a
n
n
i
s
t
e
r
s

Mum cut my hair. I hated that. First the front and then the back. It wasn't fair. I liked it long. I told her so, but she said, 'No!' I begged and cried to change her mind. Well now it's short, it looks O.K. Just wait till next year, I'd always say, 'I'll keep it long. Just you'd see.' — only I wished mum would leave it be.

Haircuts

Cam Phung Te (15)
St John Wall School,
Handsworth,
Birmingham

I do not have breakfast because I'm too
EXCITED

My arms SHAKE and SHAKE and SHAKE

My tummy TICKLES and TICKLES

OPEN IT!

can't wait!

Mark Powell (7)
Nunnery Wood Primary School, Worcester

| Term 1 | Unit 10 |

Nelson Mandela

by Richard Killeen

Part One: The young Nelson

Nelson Mandela was born on 18 July 1918. He was the son of a royal chief in Transkei, a part of South Africa. When he was only nine years old, Nelson's father died. He was sent to live with the head chief of his people, the Thembu. This man adopted Nelson as his own son.

Nelson was brought up in the traditional way of the Thembu people. He learned old customs which had been passed on from parents to children for hundreds of years. But he also got a good modern education. When Nelson was sixteen he was sent to boarding school. Then when he was twenty-one he went to Fort Hare University to study for a degree.

However, Nelson did not finish his degree at Fort Hare. He left in his third year and headed to the great city of Johannesburg. There were gold mines and diamond mines near the city which had made South Africa rich. But the white people kept all the wealth and power for themselves. White people ran South Africa, yet most of the people in the country were black and had almost nothing.

▲ Johannesburg is the biggest and richest city in South Africa.

Nelson soon met an estate agent called Walter Sisulu, who got him a job in a law firm. This gave Nelson enough money to continue his degree, which he

◄ Nelson in the village where he grew up. He lived in a hut.

finished in 1942. After this, Nelson decided to become a **lawyer**, so he began to study law at the University of Witswatersrand in Johannesburg. Nelson continued to work at the law firm while studying.

In 1945, Nelson married his first wife Evelyn. Their first child was born in 1946. He was called Thembi.

Part Two: The ANC and apartheid

Nelson's best friend at university was Oliver Tambo, who was another black law student. In 1944, Nelson and Oliver helped to start a group called the Youth League. This was part of an older organization called the African National Congress (ANC), which was working to get better treatment for black people in South Africa. By 1949, Nelson and the Youth League had taken control of the ANC.

However by then, life for blacks in South Africa had got worse because the **government** wanted to separate black people and white people completely. Its word for this was **apartheid** (pronounced "a-par-tide").

Meanwhile, Nelson's law studies were going badly because he was spending so much time working for the ANC. But he eventually became a lawyer in 1951. A year later, Nelson and Oliver Tambo set up the first-ever black law practice in Johannesburg. By now, Nelson and Evelyn had a second son.

▲ Nelson Mandela addressing a meeting.

▼ An apartheid sign at the beach. Black people were not allowed on this beach.

Term 1 | Unit 10

Nelson and Oliver Tambo help plan the Youth League.

Nelson and the other ANC leaders hated apartheid because it meant that blacks could not live in certain areas, could not vote, and could not use the same services as white people. So they organized **strikes**, **boycotts** and other **protests**. They broke apartheid laws and held noisy public meetings all over the country. The police often attacked them and there was a lot of violence. In 1952, Nelson was put in charge of these public protests for all of South Africa. He also became head of the ANC in Transvaal, the rich area which included Johannesburg.

Then the government arrested Nelson because he was a danger to its rule. It used one of the worst apartheid laws against him and **"banned"** him. This meant that Nelson could not attend any public meetings, could only meet one person at a time, and was watched closely by the police the whole time. Nelson was a prisoner in his own home.

Nelson in the office of his law practice.

Part Three: Long years in jail

On 7 November 1962, Nelson was found guilty of leaving South Africa without a passport. He was sent to jail for five years. First he went to a prison in Pretoria, then to Robben Island.

Apartheid made life very hard for black people in South Africa.

Robben Island Prison can be seen from the beaches near Cape Town. No one has ever escaped from it to this day. Nelson was not long there when he was brought back to Pretoria to be accused of leading the ANC's army. He was found guilty again and might have been hanged, but the judge sent him back to Robben Island – this time for life. Nelson was forty-six years old.

Back at Robben Island, Nelson was put in a tiny cell where he was kept for sixteen hours each day. He was allowed very little contact with Winnie (his second wife) and his family. He could only write and receive one letter every six months.

A protest against apartheid.

Every day, Nelson had to get up at 5 am. By 7 am, he was at work. This meant breaking stones, or gathering seaweed on the shore, or working with a pickaxe in a stone quarry. At noon,

70

lunch came in a big drum for the prisoners to eat. It was poor food and tasted bad. Then there was more work until the middle of the afternoon.

By 4 pm Nelson was back in his cell. He was supposed to be in bed by 8 pm, but as the years went by, he was sometimes allowed to stay up late to read, which he loved. Nelson spent nearly twenty years like this on Robben Island, over 7,000 days and 7,000 nights. Every day was the same.

Nelson stayed on Robben Island until 1982, when he was moved to Pollsmoor Prison near Cape Town. By now Nelson was the most famous prisoner in the world.

At the same time, other countries were changing their opinion about South Africa. Its government was unpopular all over the world because of apartheid. In South Africa the black **townships** were rising up in anger. The words on everyone's lips were: "Free Nelson Mandela."

A new government, under **President** F. W. de Klerk, decided that the only way to solve South Africa's problems was to release Nelson from prison.

The judge passes sentence on Nelson.

Nelson in his cell.

Glossary

African National Congress (ANC) The group who have worked to get the same rights for black people as white people in South Africa.

apartheid The system that completely separated black people from white people.

banned Under the system of apartheid, not allowed to attend public meetings, meet more than one person at a time or talk to another banned person.

boycotts Refusals to buy certain goods or use certain services. Boycotts can be used to make the people who make goods or provide services lose money.

democratic Where there are equal rights for all the people in a country. In a democracy, every adult man and woman can say who they want to be their leader.

elections The choosing of the leaders of a country.

government The group of people who rule a country.

71

Term 1 | **Unit 10**

lawyer A person who is an expert in the law.
massacre The violent killing of a large number of people.
multi-racial Including many races.
passport A document that gives permission to travel abroad.
president The leader of a country which is a republic.
protest To object strongly.
rally A gathering together of people in order to protest against something.
strikes Stopping work until certain demands have been met.
townships Under apartheid, poor areas where blacks were forced to live.
Zulu One of the principal black peoples in South Africa, mainly found in Natal and the Eastern Cape.

Books to read

Long Walk to Freedom by Nelson Mandela, (Little Brown, 1994)

Mandela for Beginners by Tony Pinchuck, (Icon Books, 1994)

South Africa: A Modern History, by T.R.H. Davenport, 4th edition (Macmillan, 1991)

Date chart

1918	Nelson Mandela is born in Transkei on 18 July.
1934	Becomes a boarder in Healdtown High School.
1939	Enters Fort Hare University College, in Ciskei.
1941	Goes to Johannesburg and works in a law office.
1942	Starts to study law at Witswatersrand University.
1944	Co-founder of the Youth League of the ANC.
1945	Marries Evelyn Ntoko Mase.
1946	Birth of Nelson and Evelyn's first child, Thembi.
1948	National Party government establishes system of apartheid.
1949	Youth League takes over the ANC.
1951	Qualifies as a lawyer.
1952	Founds the first black law partnership with Oliver Tambo. Banned by the government under apartheid laws.
1955	Founder member of the Congress Alliance.
1956	One of the defendants in the Treason Trial.
1958	Second marriage, to Winnie Madikezela.
1960	Sharpeville massacre.
1962	Arrested for leaving South Africa without a passport. Spends next twenty-eight years in jail.
1990	Released from prison on 11 February.
1994	Elected President of South Africa on 27 April.

▲ Nelson breaking stones in the prison quarry.

Term 1 | Unit 11

Blitz

by Robert Westall

Part One

As soon as the bombing of Tyneside got bad, the timber-yards down by the river moved their wood piles out into the open fields.

Albert Bowdon and I were the first to find them, on Lawson's Farm. We were cycling around as always, looking for war souvenirs and trouble.

Lawson's was a favourite calling-stop, right out beyond the edge of town. It had been sold to a house builder just before war broke out, but the farm-buildings still stood, a marvellous place for the gangs to practise street-fighting each other, shinning up the ladders into the haylofts. Though no matter how hard you machine-gunned the enemy with your wooden tommy-gun, no matter how hard you shouted "*Wa-wa-wa-wa*!" he would never admit to being dead. Just say you'd been narrowly missed and go on fighting.

Lawson's was deserted at night because it was a long walk from town, and the gangs usually saved it for weekends. But, looking through Lawson's wildly overgrown hedge, we saw a new city grown up like mushrooms overnight. A city of many streets, and pale gold and white buildings. A city of flat roofs, which gave it an eastern look, like something in the background of a Christmas crib; which was why we called it the Ruined City of Kor.

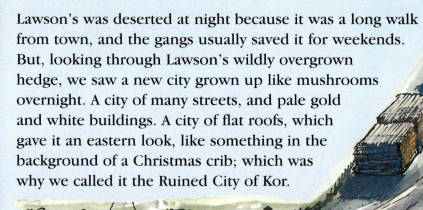

73

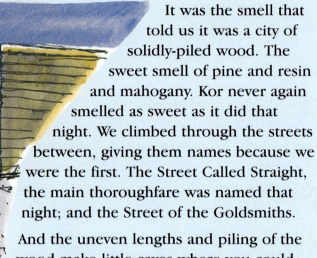

It was the smell that told us it was a city of solidly-piled wood. The sweet smell of pine and resin and mahogany. Kor never again smelled as sweet as it did that night. We climbed through the streets between, giving them names because we were the first. The Street Called Straight, the main thoroughfare was named that night; and the Street of the Goldsmiths.

And the uneven lengths and piling of the wood make little caves where you could hide and plot, or keep dry in the rain, or even, greatly daring, light camp-fires.

Later, there was a sidestreet of caves used by lads who'd got taken short or couldn't be bothered to walk home, and that got called Rotten Row. People brought chalk and paint, and labelled the streets with their names in big scrawling letters.

Of course it was a nuisance when men came with lorries during the day, when we were at school, and took our buildings away, or built new ones. But they were never there when we were, not even a night-watchman; even the old gaffers had gone for war work.

There were two games we played in the Ruined City of Kor, besides street-fighting. If several gangs got together, you had "Breakout from Stalag Luft VI" which was a marvellous chase over the piles and the long planks we laid between them, miles above the ground.

But even if there were only two of you, you could still play "Paratroops". From the tallest pile, a plank sloped down at forty-five degrees, a plank smoothed over the weeks by a hundred bums – and one or two tin trays, when the plank was new and full of splinters. But what did a few splinters in your bum matter? Britain stood alone; it was a time for courage.
You whizzed down the plank at breathtaking speed, pushed up

your kid's tin hat when it fell over your eyes, and machine-gunned everything in sight in a mad rage.

* * *

(Part Two)

Normally, in raids, I was down our shelter, with nothing to stare at but a pile of sandbags our dog had peed on more often than I care to remember. But now I could see the whole town spread out before me. The gasworks, the masts and funnels of the ships in the river.

"There they go," yelled Albert. And I caught a fleeting glimpse of a handful of long thin shapes streaking over the works chimneys down by the river. "Keeping low so the guns can't get them."

"If the guns don't get them the fighters will…"

"Hurricanes from Usworth and Spitfires from Acklington," we chorused together, with great satisfaction. "Gonna be a dogfight."

And then we began to hear the machine-guns up in the clouds; they sounded like a boy running a stick along a row of iron railings. Only lots of boys, and lots of railings.

"Goin' out for a look," said Albert.

But he never did. Because at that moment we heard the engines. Howling, screaming. Coming straight at us like the end of the world. Louder and louder and louder 'til it couldn't possibly get any louder. Only it did.

The noise pressed you flat like a huge hand. And kept on pressing. Just when I had given up all hope, and Albert's mouth kept opening and shutting and no sound came out, a great fat Jerry plane, a Heinkel, whizzed into view, all pale-blue belly and the machine-gun underneath sparking away like a firework.

And then it was just a dwindling speck, and the stink from its smoking exhausts.

"There was a British fighter after that Jerry," said Albert. "The Jerry was shooting at it."

"Where is it then?" I said.

75

It was then we heard the crash. It was like the night me mam pulled the Welsh dresser over, trying to hang up the Christmas decorations, only worse.

Then silence. Only a dog barking in the distance.

"Something's got shot down," said Albert.

"Wasn't the Jerry."

"Oh God."

We sort of screwed up, like when the opposing team score the winning goal. It was an awful feeling.

"Shall we go and look?"

"He might be trapped... He might be..."

It was unsayable. But we went.

It took a long time to search Ruined Kor. Expecting at every corner...

(Part Three)

But what we found was a surprisingly long way off. A new row of furrows in the field beyond Kor, as if a farmer with six ploughs joined together had...

And a gap in the hedge that something had vanished through. Something definitely British, because a lump of the tail had fallen off, and lay with red, white and blue on it.

We tiptoed through the gap.

It looked as big as a house.

"Spitfire."

"Hurricane, you idiot. Can't you tell a Spitfire from a Hurricane yet?"

"It's not badly damaged. Just a bit bent."

I shook my head. "It'll never fly again. It looks ... broke."

The tail was up in the air; the engine dug right into the ground, and the propeller bent into horseshoe shapes.

"Where's the pilot?"

"He might have baled out," suggested Albert, hopefully.

"What? At that height? His parachute would never have opened. Reckon he's trapped inside. We'd better have a look."

"Keep well back," said Albert. "There's a terrible smell of petrol. I saw petrol take fire once..."

There was no point in mocking him. I was so scared my own legs wouldn't stop shaking. But it was me that went a yard in front.

The cockpit canopy was closed. Inside, from a distance, there was no sign of any pilot.

"Baled out. Told ya," said Albert.

"With the canopy closed?"

"The crash could've closed it, stupid."

"I'm going to have a look."

I don't think I would have done if I'd thought there was anybody inside. I edged up on the wing, frightened that my steel toe and heel caps would strike a spark from something. The smell of petrol was asphyxiating.

He was inside.

Bent up double, with only the back of his helmet showing. And there was a great tear in the side of the helmet, with leather and stuffing ... and blood showing through.

"He's a dead 'un," said Albert, six inches behind my ear. I hadn't even heard him come – he was wearing gym-shoes. "Look at that blood."

I felt sick. The only dead thing I'd ever seen was the maggot-

77

laden corpse of a cat in the ruins of Billing's Mill.

"Let's go an' fetch the police," said Albert. "They deal with dead 'uns."

I was just edging carefully back down the wing, when a flicker of movement in the corner of my eye made me jump.

(Part Four)

The dead 'un was sitting up.

The dead 'un was looking at me with two bright blue eyes.

The dead 'un grinned at me. Made a little "hello" gesture with his gloved hand. My terror turned to rage. I was so angry with him because he wasn't dead. So I hammered on the closed canopy and shouted, "Open up, open up!" like a policeman.

His hand went up, and he undid a catch and pushed the canopy back, where it locked open.

"Hi, kids." He sounded American, or at least Canadian.

"Boy, have I got a headache! Haven't got a fag, have you?"

I didn't think. I had a fag and a half, in an old tobacco tin, that I'd pinched from my father's cigarette case. We sometimes came to Ruined Kor to smoke, in secret. And now I got it out. I mean, the RAF were our heroes, the Brylcreem Boys...

Albert gave one look at my box of matches and fled. Screaming about petrol.

It was then that I realised the dead 'un mightn't be dead, but he was in a pretty queer way. That bullet in the head must have driven him mad; his brain was not working right...

"Come on," I shouted. "Get out. You can't stay here."

He just grinned lazily again. "What's the hurry, kid? It's a lovely evening. Let's take it easy."

I looked at where the engine was. The engine-covers had crumpled up and I could see the engine. And feel it. It was so hot it was practically giving my bare knees a sunburn.

As I watched, some liquid dripped on to it and vaporised into a puff of white smoke. Then a little shower of electrical sparks...

I ran like hell. I didn't stop running for fifty yards, I was so terrified the plane was going to blow up.

We stood and watched him from a safe distance. We saw the heat-shimmer rising from the engine, the petrol oozing dark from the tank in the fuselage behind his head.

And he went on smiling at us, waving to us.

"Like he's on his holidays," whispered Albert.

I just wanted to run away. The idea of seeing him smiling one minute, then frizzling up like a moth in a candle-flame the next...

Then I had a brainwave. I took out my tobacco tin and waved the whole cigarette at him. Greatly daring, edging towards him, at a distance of thirty yards, I lit up the half-fag and blew a luxurious smoke-ring in the still evening air.

It worked. He bellowed, "For God's sake, kids," and began to heave himself out of the cockpit with a big grimace.

The first time it didn't work. The second time he managed to remember to undo his parachute and safety-harness.

Then he was weaving slowly across the grass towards us, like the town drunk. Snatched the fag off me, cupped his hands round mine, which were shaking so much I could hardly strike a match, took a big drag, and fell flat on his back, and lay there laughing up at us and blowing much better smoke rings than mine, and groaning what a headache he had.

It took fire when we were halfway back. All we could do was watch it burn. It must have been one of the earliest Hurricanes, with wooden wings as well as a wood-and-fabric body. It burnt fast; within half an hour there was just the engine and the tyreless wheels, and the machine-guns and a blackened tangle of wires, and a lot of white ash, the shape the wings had been.

All too hot to grab as souvenirs.

The Iron Woman

by Ted Hughes

The Iron Woman
A sequel to The Iron Man

The Iron Woman has come to take revenge on mankind for its thoughtless polluting of the seas, lakes and rivers. Her first target for destruction is the waste-disposal factory where Lucy's dad and most of the men in the town are employed. Lucy understands the Iron Woman's rage and she too wants to save the water creatures from their painful deaths. But she also wants to save her dad. She needs help of an extraordinary kind, and who best to ask it of but Hogarth and the Iron Man …?

Full of the power and fantastic imagery of the acclaimed modern classic The Iron Man, *this new tale by the Poet Laureate is a passionate and brilliant cry against the relentless pollution of the Earth's waterways through the dumping of industrial waste.*

"*Like* The Iron Man, *this is a superb modern myth.*"
Independent

Chapter One (Part One)

School was over and the Easter holidays had begun. Lucy was walking home, between the reed banks, along the marsh road, when it started to happen. She had just come to the small bridge, where the road goes over the deep drain. She called this Otterfeast Bridge, because once she had seen an otter on the edge of it, over the black water, eating an eel.

That had been three years before. But she still felt excitement whenever she came to this part of the road, and she always looked ahead eagerly, towards the bridge.

Today, as usual, the bridge was empty. As she crossed over it, she looked between the rails, into the black water. She always did this, just in case there might be an otter down there, in the water, looking up at her, or maybe swimming beneath at that very moment.

And today, there was something. But what was it, down there in the water? She leaned over the rail and peered.

Something deep in the dark water, something white, kept twisting. A fish?

Suddenly she knew. It was an eel – behaving in the strangest way. At first, she thought it must be two eels, fighting. But no, it was just one eel. It knotted itself and unknotted. Then it swam quickly round in circles, corkscrewing over and over as it went. At one point, its tail flipped right out of the water. Then it was writhing down into the mud, setting a grey cloud drifting. Then it was up at the surface again, bobbing its head into the air. She saw its beaky face, then its little mouth opening. She saw the pale inside of its mouth.

Then it was writhing and tumbling in a knot. Quite a small eel, only a foot long.

As it danced its squirming, circling, darting dance, it was drifting along in the current of the drain. Soon she lost sight of it under the water shine. Then, twenty yards downstream, she saw its head bob up again. Then a swirl and it vanished. Then up again, bob, bob, bob.

What was wrong with it? Seeing its peculiar head bobbing up like that, and its little mouth opening, she had felt a painful twist somewhere in her middle. She had wanted to scoop the eel up and help it. It needed help. Something was wrong with it.

At that moment, staring along the dimpled shine of the drain where it curved away among the tall reeds, she felt something else.

At first, she had no idea what made her head go dizzy and her feet stagger. She gripped the bridge rail and braced her feet apart. She thought she had felt the rail itself give her hand a jolt.

What was it?

"Garronk! Garronk! Garraaaaaark!"

The floppy, untidy shape of a heron was scrambling straight up out of the reed beds. It did not flap away in stately slow motion, like an ordinary heron. It flailed and hoisted itself up, exactly as if it were bounding up an invisible spiral stair. Then, from a great height, it tumbled away towards the sea beyond the marsh. Something had scared it badly. But what? Something in the marsh had frightened it. And seeing the heron so frightened frightened Lucy.

The marsh was always a lonely place. Now she felt the loneliness. As she stood there, looking up, the whole bluish and pinky sky of soft cloud moved slowly. She looked again along the drain, where the reeds leaned all one way, bowing gently in the light wind. The eel was no longer to be seen. Was it still writhing and bobbing its head up, as the slow flow carried it away through the marsh? She looked down into the drain, under the bridge. The black water moved silently, crumpling and twirling little whorls of light.

Then it came again. Beneath her feet the bridge road jumped and the rail jarred her hand. At the same moment, the water surface of the drain was blurred by a sudden mesh of tiny ripples all over it.

An earthquake! It must be an earthquake.

A completely new kind of fear gripped Lucy. For a few seconds she did not dare to move. The thought of the bridge collapsing and dropping her into the drain with its writhing eels was bad enough. But the thought of the marsh itself opening a great crack, and herself and all the water and mud and eels and reeds pouring into bottomless black, maybe right into the middle of the earth, was worse. She felt her toes curling like claws and the soles of her feet prickling with electricity.

Quickly then she began to walk – but it was like walking on a bouncy narrow plank between skyscrapers. She lifted each foot carefully and set it down firmly and yet gently. As fast as she dared, and yet quite slow. But soon – she couldn't help it – she started running. What if that earthquake shock had brought the ceiling down on her mother? Or even shaken the village flat, like dominoes? And what if some great towering piece of machinery, at the factory, had toppled on to her father?

And then, as she ran, it came again, pitching her off balance, so that her left foot hit her right calf and down she went. As she lay there, flat and winded, it came again. This time, the road seemed to hit her chest and stomach, a strong, hard thump. Then another. And each time, she saw the road gravel under her face jump slightly. And it was then, as she lay there, that she heard the weirdest sound. Nothing like any bird she had ever heard. It came from out of the marsh behind her. It was a long wailing cry, like a fire-engine siren. She jumped up and began to run blindly.

(Part Two)

Already the head was out. It still didn't look much like a head – simply a gigantic black lump, crowned with reeds and streaming with mud. But the mouth was clear, and after that first wailing cry the lips moved slowly, like a crab's, spitting out mud and roots.

83

Half an hour passed before the lump moved again. As it moved, the reeds away to either side of it bulged upwards and heaved, and the black watery mud streamed through them. The mouth opened and a long booming groan came out of it, as the head hoisted clear. Another groan became a wailing roar. A seagull blowing across the marsh like a paper scrap veered wildly upwards as the streaming shape reared in front of it, like a sudden wall of cliff, pouring cataracts of black mud and clotted, rooty lumps of reeds where grass snakes squirmed and water voles flailed their forepaws, blinking their eyes and squealing as they fell.

The black shape was the size of two or three elephants. It looked like a hippopotamus-headed, gigantic dinosaur, dragging itself on all fours up out of a prehistoric tar pit. But now, still like a dinosaur, it sat upright. And all at once it looked human – immense but human. Great hands clawed at the head, flinging away squatches of muddy reeds. Then, amid gurglings and suckings, and with a groaning wail, the thing stood erect. A truly colossal, man-shaped statue of black mud, raking itself and groaning, towered over the lonely marsh.

* * *

When she reached home, Lucy found everything as usual. Her mother had felt no jolts or tremors. She had no idea what her daughter was talking about. Later that evening, when her father came home, he told of the bad smash there had been on the marsh road. A birdwatcher had lost control of his car and gone off the road. He'd gone off his head, too. He had come into the village post office, jabbering all kinds of madness. Police had driven him back into town, where he was staying. Car a total wreck. Funniest thing – every speck of paint was gone off it. And the road was one mess. It looked as if he'd hit the sound barrier. Bit of a mystery.

Listening to this, Lucy wondered what kind of madness the birdwatcher had been jabbering. Maybe those shocks had jounced him off the road and out of his wits at the same moment. She kept remembering the horrible wailing cry. What was going on in the marsh? As she sat there at the table, she watched her arms go goose-pimpled.

Then she began to think about the twisting eel.

Chapter Four (Part Three)

Next morning Hogarth and Lucy were up early. They planned what they were going to do. Lucy left a note for her parents:

"When the TV people come to interview me, tell them I'll be at the factory gate at 12 o'clock sharp."

Soon they were climbing up towards the woods behind the town. They scrambled over a brambly bank and were among the trees.

"Look!" hissed Hogarth. He was pointing at the ground. Lucy gazed at the deep, huge prints in the soft mould. "The Iron Man. No toes, you see. Your Iron Woman has toes."

The track led up through the woods to the field above, that climbed to a hilltop. And there they were, sitting facing each other, two colossal figures, their backs to the boles of great cedars that grew among the ancient stones on the hill's very crown.

"We're here," yelled Lucy, and ran towards them. "It's us."

The immense heads turned.

"Iron Man!" shouted Hogarth. "I knew you'd make it."

Lucy told them everything that had happened: the fight in the offices, the journalists, the television crew coming today. The

85

enormous eyes glowed. The Iron Man's glowed amber. The Iron Woman's glowed black. But not a sound came out of either of them.

"Why don't you come and let the TV people see you?" cried Hogarth. "You could give them the screams, on television. Then they'd have to believe. Everything would have to change."

"Oh yes, you must come," cried Lucy. "Just the sight of you –"

A humming started up within the Iron Woman. "Nothing would change," came the deep, rumbling, gentle voice.

Lucy and Hogarth stared at her. What did that mean? Weren't the screams going to change everybody? And the sight of the Iron Woman, as a giant scream-transmitter – wouldn't that change everything?

"It needs something more," said the great voice, up through their shoe-soles.

Hogarth and Lucy were baffled. How could there be anything more?

"So what do we do?" asked Hogarth.

The rumbling started again. And the voice came again: "Do?" Then again, louder: "*Do*?" Then, with a roar: "DO?"

And Lucy and Hogarth almost fell over backwards as the Iron Woman, in one terrific heave, got to her feet. Branches were torn off as she rose erect among the cedars. And her arms rose slowly above her head. Her fists clenched and unclenched, shooting her fingers out straight. Then clenched again. She lifted one foot, her knee came up, then:

BOOM!

Her foot crashed down. The whole hilltop shook and the sound echoed through her great iron body as if it were a drum. Again, her other foot came up – and down:

86

BOOM!

Ripping the boughs aside, her fists clenching and unclenching, her feet rising and falling, Iron Woman had begun to dance. There in the copse, in a shower of twigs, pine cones, pine needles and small branches, she revolved in her huge stamping dance, in front of the Iron Man whose eyes glowed bright gold. And she sang, in that deep, groaning, thundering voice of hers: "Destroy the ignorant ones. Nothing can change them. Destroy them."

She went on repeating that over and over, in time to her pounding footfalls, as she turned round and round. Lucy hid her mouth behind her clenched fists. The Iron Woman was terrifying. She was overwhelming. She was tremendous.

"Give them a chance," Lucy screamed. "Let's see what they say today. They might have changed already."

She just yelled it out at the top of her voice. Her father was one of the ignorant ones, according to the Iron Woman. But it was no good. The giant dancer's eyes were glowing a dark red. She stamped each foot down as if she wanted to shatter the whole leg.

"Nothing will change. Only their words change. They will never change. Only their words change. Only their words only their words only their words ..."

Then her voice became simply a roar. And now it seemed to Hogarth that inside her roar he could hear the scream, the wailing and the crying of all the creatures, roaring out over the woods. And again he began to see the faces, large, small, tiny – the wide mouths and the terrible eyes of the SCREAM.

87

Scheherezade

By Stephen Corrin

There was once a King of Persia named Shahryar who was most devoted to his beautiful Queen. He thought she was a most faithful and loyal wife to him. She, however, only pretended to be devoted to him. One day Shahryar's brother, who used to go hunting with him, felt ill and stayed behind in the palace while the King was away. Through the window of his room he was horrified to see the Queen unveil her face in the presence of the courtiers. Now you must understand that in the Persia of those days a woman was strictly forbidden to do this and, besides, the King had expressly instructed her not to leave her rooms.

The King's brother told the King and the King realized that he had been deceived by the wife whom he had always trusted. He ordered her to be executed immediately, while he himself shut himself up in a room and refused to eat or drink for several days. At last his brother persuaded him to come out and resume his royal duties. But his fury over what had happened remained as great as ever and he made a fearsome vow, in the name of Allah, that whatever new queen he might marry should be executed the morning after the wedding. By doing this he thought he would calm his anger and at the same time avenge himself on all wives for what his own wife had done to him. He decided to keep on re-marrying and have every one of his queens executed after the marriage.

And that is what happened; and it went on for many months and every person who had a daughter of marriageable age tried to find ways and means of sending her away to a safe hiding place.

Now King Shahryar's prime minister, the Grand Vizier as he was called, had two beautiful daughters of his own, Scheherezade and Dinarzade. Scheherezade was a most unusual girl, extremely learned, incredibly beautiful and full of good common sense. She knew that one day, sooner or later, she would be compelled to become the King's wife, but in her wise and lovely head she thought of a plan that would save not only herself but all the other Persian girls whose lot it might be to become Shahryar's wife.

One day the Grand Vizier returned from the palace and told his daughters the dread news that the King had decided that Scheherezade was to be his next Queen. But Scheherezade was quite prepared for this and said, "Honoured father, let us do as the King wishes. Have trust in me and one day you will see an end to this monstrous cruelty."

When the Grand Vizier saw how firm his daughter was in her resolve, he gave way. Scheherezade put on her bridal garments. She looked so enchanting that her attendants wept to think that so magnificent a creature was walking straight to her death.

Then Scheherezade took her sister, Dinarzade, into a room by themselves and said to her, "You, dear sister, must play an important part in the plan I have devised to save myself and you and all the young women of Persia." Dinarzade looked at her in great astonishment. Scheherezade continued, "You know how much you have enjoyed the stories I have so often told you. Well, before I am to be put to death, I shall ask the King as a special favour, to allow you to come and listen to just one more story in his presence. So when I send for you, you must come to the palace."

"Yes, dear sister," replied Dinarzade, her eyes filled with tears, "of course I shall come."

After the wedding the new Queen said to her husband, "When a prisoner is condemned to death, he is allowed one last request. As I am to die tomorrow morning, may I, as my final wish on

this earth, say goodbye to my sister?" Her request was granted and Dinarzade was soon at her sister's side in the palace. She wept bitterly as she said her farewell and Scheherezade could see that even the King looked somewhat sorrowful at the scene. She cleverly took advantage of this softening in his mood and asked him whether she might be allowed to tell her sister a favourite story that she had often told her in the past. King Shahryar, it so happened, was also very fond of listening to stories and so he willingly consented.

And now Scheherezade, in her lovely low voice, began to tell a most interesting story. King Shahryar listened, quite relaxed at first, but more attentively as the story got more and more exciting. But when she got to the most breathlessly exciting part she paused and said to her sister, "I fear, dear Dinarzade, that you must leave now, for His Majesty is tired and wishes to retire to his bed."

"No, please continue," said the King.

"There is much more to come," replied Scheherezade. "I could continue tomorrow if my life were spared for one more day."

"Very well," said the King a trifle impatiently, and so Dinarzade went home but promised to come back the next day. The King thought to himself, "There is no need to have her executed tomorrow, I can always wait another day, but I must hear the end of that story whatever happens." But he was reckoning without Scheherezade's amazing gift for telling stories and, what was more important, her knack of breaking off just at the most exciting or puzzling point of the story. The Grand Vizier, you may well imagine, was astonished when he discovered that his daughter's execution had been postponed.

So the next day Dinarzade arrived at the palace and King Shahryar ordered Scheherezade to continue her story and she did, with a vengeance! She went on and on, increasing the excitement and the thrills so that when it finally came to an end the King asked her to tell another story! He was thinking to

himself, "First let me hear her tell another exciting tale, there is no great hurry for her execution."

Now Scheherezade knew more than a thousand stories and she told them to the King night after night but always breaking off at the most intriguing part and leaving her listener in such a state of suspense that he kept asking for more.

After a thousand and one nights had passed in this way, Scheherezade, instead of starting a new story, turned to the King and said, "It seems, Your Majesty, that you have not been displeased with my stories. If I have found favour in Your Majesty's eyes, may I now ask for some reward?" The King felt somewhat ashamed, for it was the custom of Persian monarchs always to reward even their humblest subjects for any small service, and yet he had given nothing, nothing at all to his own Queen!

Scheherezade took advantage of his silence to continue. "You once made a most dreadful vow," she said, "but Allah would certainly not ask from you that you should fulfil so evil a pledge."

The King had listened attentively, just as he had listened to her stories and he felt a deep guilt in his heart.

"My Queen," he began, "I now know that I have been too hasty and that I should never have made that evil vow." And he immediately caused it to be proclaimed from his palace that he had forsaken his terrible vow and praised his Queen Scheherezade as the most excellent of women and the most devoted of wives.

The people were relieved and overjoyed at this tremendous change in the King's mood and in gratitude to their wonderful Queen they renamed their capital city after her, for the name Scheherezade itself means Saviour of the City: the name given to her at birth proved truly prophetic! And the tales she told have come down to us as *The Arabian Nights* or, sometimes, *The Thousand and One Nights*.

Bedd Gelert

By Stephen Corrin

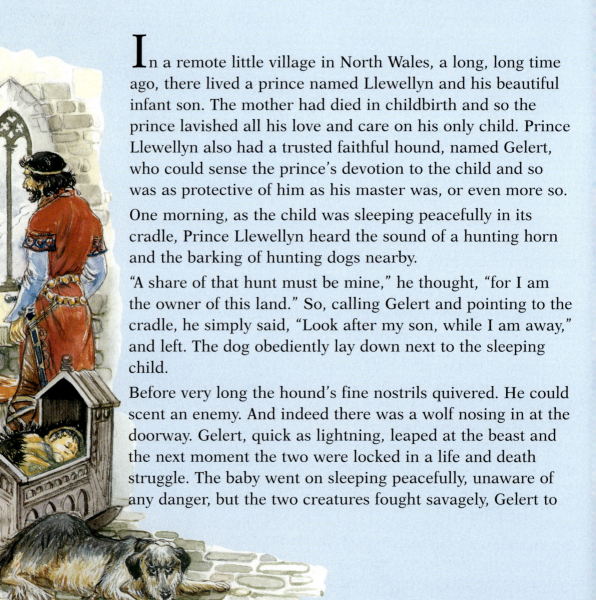

In a remote little village in North Wales, a long, long time ago, there lived a prince named Llewellyn and his beautiful infant son. The mother had died in childbirth and so the prince lavished all his love and care on his only child. Prince Llewellyn also had a trusted faithful hound, named Gelert, who could sense the prince's devotion to the child and so was as protective of him as his master was, or even more so.

One morning, as the child was sleeping peacefully in its cradle, Prince Llewellyn heard the sound of a hunting horn and the barking of hunting dogs nearby.

"A share of that hunt must be mine," he thought, "for I am the owner of this land." So, calling Gelert and pointing to the cradle, he simply said, "Look after my son, while I am away," and left. The dog obediently lay down next to the sleeping child.

Before very long the hound's fine nostrils quivered. He could scent an enemy. And indeed there was a wolf nosing in at the doorway. Gelert, quick as lightning, leaped at the beast and the next moment the two were locked in a life and death struggle. The baby went on sleeping peacefully, unaware of any danger, but the two creatures fought savagely, Gelert to

protect the infant and the wolf to devour it, for it was ravenously hungry after days of roaming the hills and forests.

As they fought, blood splattered all over the walls and floor, and the wolf, getting nearer the scent of its intended prey, pushed the brave dog closer to the cradle. Panting furiously, the wolf thrust Gelert right at its base and overturned it, bespattering the coverlets with blood. Miraculously, the baby continued to sleep soundly, ignorant of the mortal danger it was in and undisturbed by the ferocious growling and snarling of the two combatants. But Gelert, now sensing the imminent danger to his ward, fought back, drove his opponent to the opposite corner and sank his teeth into the wolf's throat. With a last dying snarl the wolf fell back and drew its last breath.

The faithful Gelert lay down, triumphant but exhausted, next to the sleeping child, now untidily covered by blood-stained blankets and coverlets.

About half an hour later Prince Llewellyn returned from his hunt and Gelert dragged himself to his feet and went to meet him. The prince was horrified at the sight that met his eyes, but most of all by the blood on Gelert's mouth and feet. He did not see the wolf's body in the far corner and he could only think that Gelert had killed the child.

He drew his sword and in a movement of blind fury he plunged it into the heart of his faithful hound. The dog gave a piteous and puzzled look up at his beloved master and sank back dead with a final wailing breath.

And then the prince heard a lusty cry from the direction of the cradle. He picked up the child and found it safe and sound, and then his eye fell on the torn and bloody carcass of the wolf in the corner. In a flash everything became clear.

The prince's grief was beyond control and for many years he could not erase the memory of that awful day from his guilty mind.

But if today you are on a visit to Colwyn Bay in North Wales, you can visit the village of Bedd Gelert and see the reputed grave of that famous dog, the actual spot where Prince Llewellyn is supposed to have buried his faithful companion. There is a tombstone there which tells the whole story and is headed: TO THE MEMORY OF A BRAVE DOG.

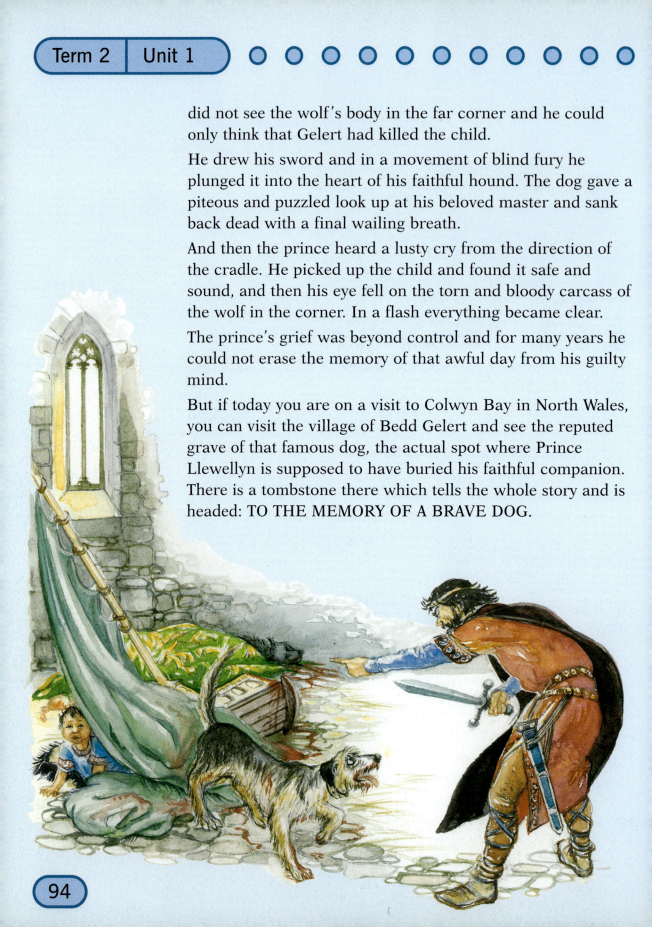

| Term 2 | Unit 2 |

Odysseus and Circe

by Stephen Corrin

Part One

When the Greeks went to war against the Trojans to try to recapture the divinely beautiful Helen, who had been stolen from her husband Menelaus by Paris, the son of Priam, King of Troy, Odysseus was one of the many great warriors in their ranks. And when the Greeks were finally the victors, thanks mainly to the cunning device of the Wooden Horse which Odysseus had thought of, most of them sailed back home in their long ships, weary and homesick after their ten long years of battle.

Odysseus was not allowed a safe return home because he angered Poseidon, god of the seas, by killing his son Polyphemus, the hideous man-eating Cyclops. Poseidon played all sorts of tricks on Odysseus to hinder him, and his many adventures are related by Homer in his great epic poem the *Odyssey*.

One of these adventures was with the enchantress Circe.

One morning, weary with day after day of hard rowing under a mercilessly blazing sun, Odysseus and his men arrived at the island of Aeaea. Too tired even to land, they all went to sleep and did not wake up for two whole days. As they were short of provisions, Odysseus decided to go and explore the island to see what it offered in the way of food and shelter. He found any number of streams of fresh water and many stretches of fragrant woods and, most important of all, a long column of bluish

95

Term 2 | Unit 2

smoke rising from somewhere in the middle of the island. Back he went to his men and reported what he had found, but having already survived so many perilous situations the men decided it would not be wise for all of them to go ashore. Odysseus agreed that the crew should be divided into two parties, each with a leader, and that one party should stay behind to guard their only remaining ship. Then they drew lots as to which one should go on land. The lot fell to Eurylochus, a friend of Odysseus, and so he, with twenty-two rather unwilling companions, went ashore and made straight for the direction of the column of blue smoke.

Eventually they came to a clearing in the midst of which stood a magnificent palace of gleaming white marble, and as they drew nearer a band of wild beasts, lions, tigers, wolves and bears, came running towards them. The men stood rooted to the spot, petrified with fear, expecting to be torn to pieces immediately. But to their great relief and amazement these apparently savage beasts behaved just like affectionate dogs, rubbing themselves against the men and wagging their tails. So they plucked up courage and walked through the marble pillars into the palace itself. Now they could hear the sound of sweet singing and the whirr of a loom and they called out a greeting to announce their presence. Presently two great polished doors opened wide and a tall woman appeared, smiling invitingly. This was the

96

sorceress, Circe. Eurylochus felt in his bones that there was some kind of trap awaiting them and he refused Circe's invitation to partake of food and drink, but all the other men, faint and famished as they were, accepted eagerly. Eurylochus managed to slip away and hide in a spot from where he could watch what was happening without being seen. He saw Circe lead the men into a stately hall and seat them at a table laden with tempting bowls of mouth-watering food, into which four fair maidens poured wine and honey and a sort of barley-meal. The men ate and drank greedily, for not a morsel of food had passed their lips for several days, let alone such luxurious fare. Eurylochus looked on hungrily, hardly able to resist rushing forward and grabbing something to stuff into his parched mouth. Then he saw Circe walk round the table behind the men and strike each one lightly with a wand. And lo and behold! the men's heads turned instantly into pigs' heads, their bodies into pigs' bodies and they dropped from their benches on all fours and grunted and snorted like swine. Then she shooed them out of the stately hall and ushered them unceremoniously into pigsties where she threw them handfuls of acorns and beech nuts.

Eurylochus, thankful that he had escaped this terrible transformation, slipped quietly from his hiding place and returned to the ship to report these sad happenings to Odysseus. The wily warrior immediately took up his great bow and sword and, despite all Eurylochus's earnest pleadings, made him lead the way back to Circe's palace. But half way there Eurylochus became so frightened that Odysseus allowed him to return to the ship and went on alone, determined to confront the sorceress and force her to restore his men to their human shape. But how? Fortunately for him, the god Hermes suddenly appeared in his path in the form of a handsome young man, wearing winged sandals and carrying a golden wand.

Odysseus was about to walk past him, so eager was he to hasten to the aid of his men, when the god spoke.

Term 2   Unit 2

"I know, Odysseus, that you are on your way to the palace of the enchantress Circe, but I fear that without my help you will be of little service to your companions in their pigsties. And do you too wish to be changed into a pig?"

Odysseus was so startled to find that the stranger knew so much about his plight that he paused to listen further.

"You must do as I instruct you," continued Hermes, and he handed Odysseus a milk-white flower with a black root which he plucked from below an oak tree. "Take this," he said, "and guard it carefully, for it has powers far stronger than those possessed by Circe. As long as you have this plant in your possession, none of her spells can harm you. Her wine will not transform you into an animal, her sword cannot wound you nor her wand enchant you. And when she sees that she is powerless to do anything to you, you can compel her to restore your companions to their human form. But I must warn you that she will do all she can to charm you into staying in her palace until she can find an opportunity to rob you of your courage. Do not be beguiled!" And with those words the messenger of the gods winged his way into the blue sky.

Odysseus now walked into the palace and was warmly welcomed by the smiling Circe. She treated him with great honour, led him to a golden seat and offered him wine in a golden cup. As soon as he had drunk it, Circe's expression changed. She struck Odysseus lightly with her wand and cried out, "Now go and join your friends in the pigsties!" To her disappointment and surprise, however, no change came over Odysseus. He sprang nimbly from his golden chair and drew his sword as if to attack her. Circe fell to the ground, clasped Odysseus round the knees and pleaded for her life.

"I do not know what manner of mortal man you are," she cried. "No human being has ever before withstood my spells. Only the renowned Odysseus, wisest of all men, could have resisted me thus ... but perhaps you are indeed Odysseus!"

98

"I am he," replied the warrior sternly, "and I will spare your life if you restore my men to their human shape and solemnly swear never again to use your evil spells against us!"

The sorceress rose to her feet and once again she was all sweetness. She placed her hand upon the warrior's sword and swore that never more would she plan mischief against him or his companions. She then ordered a bath to be prepared for him, and when he had refreshed himself in the sweet-scented waters her attendants arrayed him in a fresh cloak and tunic and led him into a splendid banqueting hall, where a great feast had been prepared in his honour. But Odysseus refused to partake of anything until all his men had joined him at the table. Within a few seconds they came in, newly bathed, clad in fresh robes, and glad to see their leader safe and sound. Then Circe confessed to them that the god Hermes had told her that Odysseus would indeed visit her island on his journey home from Troy and she drank a toast to their eternal friendship.

When the feast was over Odysseus went back to his ship and told the men who had been guarding it everything that had taken place on the island. He led them back to Circe's palace, where they were joyfully reunited with their companions.

They were treated royally by the enchantress (for she never broke her oath) and were invited to stay for a whole year.

Term 2 | **Unit 2** ○○○○○○○○○○○○

Theseus and the Minotaur

Greek Myths retold by Jacqueline Morley

But the secret of the Minotaur could not be kept for long. As it grew up the beast proved terrifyingly savage. It soon began demanding human flesh to eat. Minos declared that all the conquered cities that paid him tax should in future send healthy young people to feed the Minotaur. From Athens he demanded seven youths and seven maidens, to be paid every ninth year.

Aegeus, the king of Athens, was a weak man who only bewailed the calamity. Twice the terrible payment was made, accompanied by hopeless weeping as the young people sailed for Crete in a boat carrying a black sail. In the year that the third payment fell due a stranger arrived at the Athenian court – a young man, Aegeus's unknown son Theseus. When he heard the story of the seven youths and maidens he bravely demanded to go as one of them, to kill the Minotaur. His father was dismayed at the thought of losing his new-found son, but he yielded at last. Aegeus asked his son to promise one thing.

"If you return victorious," he said, "order the black sail to be lowered and raise a white one. Then I shall know at once that you are safe." And Theseus promised that he would.

100

Watching the horizon, the young Athenians saw the island of Crete appear, and looked at it with dread. But they had a shred of hope, for no one who saw Theseus could doubt that he was a favourite of the gods, both for his courage and his beauty. Minos's daughter Ariadne thought so, when she saw him leading the young Athenians to the king. Even Minos was unwilling to fling such a noble prince to the monster. He urged him to think again and go home. Theseus laughed at this suggestion.

"Then you must be my guest for a fortnight and I will sacrifice you last," said Minos. But Theseus insisted that he should be the first to meet the monster.

Minos grew irritated. "If that's your wish," he said, "tomorrow you can get to know him well." That night the princess Ariadne tiptoed to the room where Theseus lay and whispered, "I want to save you. But if I help you, you must swear to take me to Athens with you as your wife, for my father will kill me when he learns what I have done."

Theseus readily agreed. Ariadne gave him a sword which she had obtained from Daedalus, and told him what the cunning Athenian had advised. "This sword is the only weapon that can harm the monster. Take it, and take this ball of thread to guide you through the maze." Then in the dark she led him to the entrance to the maze, tied the end of the thread to the huge ring in the centre of the door and told him to always keep the ball in his hand.

Theseus felt his way cautiously in the dark. He would have wandered aimlessly if the thread had not shown him the ways he had already taken. He had unrolled the last of the thread when he heard ahead of him a steady pounding. The Minotaur was pacing round and round in some open space, quite close to him. The moment had come. Theseus stepped into the dim light of a courtyard. The Minotaur saw him and charged.

101

Theseus darted aside and swung the sword with all his force into the creature's belly. With a bellow of rage the monster fell to the ground, grasping Theseus so that he fell upon it. He felt the soft skin underneath its throat and drove the sword in deep. The monster groaned and died.

Shaken but triumphant, Theseus followed the thread back to Ariadne who was waiting at the gate. She flung her arms around him, then through the sleeping city she guided the Athenians to the harbour. They stole aboard their ship and sailed for Athens. During the voyage they sheltered for the night upon the island of Naxos. Next day, when Ariadne awoke, she found herself alone. The ship had sailed without her. Some say that Theseus had never loved her and had left her on the island. But others tell how the wine god Dionysus had come to him that night in a dream and commanded him to go. This surely is the truth, for while Ariadne wept, Dionysus, with his band of laughing satyrs, came tumbling from the sky and carried her off to be his wife.

Theseus sailed on, and sorrow for Ariadne made him forget to put up the white sail as he had promised. Aegeus, who had gone every day to the cliff top to watch for his son's boat, saw the black sail returning and cast himself into the sea for grief. So Theseus came home to mourning and became king of Athens, which he ruled long and well.

(alternative ending retold by Nathaniel Hawthorne)

Now, some low-minded people, who pretend to tell the story of Theseus and Ariadne, have the face to say that this royal and honourable maiden did really flee away under cover of the night, with the young stranger whose life she had preserved. They say, too, that Prince Theseus (who would have died sooner than wrong the meanest creature in the world) ungratefully deserted Ariadne on a solitary island, where the vessel touched on its voyage to Athens. But had the noble Theseus heard these falsehoods, he would have served their slanderous authors as he served the Minotaur! Here is what Ariadne answered, when the brave Prince of Athens besought her to accompany him:

"No, Theseus," the maiden said, pressing his hand, and then drawing back a step or two, "I cannot go with you. My father is old, and has nobody but myself to love him. Hard as you think his heart is, it would break to lose me. At first, King Minos will be angry; but he will soon forgive his only child; and, by and by, he will rejoice, I know, that no more youths and maidens must come from Athens to be devoured by the Minotaur. I have saved you, Theseus, as much for my father's sake as for your own. Farewell! Heaven bless you!"

All this was so true, and so maiden-like, and was spoken with so sweet a dignity, that Theseus would have blushed to urge her any longer. Nothing remained for him, therefore, but to bid Ariadne an affectionate farewell, and go on board the vessel, and set sail.

Italian Recipes

Classic Italian (foreword by Valentina Harris)

Introduction

Italian food is imaginative, colourful and bursting with flavour. It is in harmony with today's thoughts on healthy eating and the "Mediterranean diet", with its emphasis on energy-giving foods, olive oil and plenty of fruit and vegetables. Italy is a country of changing climates and landscapes, and so too is its cooking, varying according to the region from which a particular dish comes. From the cool and mountainous north come hearty, warming dishes. Among these are polenta, a gorgeous, golden yellow porridge made from cornmeal; wonderful baked pasta dishes such as lasagne; and rich risottos, with locally grown arborio rice, of which northern Italians eat rather a lot. From the south, where the climate is warmer, we find more colourful dishes, such as pizza and simple meat dishes made with additional ingredients such as peppers, olives and herbs that thrive in the hot Mediterranean sun. Southern Italians like their pasta served simply; with oil, and herbs. The land is rich in produce: from the forests come game; sheep and goats graze in the foothills; wheat for pasta grows in the plains; and there is a wealth of vegetables and fruit in every field and orchard. Veal, beef and dairy foods are produced, the seas and lakes are brimming with all sorts of fish and shellfish, and in the hills, vines and olive trees are cultivated.

Olive oil is one of the most important ingredients in Italian cooking and although it may seem expensive, it pays to use the best that you can afford. Most recipes only need a little and it makes all the difference to the flavour of a dish. Extra virgin olive oil, produced from the first cold pressing of the olives, is excellent for dressings or pouring on to pasta, while pure olive oil is perfect for cooking.

Vegetables play a vital role in Italian cuisine and among those most often used are courgettes, aubergines, broccoli, peppers, spinach and tomatoes. Other favourite Italian ingredients include garlic, freshly grated nutmeg, capers, olives and pine nuts, all adding enticing flavours to savoury dishes.

Cheese is used in small amounts as an ingredient in many recipes. Italians make a large variety of cheeses and these are becoming increasingly easier to find in other countries. There are many varieties of cheese ranging from soft, crumbly and mild, to hard, creamy and full-flavoured. The most well-known is Parmesan, the undisputed king of Italian cheeses. Genuine Parmesan cheese is only made in Emilia and an authentic cheese always has the title "Parmigiano-Reggiano" stamped on its rind. Always buy fresh Parmesan for grating – the flavour of ready-grated Parmesan is a poor substitute.

Italian food is simple and rustic, lovingly prepared and well-presented. Cooking as the Italians do is easy and fun. They love to cook, but above all, Italians enjoy sharing food with friends and family, turning even the simplest meal into a celebration. With the help of these delicious and authentic recipes, you will be certain to do the same.

◀ A colourful roadside stall in a street market in Rome shows just a small selection of Italy's tempting produce.

Term 2 | Unit 3

Soups, starters and salads

MINESTRONE WITH PESTO
Minestrone con Pesto

Minestrone is a substantial mixed vegetable soup made with almost any combination of fresh seasonal vegetables. Short pasta or rice may also be added. This version includes pesto sauce.

Ingredients
1.5 litres/2½ pints/6¼ cups stock or water; or a combination of both
45ml/3 tbsp olive oil
1 large onion, finely chopped
1 leek, sliced
2 carrots, finely chopped
1 celery stick, finely chopped
2 garlic cloves, finely chopped
2 potatoes, peeled and cut into small dice
1 bay leaf
1 sprig fresh thyme, or 1.5ml/¼ tsp dried thyme
115g/4oz/¾ cup peas, fresh or frozen
2–3 courgettes, finely chopped
3 tomatoes, peeled and finely chopped
425g/15oz/2 cups cooked or canned beans, such as cannellini
45ml/3 tbsp pesto sauce
freshly grated Parmesan cheese, to serve
salt and ground black pepper

SERVES 6

1 In a large saucepan, heat the stock or water until it reaches simmering point.

2 In another saucepan heat the olive oil. Stir in the onion and leek, and cook for 5–6 minutes, or until the onion softens.

3 Add the carrots, celery and garlic, and cook over a moderate heat, stirring often, for a further 5 minutes. Add the potatoes and cook for a further 2–3 minutes.

4 Pour in the hot stock or water, and stir well. Add the bay leaf and thyme and season with salt and pepper. Bring to the boil, then reduce the heat slightly, and leave to cook for 10–12 minutes more.

5 Stir in the peas, if fresh, and the finely chopped courgettes and simmer for a further 5 minutes. Add the frozen peas, if using, and the chopped tomatoes. Cover the pan, bring slowly to the boil, then simmer the mixture for about 5–8 minutes.

6 About 20 minutes before serving the minestrone, remove the lid, and stir in the beans. Simmer for 10 minutes. Stir in the pesto sauce. Taste and adjust the seasoning if necessary. Simmer for a further 5 minutes, then remove the pan from the heat. Allow the soup to stand for a few minutes, to bring out the flavours, then serve in warmed bowls. Serve the grated Parmesan separately.

Pasta and pizza

CALZONE
Calzone

Calzone are simply pizzas with the topping on the inside. This vegetable filling is delicious but you could change the ingredients if you like.

INGREDIENTS

For the Pizza Dough
450g/1lb/4 cups plain flour
1 sachet easy-blend dried yeast
about 350ml/12fl oz/1½ cups warm water

For the Filling
5ml/1 tsp olive oil
1 red onion, thinly sliced
3 courgettes, sliced
2 large tomatoes, diced
150g/5oz mozzarella, diced
15ml/1 tbsp chopped fresh oregano
skimmed milk, to glaze
salt and ground black pepper
fresh oregano sprigs, to garnish

Makes 4

Cook's Tip
Don't add too much water to the dough when mixing otherwise it will be difficult to roll out – the dough should be soft, but not at all sticky.

1 To make the dough, sift the flour and a pinch of salt into a bowl and stir in the yeast. Stir in just enough warm water to mix to a soft but not sticky dough.

2 Knead for 5 minutes until smooth. Cover with clear film or a dish towel and leave in a warm place for about 1 hour, or until doubled in size.

3 Meanwhile, make the filling. Heat the oil and sauté the onion and courgettes for 3–4 minutes. Remove from the heat and add the tomatoes, mozzarella and oregano and season to taste with salt and pepper.

Preheat the oven to 220°C/425°F/Gas 7 for at least 20 minutes.

4 Knead the dough lightly and divide into four. Roll out each piece on a lightly floured surface to a 20cm/8in round. Place a quarter of the filling on one half of each round. Brush the edges with milk. Fold over the filling. Press the edges firmly. Brush with milk. Bake for 15–20 minutes until golden. Garnish with oregano sprigs.

The Food of Italy (Claudia Roden)
Planning a Meal

I have grouped the recipes by region, but you are meant to pick from all over when you plan a meal. To make it easier for you to choose, the dishes are listed here in sequence, but bear in mind that they are flexible. Many *antipasti* make a perfect second course or a side dish or they can be part of a buffet, and many dishes can be served on their own as a meal in itself.

A formal meal in Italy is a succession of courses, with no main course, starting with an hors d'oeuvre or appetiser (*antipasto*), followed by a first course (*primo*) of either pasta, risotto or soup, and a second course (*secondo*) of meat, poultry or fish, accompanied by one or two vegetable side dishes (*contorni*). Then there is salad (*insalata*), sometimes cheese, and the meal ends with fruit or dessert (*dolce*).

Antipasti used not to play an important part in Italian eating. Not long ago they would consist only of a few slices of cured meat or salami, and these are still the favourites. Antipasti are meant only the whet the appetite, so do not make too much. For most people in Italy the first course is the most important, and pasta is the favourite food. Although most favour the simplest treatment – olive oil and garlic with fresh raw tomato and basil or a dressing of butter melted with sage leaves, sprinkled with freshly grated black pepper and parmesan, the versatility of pasta is extraordinary. Risotti and other rice dishes, gnocchi and canederli (bread dumplings) are also versatile. Soups can be a meal in themselves or light and delicate.

With so much coast, Italy has a wide range of fish and seafood. Until recently fish was considered to be a Friday dish only, and not grand enough to serve to guests, but now it is one of the most popular foods.

Meat and poultry dishes are mostly grills, roasts and stews; there are lovely game dishes and offal is particularly good. Egg or vegetable dishes can also be served as a second course. Vegetable dishes are an important part of every meal so make good use of the repertoire. Salad can be green leaves or boiled vegetables dressed with olive oil and lemon juice. Then cheese may be served. The usual way to end a meal is with fruit. In Italy, desserts are rarely served at home, but if I did not offer a sweet, I believe my guests would feel cheated.

Sardinia

CULINGIONES
Cheese ravioli

Natalina Laconi and her sister make these beautifully crafted little ravioli at their restaurant Su Meriagu at Quartu Sant Andrea, Cagliari, with a variety of different fillings (including mashed potatoes or spinach).

Serves 4

Fresh egg pasta

600g (1lb 6oz) fresh pecorino or well-drained mashed cottage cheese

2 eggs

Bunch of mint, finely chopped

Salt and pepper

Zest of half an orange (optional)

Grated nutmeg (optional)

½ packet saffron powder dissolved in a drop of hot water (optional)

2 tablespoons or more melted butter

Grated pecorino

Mix the cheese, eggs, mint, salt and pepper, zest, nutmeg and saffron in a bowl. Roll out the dough to a thin sheet on a lightly floured surface. Cut into 6.5cm (2½ in) rounds with a pastry cutter. Put a heaped teaspoonful of filling in the centre (a little to one side) of the rounds. Fold over to make a half-moon shape then pinch the edges together and twist to make a tight, festooned edge. Boil the ravioli in plenty of boiling salted water for five minutes and drain as soon as they are done. Coat with butter and serve with grated pecorino cheese, or with fresh tomato sauce and grated cheese.

PASTA CON FRUTTI DI MARE

Seafood pasta
Serves 6

1kg (2lb) mussels or clams

4 scallops (optional)

250g (½lb) small squid or cuttlefish

250g (½lb) scampi or prawns

3 cloves garlic, finely chopped

3 tablespoons olive oil

1 hot red chilli, fresh or dried, finely chopped or crumbled or a pinch of powder (optional)

4 tomatoes, peeled and chopped (optional)

300ml (½ pint) dry white wine

Salt and pepper

Bunch of parsley, finely chopped

600g (1¼lb) spaghettini, tagliolini (thin noodles) or tagliatelle

---

Clean the shellfish and steam them open. When they are cool take them out of their shells and filter the remaining liquid in the pan (keep it for the sauce). Cut the scallops into 2–4 pieces. Clean the squid and cuttlefish and cut the bodies into rounds. Shell the prawns.

Fry the garlic in oil till it just begins to colour. Add chilli and tomatoes if you like, the liquid from the shells and the wine. Season with salt and pepper and simmer for 10 minute to reduce a little. Then add the squid and prawns and cook a few minutes only until the prawns turn pink and the squid turns opaque. Add the mussels or clams and scallops and the parsley and heat through when the pasta is ready to serve.

Cook the pasta in plenty of boiling salted water until *al dente* and serve with the sauce.

VARIATION *A pinch of saffron occasionally gets into the sauce. In Venice at Cipriani's they make a shellfish sauce with champagne and add cream.*

Grimm's Fairy Tales

The highly evocative stories in this treasury of tales have become part of our heritage and culture and are an essential part of every child's imaginative upbringing.

In bringing to life a host of unforgettable characters such as Tom Thumb, the Frog-Prince and Ashputtel, the Brothers Grimm created a feast of stories to stimulate the mind and emotions of readers of all ages. Some of the tales are sinister, some funny; others teach us about love, compassion or revenge, greed, cruelty or kindness. Because of their enormous range and scope, they form a vital part of our understanding of the world.

As popular today as they were when they were first published, these stories should find a place on the bookshelf of every home. As well as leading us to strange lands where birds and beasts dwell with dwarfs, giants, princesses and peasants, they will continue to delight, terrify and educate readers, young and old.

Red Riding Hood

By the Brothers Grimm

Version A

Part One

Once upon a time there was a sweet little maiden. Whoever laid eyes upon her could not help but love her. But it was her grandmother who loved her most. She could never give the child enough. One time she made a present, a small, red velvet cap, and, since it was so becoming, she always wanted to wear only this. So she was simply called Little Red Cap.

One day her mother said to her, "Come, Little Red Cap, take this piece of cake and a bottle of wine and bring them to your grandmother. She is sick and weak. This will strengthen her. Be nice and good, and give her my regards. Don't tarry on your way, and don't stray from the path, otherwise you'll fall and break the glass. Then your sick grandmother will get nothing."

Little Red Cap promised her mother to be very obedient. Well, the grandmother lived out in the woods, half an hour from the village. And, as soon as Little Red Cap entered the woods, she encountered the wolf. However, Little Red Cap did not know what a wicked sort of an animal he was and was not afraid of him.

"Good day, Little Red Cap."
"Thank you kindly, wolf."
"Where are you going so early, Little Red Cap?"
"To Grandmother's."
"What are you carrying under your apron?"

111

"My grandmother is sick and weak, so I'm bringing her cake and wine. We baked yesterday, and this will strengthen her."

"Where does your grandmother live, Little Red Cap?"

"Another quarter of an hour from here in the woods. Her house is under the three big oak trees. You can tell it by the hazel bushes," said Little Red Cap.

The wolf thought to himself, this is a good juicy morsel for me. How are you going to manage to get her?

"Listen, Little Red Cap," he said, "have you seen the pretty flowers which are in the woods? Why don't you look around you? I believe that you haven't noticed how lovely the birds are singing. You march along as if you were going straight to school in the village, and it is so delightful out here in the woods."

Part Two

Little Red Cap looked around and saw how the sun had broken through the trees and everything around her was filled with beautiful flowers. So she thought to herself: Well, if I were to bring grandmother a bunch of flowers, she would like that. It's still early, and I'll arrive on time. So she plunged into the woods and looked for flowers. And each time she plucked one, she believed she saw another one even prettier and ran after if further and further into the woods. But the wolf went straight to the grandmother's house and knocked at the door.

"Who's there outside?"

"Little Red Cap. I'm bringing you cake and wine. Open up."

"Just lift the latch," the grandmother called. "I'm too weak and can't get up."

The wolf lifted the latch, and the door sprung open. Then he went straight inside to the grandmother's bed and swallowed her. Next he took her clothes, put them on with her nightcap, lay down in her bed, and drew the curtains.

Little Red Cap had been running around after flowers, and, only when she had as many as she could carry, did she continue on her way to her grandmother. Upon arriving there she found the door open. This puzzled her, and, as she entered the room, it seemed so strange inside that she thought, Oh, oh, my God, how frightened I feel today, and usually I like to be at grandmother's. Whereupon she went to the bed and drew back the curtains. Her grandmother lay there with her cap pulled down over her face so that it gave her a strange appearance.

"Oh, grandmother, what big ears you have!"

"The better to hear you with."

"Oh, grandmother, what big eyes you have!"

"The better to see you with."

"Oh, grandmother, what big hands you have!"

"The better to grab you with."

"Oh, grandmother, what a terrible big mouth you have!"

"The better to eat you with."

Part Three

With that the wolf jumped out of bed, leapt on Little Red Cap and swallowed her. After the wolf had digested the juicy morsel, he lay down in bed again, fell asleep, and began to snore very loudly. The hunter happened to be passing by and wondered to himself about the old lady's snoring. He decided he had better take a look. Then he went inside, and, when he came to the bed, he found the wolf whom he had been hunting for a long time. He had certainly eaten the grandmother. Perhaps she can still be saved. I won't shoot, thought the hunter. Then he took a shearing knife and slit the wolf's belly open, and, after he had made a couple of cuts, he saw the glowing red cap, and, after he had made a few more cuts, the girl jumped out and cried, "Oh, how frightened I was! It was so dark in the wolf's body." And then the grandmother came out alive. So now Little Red Cap fetched large heavy stones with which they filled the wolf's body, and, when he awoke, he wanted to jump up, but the stones were so heavy that he fell down dead.

So all three were pleased. The hunter skinned the fur from the wolf. The grandmother ate the cake and drank the wine that Little Red Cap had brought, and Little Red Cap thought to herself: Never again in your life will you stray by yourself in the woods when your mother has forbidden it.

Red Riding Hood Version B

Part One

In the far north, beside a river which froze hard as rock in the dark days of winter, there stood a great timber mill and a town built out of wood. The wood came from the trees of the deep forest which surrounded the town and stretched into the far distance.

In this town lived a quiet and shy little girl, called Red Riding Hood. Her real name was Nadia but everyone called her Red Riding Hood because when the cold came she always wore a thick red cloak with a hood. It had been given to her by her great-grandmother who had worn it herself, long ago, when she was a child.

Her great-grandmother still lived in a cottage in the forest and Red Riding Hood loved to visit her more than anything in the world; but she would never go alone because she was frightened to walk through the forest.

Red Riding Hood was frightened of many things. She was frightened of going to bed by herself, she was frightened of dogs and of thunder and of people she did not know. But she was most frightened of the forest. The forest seemed strange to her for she had been born far away in a city in the south, where her mother and father had gone to be trained for their work in the great timber mill.

"Why do you never play in the forest like we did when we were children?" they asked her.

"It is dark under the trees," said Red Riding Hood, "and in winter the wolves howl in the distance."

"There have been no wolves in the forest since anyone can remember," said her parents, laughing.

But her great-grandmother took the child to one side and said to her quietly, "Not everyone can hear that howling; they think it is only the wind in the trees. One winter day when I was a girl, out alone chopping wood for the stove, I was attacked by one of the grey wolves which speak."

"Oh, great-grandmother!" whispered Red Riding Hood. "What did you do?"

"I fought the wolf with my hatchet and killed it," replied the old woman, "for I was strong and agile when I was young."

But now the great-grandmother was very old and frail, and almost every day when school and work were over, Red Riding Hood went with her mother and father, or with some of the other children, to cook supper for her and to sit and talk.

Winter was coming. Snow fell. It was dark before the children came out of school and the wind grew icy cold.

In the school the children were hard at work finishing the fur jackets which they had been making to wear during the bitter weather. They were very proud of these jackets, for all of them had cut out their own with great sharp knives and were sewing pieces together with special strong needles and

115

Term 2   Unit 4

thread. Only Red Riding Hood was not making a jacket. She wanted to wear a red cloak and hood and besides she was frightened that she might cut herself on one of the sharp knives.

Her mother and father worried that she would be cold without a jacket, for the red cloak was growing worn.

"We can see to that," said the great-grandmother, as they all sat around her stove one evening. "Bring the special sewing things with you after school tomorrow and I will help you make a sheepskin lining for your cloak."

"What a good idea," said Red Riding Hood's parents and Red Riding Hood thought happily about tomorrow as she walked home between them through the forest.

"Why don't you take some presents to great-grandmother?" said the father the next morning. "Here are some brown eggs and some chocolate and a pot of the blackberry jam you helped us make."

"We shall be busy this evening," said her mother, "but you can easily walk to great-grandmother's on your own. The path through the forest is cleared of snow every day and there will be a full moon tonight."

Red Riding Hood said nothing. She took a basket and carefully put into it the eggs, the chocolate and the jam. She did not feel happy any more. The other children were going to stay late at school to finish their jackets. She would have to walk through the forest to her great-grandmother's cottage all alone.

Red Riding Hood was frightened. All day at school she could think about nothing but whether she dared to walk through the forest alone. At dinnertime she did not want to eat because she felt sick. She borrowed a special needle and thread and a sharp knife and put them in the basket with the presents, but when school was over she did not set out for her great-grandmother's, although she was longing to see her. She turned her back on the forest and started to walk into the town towards home.

It was dark and quiet outside the school. The other children were still inside sewing their jackets. In the distance Red Riding Hood could hear the noise of sawing from the timber mill. Then she heard another sound, from quite close, somewhere near the edge of the forest. It was the howling of a wolf.

Red Riding Hood stood listening. She knew it was one of the grey wolves. But who would believe her? They would laugh and say she had imagined it. She thought of her great-grandmother, all alone.

Part Two

What if a wolf had come again for great-grandmother now that she was no longer young and agile? Red Riding Hood turned around and ran into the forest and along the path to the old woman's cottage.

She ran and ran until her side hurt and her heart thumped so fast she had to stop to get some breath.

The moon shone through the bare branches of the trees onto the snow and the frozen earth. It was very still. Then a gust of wind blew snow into the air and through the wind Red Riding Hood thought she heard a cold voice calling, "Run home, little girl, run home. This is the night of the wolf."

Then she heard a low growl, and staring through the flurry of snow she saw a streak of grey moving toward her great-grandmother's cottage. Her mouth went dry and her legs felt as if she could not move them, but she made them walk on until at last she reached the cottage.

"Great-grandmother, great-grandmother!" she cried, rattling the door latch. "I'm here!"

"Lift up the latch and walk in," called a thin and quavering voice.

"Great-grandmother, are you ill?" cried little Red Riding Hood, and she opened the door and ran into the bedroom.

In the high, wooden bed there was a shape huddled down under the bedclothes. It was hard to see with only the moonlight coming through the window. Red Riding Hood peered at the shape and moved closer to the bed.

"What big eyes you have, great-grandmother," she said.

"All the better to see with, my dear," said the thin, quavering voice.

"And what big ears you have, great-grandmother."

"All the better to hear you with, my dear," said the voice.

"And what a strange nose you have, great-grandmother," said Red Riding Hood, moving a little closer.

"All the better to smell you with, my dear," said the voice, and Red Riding Hood could see a mouth full of yellow pointed teeth.

"And what big teeth you have!" she cried, backing away.

"All the better to eat you with!" snarled the shape, leaping from the bed. It was a grey wolf.

Part Three

Red Riding Hood screamed and as she screamed she heard her great-grandmother calling. "Quick, child, quick! Let me in!"

Red Riding Hood flung open the door into the kitchen and there was her great-grandmother pulling a blazing branch from the stove. With this branch she advanced on the growling wolf, old and bent though she was.

The wolf was frightened by the flame. It circled fiercely around the old woman, trying to get behind her and spring on her. Red Riding Hood shrank back against the wall. She could see that soon the branch would be burnt out and then the wolf would spring on her great-grandmother. Suddenly she remembered how easily the other children had cut through skins to make their jackets. She reached into her basket and pulled out the great sharp knife. Just as the branch burnt out and the wolf gathered itself for the kill, Red Riding Hood leapt forward and plunged the knife deep into its heart. The wolf gave one terrifying snarl and fell dead on the ground in a pool of blood.

With the help of her great-grandmother Red Riding Hood skinned the wolf and together they made a lining of its fur. "Listen, great-granddaughter," said the old woman, as they worked together stitching the lining into the red cloak, "this cloak now has special powers. Whenever you meet another child who is shy and timid, lend that child the cloak to wear as you play together in the forest, and then, like you, they will grow brave."

So whenever she met such a child, Red Riding Hood did as her great-grandmother had said, but the rest of the time she wore the coat herself and for many years it kept her warm as she explored deeper and deeper into the great forest.

Term 2 | **Unit 5** ○ ○ ○ ○ ○ ○ ○ ○ ○ ○ ○ ○

Landmarks from the Past

Periods in history

Archaeologists and historians divide the time people have lived in Britain into different periods:

Palaeolithic: 1,000,000–10,000 BC

The first people came to live in Britain. They probably came from Europe, as Britain was connected to the European continent at this time. Palaeolithic people made simple tools of wood and stone. They were nomadic, following around the animals they hunted for food. The Ice Age occurred during this period.

Mesolithic: 10,000–4,000 BC

People made more complicated tools than their Palaeolithic ancestors (using, stone, wood and bone); but they were still nomadic hunters and gatherers.

Neolithic: 4,000–2,500 BC

People knew how to cultivate wild cereal grasses for food and how to domesticate and herd the animals their Mesolithic ancestors had hunted. This meant they could live in one place all the time, and build more permanent homes.

Bronze Age: 2,500–600 BC

People learnt how to make tools from the metal bronze, a combination of copper and tin.

Iron Age: 600 BC–AD 43

Iron largely replaced bronze as the metal used for weapons and tools. (Iron is stronger than bronze.)

Roman: AD 43–410

The years when Britain was part of the Roman Empire.

Saxon: 410–1066

Saxons from Germany and other people, such as the Vikings from Scandinavia, settled in Britain.

120

Medieval: (also known as the Middle Ages): 1066–1485
The Saxons were defeated by Norman invaders from northern France in 1066. England was then ruled by a Norman king (William I) and his barons. For the next 400 years England (and later Wales) was run on a feudal system – with peasants at the bottom ruled by lords of the manor, who were, in turn, ruled by the barons, and the king.
Later times are generally described in centuries. For example, the seventeenth century refers to the hundred years leading up to the century number: from 1600 to 1699.

▼ These crop marks, invisible from the ground, show the position of an ancient site.

What can be seen from the air

Photographs taken from the air often show the location of earthworks (such as mounds, banks and ditches) and old buildings from crop marks. When the weather is very dry, crops grow better over old pits and ditches, which stay damp, and less well over old walls where the soil is dryer. Photographs taken at the right time of year can show the perfect outline of an old building or other things which lie below the ground, but which cannot be seen from ground level.

How to use maps

To start looking for old marks on the land, it is a great help to have a good map. Large-scale maps – which show a small number of kilometres to each centimetre on the map – are best, because they contain the most detail. The most detailed maps available are the Ordnance Survey Pathfinder and Landranger series.

▲ This part of an Ordnance Survey Landranger map for Northumberland shows Roman roads, camps and forts, and a tumulus – a prehistoric burial mound.

Pathfinder maps are 4cm to 1km in scale (1:25,000). Landranger maps are 2cm to 1km (1:50,000).

At the beginning or on the edge of the map you will find a guide to the symbols the map uses to show different things. Unfortunately, different maps use different symbols, but a common symbol is a large red M meaning a monument. Some maps write the names of ancient things in gothic letters like this: 𝔄𝔟𝔟𝔢𝔶. Some use a different colour ink to name ancient sites.

121

Term 2 | Unit 5

Homes, Villages and Towns

by Gillian Clegg

The first homes were little more than simple shelters and caves. Then huts were built and homes gradually became larger and more comfortable. Small groups of people living in the same place grew into the villages and towns we know today.

The first people to live in the British Isles arrived approximately 440,000 years ago, during the last Ice Age (which occurred during the Palaeolithic period). The climate wasn't always cold in the Ice Age, though. There were warm spells, lasting thousands of years, when animals such as elephants, lions, hippopotamuses and rhinoceroses roamed the country.

▼ Very old bones, found in caves, suggest that some people lived there during the Ice Age.

Caves

There were times when Britain was as cold as the Arctic is today. During these periods, people would shelter in the mouths of caves or under overhanging rocks. The animals in Britain then included bison, mammoth, horse and reindeer, and bones that have been found in caves tell us that early people hunted and ate these animals.

Caves used by early people that can still be seen today are Kent's Cavern, near Torquay in Devon; Paviland Cave, at Gower in Glamorgan; and five caves on the Cresswell Crags in Derbyshire.

Caves were not only used in the cold Palaeolithic period. Some people, such as hermits in the medieval period, have always preferred them to houses. Well-known caves you can visit are Wookey Hole in Somerset, which was lived in during prehistoric and Roman times; and the cave in Knaresborough, Yorkshire, which was occupied in the fifteenth century by Mother Shipton, who predicted the invention of motor cars and aeroplanes.

Huts

The people of the Palaeolithic and Mesolithic periods were hunters. Because they needed to follow the animal herds, they were always on the move and only put up temporary huts, made of branches, with roofs made of thatch or animal skin. Sometimes they lived in hollow scoops in the ground covered by branches, bracken or turves.

▲ Neolithic people lived in these stone huts at Skara Brae. As there were no trees there, the furniture was also made of stone.

By 4000 BC, people had learnt to farm, so they could live in one place all the time. Neolithic, Bronze Age and Iron Age people usually lived in round or rectangular huts. These were normally made by weaving branches together and filling the holes between the branches with clay to make a wall. Since wood decays, the huts themselves no longer survive, but archaeologists recognize them on excavations from the stains in the soil left by the posts that supported the walls and roof. Examples of how these wooden huts may have looked can be seen in some open-air museums: the Ulster History Park at Omagh, County Tyrone, has rebuilt Neolithic huts, and there are Iron Age huts at Butser Hill, near Petersfield in Hampshire, which is a recreated Iron Age farm.

In hilly areas, homes were built in stone, which is lucky for us as some still survive today. The best examples of very early (Neolithic) stone huts are in the Orkney Islands, Scotland. Those at Skara Brae are well worth visiting. Very ruined remains of Neolithic stone huts can also be seen in England, for example at Carn Brae, near Redruth in Cornwall.

Later (Bronze Age and Iron Age) stone huts can be found in Cornwall, Devon, Yorkshire, Wales and Scotland. Good examples are Grimspound on Dartmoor, where there are several huts surrounded by a circular wall, and Jarlshof in the Shetland Isles. In Jarlshof, the most unusual remains are the wheelhouses. These are circular huts divided by walls forming shapes like segments in an orange. Wheelhouses were built in the Iron Age, and are only found in Scotland.

Iron Age huts can also be seen at Chysauster near Penzance, and Carn Euny, Cornwall. At both these places there are underground passages with rooms leading off them. These are called *souterrains* or *fogous*. Nobody knows what they were used for. Perhaps they were for storing food, for sheltering animals, or they might have been where people could hide in times of trouble.

Early Saxon huts were a bit like a tent: rectangular, with a post at either end and a sunken floor. None of these survive intact today, but reconstructed Saxon huts can be seen at West Stow in Suffolk. Many Viking huts were shaped like a boat.

Houses

The first really grand houses in Britain were built in the Roman period. Rich people owned large estates of many farms, and the landowner's home, or villa, in the countryside was often modelled on houses in Italy. These had a number of rooms connected by a covered corridor, or arranged around a courtyard.

Some of these villas were very luxurious with bathrooms, central heating, and floors decorated with mosaics (patterns made with tiny squares of coloured stone). A visit to the Roman villas at Lullingstone in Kent, Bignor and Fishbourne Palace in Sussex and

Chedworth in Gloucestershire shows how sophisticated Roman society must have been. Most homes didn't have bathrooms and central heating again until this century.

Many of the houses lived in by richer people in the medieval period were surrounded by a moat, a wide, water-filled ditch. Early moats were oval and were intended to keep enemies out. Later moats were square or rectangular and not built for defence, but as a sign of the owner's importance. Moats were probably also used for storing water for keeping fish.

▲ Part of the mosaic floor from a Roman house in Cirencester. In Roman times, mosaic floors were a status symbol. Firms of mosaic artists created the designs, which could be patterns, or pictures, often taken from classical stories.

Villages

From the earliest times, groups of huts were clustered together and often surrounded by a bank of earth or a wall for protection against attack. What is thought to be the oldest village street in Britain is in Chysauster Ancient Village. It was lived in during the Iron Age and Roman periods. It was excavated some years ago and is now open to the public.

Many of today's villages probably date from the twelfth century AD or earlier. By this time, the large farming estates of Roman times had been broken up into smaller units controlled by a lord of the manor.

Although villages have changed over the years, many still have remains of their medieval past. These are the signs to look for: an old church near the centre of the village; the lord's manor house or castle; a pump or well for drinking water; a village green where the villagers would graze their animals, often with a pond.

Term 2 | Unit 5

Places of Defence

by Gillian Clegg

There have always been enemies, whether a neighbouring tribe or invaders from overseas. Many different types of fortification have been built to keep people safe.

Causewayed camps

Neolithic farmers built huge enclosures ringed by banks and ditches. The banks had gaps for entrances. These causewayed enclosures might have protected huts where people lived, but they seem to have been used for other purposes too: places where people met, and where cattle were kept or killed. The remains of causewayed enclosures can be seen on Knap Hill and Windmill Hill, both in Wiltshire. You will have to look carefully for these – the banks are now very low and the ditches are shallow.

Hillforts

By the time of the Iron Age, Britain was split up between many different tribes who often fought each other. For protection against raids, groups of huts were surrounded by huge banks and ditches on the top of hills.

▼ The hillfort at Maiden Castle, Dorset. It was built during the Iron Age, with rows of banks and ditches to make attacks difficult.

The earliest hillforts had just one bank (rampart), but later hillforts often had several ramparts. Hillforts are a very distinctive feature on the landscape and many can still be seen, especially on hills in south and west England. Good examples are Maiden Castle in Dorset, and Cissbury in Sussex.

To identify a hillfort, look for the tops of hills which are a different shape from the hills around (not so smooth) and hills which appear to go up in a number of ridges.

Forts

Instead of hillforts, the Iron Age people in Scotland and Wales built small circular stone forts for defence. (An example is Rahoy, on Loch Teacuis in Argyll.) In the north of Scotland and the islands, chiefs defended their homes with tall circular towers. These are called brochs and many can still be seen. The best example is on Mousa Island in the Shetland Isles.

The Romans, who invaded Britain in AD 43, built forts as permanent bases for the army. There were lines of forts in Wales, the north of England and southern and eastern Scotland. The forts, large and small, were all of a similar design: rectangular with rounded corners, like a playing card. Caerleon in Gwent, designed to hold over 5,000 soldiers, is one of the best examples.

▲ The remains of Carloway Broch in Lewis, Western Isles. Originally it would have been about 10m tall.

Castles

The Normans, who conquered England in 1066, built castles to protect themselves from attacks by the English. The first castles consisted of a motte and bailey. The motte was a mound made by digging a circular ditch and piling up the soil in the centre. The mound was flattened on the top and surrounded by a fence. A wooden watch tower was built on the mound. The bailey was an area next to it, protected by a ditch and bank, which contained the wooden buildings where the owner and his soldiers lived. There are remains of motte and bailey castles all over Britain (particularly on the border between England and Wales). The wooden buildings haven't survived, so often all you can see is the motte, and if this is in country fields it can be confused with a Bronze Age burial mound. Mountfichet Castle near Stansted, Essex, is a reconstructed motte and bailey castle. Stone castles have been built on some mottes, for example Cardiff Castle and Windsor Castle.

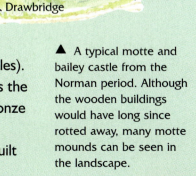

▲ A typical motte and bailey castle from the Norman period. Although the wooden buildings would have long since rotted away, many motte mounds can be seen in the landscape.

127

Term 2 | Unit 5

▼ Caerphilly Castle, Wales, was built in the thirteenth century. Cromwell's troops tried to blow it up with gunpowder during the Civil War (1642–48) which is why the tower on the right is leaning.

Later, castles were built in stone with strong walls and towers, often surrounded by a moat (don't muddle this with a motte). The entrance to the castle was by a drawbridge: a bridge across the moat which could be raised to prevent people getting into the castle. Inside the walls were the living quarters, called the keep.

There are stone castles all over Britain. Good examples of castles that date from the medieval period are Bodiam in Sussex, Bamburgh in Northumberland and Harlech in Wales.

Some castles of a completely different shape – squat and very round – were built in the sixteenth century to defend the shores of Britain against the French. Their round walls were much better for deflecting cannon-balls than the rectangular walls of most medieval castles. Deal Castle in Kent is a good example of this type.

▲ An ancient packhorse bridge at Wycoller, Colne, in Lancashire. It is so narrow that only one horse would be able to go over it at a time. See how the stones are worn down by centuries of use.

Travel
Fords and bridges

People first crossed rivers at fords: places where the river was shallow. There were many fords in Britain, as you can tell from the large number of places with names ending in 'ford' (such as Stamford, Ashford). Fords were gradually replaced by bridges. Early wooden bridges have not survived, but you can still see some simple, early stone bridges such as the Tarr Steps over the River Barle on Exmoor and the Post Bridge on Dartmoor.

From the thirteenth century, wooden bridges were replaced by stone ones. Look out for packhorse bridges, which usually have just a single, high arch over a river and are very narrow. Later in medieval period, every bridge had its own cross and many had chapels for blessing travellers. The chapels at St Ives, Cambridgeshire, Wakefield, Yorkshire and Bradford-on-Avon, Wiltshire, still survive.

The first bridge in the world to be made of cast iron was put up at a place now called Ironbridge, in Shropshire, in 1779 – and it's still there. The use of materials like iron and concrete enabled bridges to span wider stretches of water and to be built in different ways. The Clifton 'Suspension' bridge in Bristol, Avon, opened in 1864, is an early example of new engineering methods.

Canals

People have always used rivers to get from place to place and to transport the goods they traded. But rivers are not very straight, and don't necessarily go where you want them to. The problem was solved by digging artificial waterways called canals. The first canals were probably made by the Romans, such as the Fossdyke linking the rivers Trent and Witham in Lincolnshire. Most canals, though, were cut between 1760 and 1850. There was more industry in Britain by this time, and canals were mainly used to transport coal and other materials from mines to factories, and goods from factories to towns and ports.

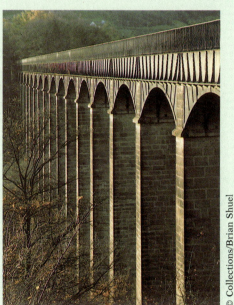

▲ The Pontcysyllte aqueduct in Clwyd, Wales, which carries the Llangollen canal over the River Dee. It was built in 1805 and is nearly 39m above the river.

Canals have another function too – to drain water from marshy land – which is why there are so many canals in the fenlands around Lincolnshire and Norfolk.

Canals involved complicated engineering works. To remain level in areas where there are hills and valleys they often go through long tunnels, and over big aqueducts: high bridges which carry water. A well-preserved aqueduct is Pontcysyllte in Clwyd, Wales. Locks (gates to allow boats to move from one level of water to another) had to be built. The first canal boats were pulled by men, then by horses, walking along the towpath beside the canal.

After railways were developed, canals were no longer so important since railways can take goods from place to place more quickly. Many canals went out of use altogether. If you see a wide, damp ditch running in a fairly straight line it may well be the remains of an old canal. You can still see old canals in cities, for example the Manchester

129

Term 2   Unit 5

Ship Canal, and the Grand Union Canal in north London. There is also a canal museum at Stoke Bruerne near Towcester in Northamptonshire.

Railways

The earliest railway track was laid in Nottinghamshire in 1597. The first railways had wooden tracks and trucks pulled by horses. They were mainly used to transport coal from mines to rivers or the sea, where the coal was loaded on to ships. When locomotives powered by steam were invented at the beginning of the nineteenth century, railways with steel tracks were built all over the country, mainly between 1830 and 1850.

▼ Blasting rocks at Linslade, Bedfordshire, to build the railway from London to Birmingham in 1837.

The building of railways was a very important event in British history, and made many changes to the wealth of the country and its way of life. Not only did the railways carry goods speedily to and from mines and factories, but they also carried people. Long-distance travel by coach and horses went out of fashion and many of the main roads were not used very much again until the arrival of the motor car in the twentieth century.

As railways can't climb steep hills, building railway lines was very complicated. Vast mounds of earth were dug to make embankments, long tunnels to take the lines through hills, and viaducts to take the line on a bridge over valleys and rivers.

In the 1960s, with more and more people and goods travelling by road, many railway lines were closed, their metal rails removed and the railway stations turned into houses. You can still see where many of these railways ran and their straight, level tracks are pleasant places to go walking or cycling.

Some short lengths of railway line have been restored so that people can experience riding on an old train pulled by a steam engine. Steam railways include the Bluebell Railway in Sussex and the Severn Valley Railway in Shropshire.

◀ This lawn covers an old railway line, and the station buildings (Barcombe Mills, Sussex) are now a restaurant. Many British railway lines were closed in the 1960s.

Glossary

AD The years after the birth of Christ. AD is an abbreviation of the Latin words *Anno Domini*, which mean "the year of our Lord".

Aqueduct A structure like a bridge which carries water over a piece of lower ground.

Archaeological excavation Digging into the ground to find evidence of how people lived in the past.

Arctic The ice-covered region at the North Pole.

BC Means "before Christ" and is used to describe the centuries and years before Christ's birth. The years number backwards, so 1000 BC is much earlier than 100 BC.

Barrow A large mound of earth under which people were buried in prehistoric times.

Boundary A line which divides areas of land belonging to different people, or different countries.

Bronze Age The years between 2500 BC and 600 BC, when people learned how to make tools from the metal bronze, a combination of copper and tin.

Celts Celtic people came from western and central Europe, and lived in Britain during the Iron Age.

Cremation Disposal of dead bodies by burning, rather than by burial in the ground.

Enclosure The process of dividing and fencing open, common land by wealthy landowners, which occurred in Britain mainly between 1740 and 1850. Before then, most country people had been able to use land for grazing animals and growing crops. After enclosure, many people were cut off from their way of making a living, or had to pay money to use the land.

Flint A hard stone which forms sharp pieces when it is broken. It was one of the first

Term 2 | **Unit 5**

materials used to make tools and weapons.
Iron Age The years from 600 BC to AD 43 when iron was first used to make weapons and tools.
Medieval period The period in British history which lasted from 1066 to 1485.
Mesolithic period The time between about 10,000 BC and 4000 BC, when people in Britain made stone stools and weapons using small flakes of flint, sometimes set in bone or wooden handles.
Mill A building fitted with machinery for grinding. Early mills were driven by wind or water. They ground grains for flour, made gunpowder and drove machinery.
Mine A hole dug in the earth, for taking out minerals such as copper, iron, coal or salt. Mines can either be tunnels under the ground, or big, open holes. The process of taking out the minerals is called mining.
Moat An area of water surrounding a house or castle, originally designed to keep unwanted people out. Moats were also used as places to store water and keep fish.
Mosaic A pattern of tiles of different shapes and colours, used as a floor covering in Roman times.
Neolithic period The years from about 4000 BC to 2500 BC when people learned how to cultivate wild cereal grasses for food and how to keep animals. This meant they could live in one place all the time.
Nomads People who move around from place to place, to look for animals or plants for food.

Palaeolithic period The years from about 1,000,000 BC to 10,000 BC when the first people came to live in Britain, probably from Europe. These people were hunters, and made simple tools of wood and stone.
Plough A tool for cutting furrows in soil, so that crops can be planted. Early ploughs were made of wood, and were pulled by oxen or horses.
Prehistoric A general word referring to the period before history was written down. In Britain this goes up to AD 43, the beginning of the Roman period.
Quarry A place where stone is dug out of the ground.
Roman period The years from AD 43 to AD 410, when Britain was part of the Roman Empire. The Romans came from Italy, and the empire stretched from Egypt to Scotland.
Saxons People from northern Europe who invaded Britain in the fourth and fifth centuries AD. They set up their own kingdoms, which eventually became England. The Saxon period lasted from AD 410 to 1066.
Turves Lumps of grass (including the roots and soil it grows in), cut out of the ground and used for building roofs, walls or mounds.
Viaduct A long structure like a bridge for carrying a road or a railway over a valley.
Vikings Warriors and traders from Norway, Sweden and Denmark who raided and settled in Britain in the eighth to eleventh centuries AD.

132

Term 2 | **Unit 6**

The Dare

by Judith Nicholls

From: Midnight Forest

Go on, I dare you,
come on down!

Was it *me* they called?
Pretend you haven't heard,
a voice commanded in my mind.
Walk past, walk fast
and don't look down,
don't look behind.

Come on, it's easy!

The banks were steep,
the water low
and flanked with oozing brown.
Easy? Walk fast
but don't look down.
Walk straight, walk on,
even risk their jeers
and run...

Never go near those dykes,
my mother said.
No need to tell me.

I'd seen stones sucked in
and covered without trace,
gulls slide to bobbing safety,
grasses drown as water rose.
No need to tell me
to avoid the place.

She ca-a-a-n't, she ca-a-a-n't!
Cowardy, cowardy custard!

There's no such word as "can't",
my father said.
I slowed my pace.
The voices stopped,
waited as I wavered, grasping breath.
My mother's wrath? My father's scorn?
A watery death?

I hesitated then turned back,
forced myself to see the mud below.
After all, it was a dare...
There was no choice;
I had to go.

133

Muffin - my Dog

Muffin the mongrel
Has long, droopy ears,
A fringe that covers his eyes,
And a tail like a fan.
He has eyes that shine
In the night.
When I come downstairs
They sparkle – greeny black
Like cat eyes.
He has bits of hair
That stick up – spiky
Like a punk rocker's.
When he opens his mouth,
His tongue hangs out
Between his teeth.
He looks like
He is laughing.

Hayley Morris (7)

St Brigid's RC J & I School, Northfield, Birmingham

A Poem for the Rainforest

by Judith Nicholls

Amazonian Timbers, Inc.

This can go next –

here, let me draw the line.

That's roughly right,

give or take

a few square miles or so.

I'll list the ones we need.

No, burn the rest.

Only take the best,

we're not in this

for charity.

Replant? No –

you're new to this, I see!

There's plenty more

where that comes from,

no problem! Finish here –

and then move on.

Song of the Xingu Indian

They have stolen my land;

the birds have flown,

my people gone.

My rainbow rises over sand,

my river falls on stone.

Dusk

Butterfly, blinded

by smoke, drifts like torn paper

to the flames below.

The Coming of Night

Sun sinks

behind the high canopy;

the iron men are silenced.

The moon rises,

the firefly wakes.

Death pauses for a night.

Song of the Forest

*Our land has gone,
our people flown.
Sun scorches our earth,
our river weeps.*

Tiger

Tiger, eyes dark with half-remembered forest night, stalks an empty cage.

Shadows

Spider,

last of her kind,

scuttles underground, safe;

prepares her nest for young ones. But

none come.

Wolf

still on his lone rock

stares at the uncaged stars and

cries into the night.

I love me mudder

I love me mudder and
me mudder love me
we come so far from over de sea,
we heard dat de streets were paved
    with gold
sometime it hot sometime it cold
I love me mudder and me mudder
    love me
we try fe live in harmony
you might know her as Valerie
but to me she is my mummy.

She shouts at me daddy so loud some
    time
she stays fit and she don't drink wine
she always do the best she can
she work damn hard down ina
    England,
she's always singing some kind of
    song
she have big muscles and she very
    very strong,
she likes pussy cats and she love
    cashew nuts
she don't bother with no if and buts.

I love me mudder and me mudder
    love me
we come so far from over de sea
we heard dat de streets were paved
    with gold
sometime it hot sometime it cold,
I love her and she love me too
and dis is a love I know is true
my family unit extends to you
loving each other is the ting to do.

Benjamin Zephaniah

My Uncle Paul of Pimlico

My Uncle Paul of Pimlico
Has seven cats as white as snow,
Who sit at his enormous feet
And watch him, as a special treat,
Play the piano upside-down,
In his delightful dressing-gown;
The firelight leaps, the parlour glows,
And, while the music ebbs and flows,
They smile (while purring the refrains),
At little thoughts that cross their brains.

      Mervyn Peake

From:
Spring

Nothing is so beautiful as Spring
  When weeds, in wheels, shoot long and lovely and lush;
  Thrush's eggs look like low heavens, and thrush
Through the echoing timber does so rinse and wring
The ear, it strikes like lightnings to hear him sing;
  The glassy peartree leaves and blooms, they brush
  The descending blue; that blue is all in a rush
With richness; the racing lambs too have fair their fling.

      Gerard Manley Hopkins

Something told the Wild Geese

Something told the wild geese
　　It was time to go,
Though the fields lay golden
　　Something whispered, "Snow!"
Leaves were green and stirring,
　　Berries, lustre-glossed,
But beneath warm feathers
　　Something cautioned, "Frost!"

All the sagging orchards
　　Steamed with amber spice,
But each wild breast stiffened
　　At remembered ice.
Something told the wild geese
　　It was time to fly –
Summer sun was on their wings,
　　Winter in their cry.

Rachel Field

The Experiment

I want you to think,
said sir
about *nothing*,
sir said.
Empty your head;
sit dead still,
don't move a toe
until I say go.
Ready? – Go!

It's easy not to blink –
you'd think.
First I blinked.
Then I saw Gary Flynn
pinching his lips
to keep the giggle in.
My big toe wiggled
Kevin Nuttall wriggled,
Mary Bollom sneezed,
the clown!
I could see sir
trying hard to frown
without moving his face.
I squeezed my toes,
Kevin Nuttall froze
and Mary Bollom went red.
I tried hard to sit still
and c-o-n-c-e-n-t-r-a-t-e
as *nothing*
rushed through my head.

by Judith Nicholls

Partners

Find a partner

says sir, and sit

with him or her.

A whisper here,

a shuffle there,

a rush of feet.

One pair,

another pair,

till twenty-four

sit safely on the floor

and all are gone

but one

who stands,

like stone,

and waits;

tall,

still,

alone.

by Judith Nicholls

Term 2 | Unit 7

The Good Fortunes Gang

by Margaret Mahy

"Being a Fortune isn't just being *called* Fortune," Tracey declared. **"You get to be a Fortune by going through a TEST..."**

When his parents moved to the small town in New Zealand where his father grew up, ten-year-old Pete can hardly wait to meet all his relatives who live there – especially the four cousins his own age. Will he like them? And, more importantly, will they like him?

But his cousins – Tracey, Jackson, Tessa and Lolly – decide that Pete must pass a test before he can join their gang: the Good Fortunes Gang. Now Pete must face a scary ordeal that means facing up to his very worst fears – alone in the dark ...

THE FIRST OF FOUR RIVETING NOVELS ABOUT THE FORTUNE COUSINS – THE COUSINS QUARTET.

"Readable, appealing and well-written"
School Library Journal

"Makes some important points about friendship in the eight to eleven age group"
Daily Mail

Part One

Chapter One

"Ice cream!" cried Pete's father, Toby, unexpectedly slowing the car as they drove into town. "I need instant ice cream." He glanced towards the back of the car where his sons, Simon and Peter, sat on either side of Bombshell, the baby, in her car seat. They were snugly packed in with sleeping-bags, windcheaters, pillows, and plastic bags of nappies. All the big stuff had gone on ahead of them in packing cases and was supposedly waiting for them in the new house.

"Shops!" cried Maddy, their mother, as if they had not seen shops for years. "I'm going to buy flowers, Toby." She opened the door of the car and scrambled out, talking as she did so. "Then, when your mother actually sees me for the first time ever, I'll be carrying a big bunch of flowers for her. And I'll get some apples. Forget the ice cream! Ice cream's just junk food."

"Oh, come on, Mum," groaned Simon, impatiently flinging himself back among the sleeping-bags. He was wearing black jeans and a black T-shirt, and had spent his Christmas money having his hair dyed black. His eyebrows, however, were still fair ... so fair that from some angles it looked as if he did not have any eyebrows at all. A thin gold earring shone in one ear. Simon looked like a teenage vampire with pimples. "We're healthy *enough*," he cried, "And there's a milk bar, right there!"

"That is not a milk bar," said his father, thrusting a red five dollar bill at Pete. "It might be a milk bar in Australia, but we're in New Zealand now, and in New Zealand it's a dairy. Your mother can buy flowers at that shop down the road, but Pete will infiltrate the dairy and buy us ice creams. Your mother doesn't have to have one."

Term 2 | **Unit 7**

"I will have one, after all," said Maddy quickly, bending down to look through the window. "A vanilla ice cream. Not one of those lurid ones that looks as if it's all bruised and bleeding. And no chocolate chip! Nothing speckled. They make me think huge flies have been sitting on them."

"You certainly know how to take the fun out of an ice cream," Toby grumbled as Pete climbed out of the car, holding the five dollar note tightly in case the wind tried to snatch it away from him. He slammed the car door behind him. He was on his own in a new world.

Part Two

Pete stood for a moment, glancing left and right. Although the shops looked ordinary enough, they were still shops in another country – a land of legend – for he was standing in Fairfield, his father's home town. "I remember, back in Fairfield …" his father would say, beginning a hair-raising story of his own childhood. And now the shops were Fairfield shops, those hills beyond them were the Fairfield hills, and the sky overhead was Fairfield sky. In a few minutes he would be meeting his New Zealand grandparents for the first time and, that afternoon, relations from all over Fairfield would be gathering for a Fortune family reunion. The reunion, it was agreed, had to come before anything else. After that, Pete and his family would be free to begin unpacking and moving into their new house – which was also an old house … the very house his father had lived in when he was a boy.

The dairy, Pete found, turned out to be one of those shops that sells everything you might run out of over the weekend and can't possibly do without. There was even a rack of videos for hire.

"*Zombie vengeance: the dead arise and take revenge on the living,*" proclaimed the one nearest to him in slimy green lettering.

"Four vanilla ice creams, please," said Pete to the woman behind the counter, and then looked doubtfully at the five dollar note. It didn't look like real money you could actually buy anything with. Pete knew he would get used to it, though. A traveller learned to get used to anything.

But then, as the woman reached for the ice cream scoop, Pete heard a dreadful sound – half whoop, half howl – coming from somewhere behind him. Zombie vengeance, he thought, and spun round, clenching his fists and gritting his teeth, prepared to go down fighting all the way. The wild whoop became a fiendish shriek, rushing towards the shop, growing louder and louder every moment. There was a whirr of wheels and, just as the shriek dissolved into crackling, wicked laughter, two figures streamed past the shop ... a boy and a girl, both yelling and laughing as they shot by on skateboards. Pete saw the girl most distinctly. He stood staring, even when there was nothing more to look at, as chilly as if he had seen a ghost.

"Watch where you're going!" someone shouted angrily.

"I swear those kids'll come to grief one of these days," said the woman behind the counter, patting generous scoops of ice cream into the cones.

But Pete was still staring at the space where the skateboarding-girl had suddenly appeared and grinned at him. He had recognized her.

145

| Term 2 | Unit 7 |

Although he had only been in town ten minutes, he had recognized her ... the girl from his worst nightmare.

Pete had been having this particular nightmare for as long as he could remember, but he had never got used to it. While he was dreaming, it was always as if it were happening for the first time, and it was always terrible. As he dreamed, every single thing he was fond of – everything that made home home – crept out of his room, while other unfamiliar things crept silently in and settled down as if they had always been there. Even the windows would slide around the walls, opening in different directions onto strange new views. His parents slid, too, tiptoeing around, picking up Bombshell the baby, and waking Simon. Finally, all four of them would steal off through the front door, while two different parents, and a strange, scowling big sister, with long fair hair and sharp blue eyes, tiptoed in through the back door. In his dream, Pete would suddenly wake up and find himself surrounded by alien furniture and alien people. "Where are Mum and Dad?" he would ask the aliens. "Here we are, you silly boy," the aliens would say with terrible smiles. "We're your *real* parents and this is your sister. That other family, the ones you *think* you remember, were nothing but dreams."

The face that had flashed in and out of sight at the shop window – the face with the fierce smile and the wild, fair hair tossing around it – had been the face of the nightmare sister. Even though his hands were by now full of ice-cream, Pete felt as if the wide-awake everyday world around him had actually become frail and thin, a curtain of cobwebs which he might accidentally brush away at any moment. He was here in Fairfield, the centre of Fortune family stories. He was here, where, according to his father, they were

146

going to stop travelling and settle down at last. But now it seemed that not only his father's family, but Pete's own worst nightmare might be waiting for him here.

Part Three

Chapter Seven

Jackson slowly stood up.

"This is a mystical Fortune song," Tracey announced. "Every Fortune who is a true Fortune knows the words of this song. Go on, Jackson."

Jackson looked as if he weren't too sure of the words himself. All the same, after a moment he began to sing.

"No matter how old a prune may be, It's always full of wrinkles ..."

"Stop!" shouted Tracey. She looked at Pete challengingly.

"Finish that song!" she ordered. "Every true Fortune can finish that song."

Pete had known the song for so many years that the words were part of his memory. But just for the moment he couldn't think of one of them.

"Shall I sing it again?" Jackson asked.

"No! Once is enough," Tracey replied quickly.

But suddenly Pete remembered standing at the bottom of the stairs only half an hour ago, teasing Simon. Every single word of the song rushed back into his head, all jostling and anxious to be sung.

"It's 'young'!" he said. "Not 'old'. *No matter how young a prune may be ...*" He began to sing.

"It's always full of wrinkles. We may get them on our face. Prunes get them every place."

He sang the first verse and chorus, then the second verse and chorus. The three cousins listened intently until Pete had finished the song.

"He got it right," said Tessa, sounding surprised.

"Yes, but that's just one song," said Tracey quickly. "Anyone can accidentally know *one* song. Jackson ... do another."

"I scream, you scream, we all scream for ice cream," Jackson sang obediently. But after the first few words Pete joined in and sang, too. When it came to the second verse Jackson hesitated, pretending he was getting tired of singing, but Pete could easily see he had forgotten the words. Jackson might be able to sing in tune but he didn't know things by heart, the way Pete did.

"What about 'Shut the Door, They're Coming Through the Window'?" suggested Tessa. She began to sing herself. Jackson and Pete joined in.

"Shut the door, they're coming through the window. Shut the window, they're coming through the door. Shut the door, they're coming through the window. Oh, the place is full, and won't hold any more!"

Tracey did not sing along. Pete had said he couldn't sing, and she had been tricked into thinking that someone who couldn't sing wouldn't know the words. As Pete, Jackson and Tessa sang the first verse and the chorus, and then the second verse and the chorus, Tracey looked more and more like the false sister of Pete's nightmare. Both Jackson and Tessa stopped singing at the end of the second chorus. They seemed the think the song was over. Pete hesitated.

"What about the third verse?" he asked.

"There isn't a third verse," said Tracey.

"Yes there is," Pete cried. "I thought every single Fortune would know the third verse. If you don't know the *third* verse you can't be a real Fortune."

Tracey looked sharply at Jackson. "Is there a third verse?" she asked.

Jackson shrugged so hard that his shoulders came right up to his ears.

"There is, and I know it, so that means I must be *more* of a Fortune than you because I know the songs better," cried Pete triumphantly.

Tracey's blue eyes seemed to drill through Pete.

"You can't possibly ever in this world be more of a Fortune than we are!" she cried.

"You said words were the test, and I know more words than you kids," Pete pointed out.

"Words are only *part* of the test," cried Tracey.

"Hey, Trace! Come off it," said Tessa. "Be fair!"

"Words are only the *first* part of the test," Tracey persisted. Anyone could tell she was thinking quickly, inventing a new test as she went along. "It's like taking a driver's test ... you answer questions and then you do the *practical* part ... the actual driving. He's still got to do the *practical* part."

Part Four

"Shall I do it now?" asked Pete, feeling full of confidence.

"Listen," said Tracey, "this reunion's probably going on for

hours and hours. We've got sleeping-bags and we'll be sleeping over at the old place (*our* old place that is. It's a new place to *you*) while the grown-ups have a bit of a rave-up. That's when we'll tell you what the *practical* test is. If you get through it, we'll count you as a real Fortune."

"Not fair!" began Tessa doubtfully. "We should vote. That's democratic."

"Jackson agrees with me," said Tracey. "That's democratic enough." Jackson wiggled his eyebrows up and down, and swayed a little.

"Ai, ai, ai!" he sang softly.

"I'm not scared," Pete said. "I'll do any old test for fun. But I'm a real Fortune – no matter how it turns out."

Just for a moment, he saw a flash of respect in Tracey's blue eyes. Just for a moment, he saw the beginning of a smile.

"We'll see about that tonight," she said, looking tough once more. "All right, then! Let's go back to the great reunion barbecue. I'm hungry."

"The meeting of the Good Fortunes Gang is now adjourned," said Tessa, sounding grown-up and important. "Now, we'll go to the grandys' for the barbecue and make out we're ordinary." She looked at Pete. "That's what we do," she said. "Pretend to be ordinary. But secretly we're radical, especially Jackson. He's radical *and* musical, too."

"If anyone says anything bad about a Fortune, we get our gang on to them," Jackson said. "That's a gang rule. We even stick up for Lolly, though she's only a Bancroft and goes to the Catholic school. Come on ... let's go!"

Term 2 Unit 8

A Fight between Lizards at the Centre of the Earth

by Jules Verne

Professor von Hardwigg, who knows all about rocks, has discovered an old document suggesting that an explorer who descended into a crater in Finland would be able to make his way to the very centre of the Earth. He sets out with his nephew, Harry, and a Finnish guide, Hans, and they do indeed find their way downwards, mile by mile, adventure by adventure, down shafts and through galleries and tunnels, to a deep ocean. They make a raft and set out to find the other side of the water. Harry keeps a diary of what happens.

Chapter One

Sunday, August 18. Nothing new to report. The same intense light as before. I can't help being afraid that it will disappear and leave us in darkness. But it is like some immense lamp and we see perfectly. The shadow of the raft stands out clearly on the surface of the water.

This sea must go on for ever. Well, it's at

151

least as wide as the Mediterranean is long, and perhaps as wide as the Atlantic. My uncle has made several attempts to discover how deep it is by tying one of our heaviest crowbars to a cord and allowing it to run out as far as it will go. But at two hundred fathoms it still hasn't reached the bottom.

This morning, when the crowbar is dragged back on board, Hans points out some strange marks to be seen on its surface. *"Tänder,"* he says. Of course, I don't understand him; but he opens his mouth, and closes it again, as if he were biting something, and I see what he means. "It's been bitten by *teeth!*" I cry.

No doubt about it! The marks on the iron bar are those of teeth! But what jaws the owner of such teeth must have! The bar, which is of solid iron, is almost bitten through!

Are there fearful creatures at the bottom of this sea, so close to the centre of the Earth? Will they surface? Doing what they have done to the crowbar, what would they do to our raft? Or to us?

But it is Sunday, and we try to spend a quiet and hopeful day.

Monday, August 19. I have been thinking about the great creatures that used to inhabit the surface of the Earth, the saurians! Is it possible that such hideous monsters still exist down here, deep inside our planet? The saurians who still remain with us, the lizards and crocodiles and alligators, up there in the rivers now so far above our heads, are feeble imitations of those great creatures of the past! I shudder when I think of meeting one of those original giants: thirty feet, perhaps, from nose to tail, and colossally strong.

No, no, I think to myself, there can no longer be such creatures, either on the face of the Earth or inside it ...

And yet ... can those toothmarks on the crowbar be made by any living thing if it is not a crocodile ten times as huge as any that survive on the Earth's surface?

I find I am staring across this deep sea with wild and terrified eyes. Every moment, I expect some immense monster to rise from the depths!

How strange this light is, I continue to think. It is like being in the most enormous room imaginable, lit by a great lamp one cannot see!

For fear that the worst might happen, I pick up our weapons, one by one, making sure each is ready to be used. My uncle sees what I am doing, and nods. So he, too, fears the worst!

On the surface of the water there are bubblings, splashings, sometimes more than that. The water swells and then is sucked down again. Something must be moving below. It happens more and more often. The sea is more and more disturbed. We must be on our guard.

Tuesday, August 20. At last it is evening – the time of day when we feel a great need to sleep. Of course, in this continuing light there is no night, but we are very tired. Hans remains at the rudder, his eyes never closed. I don't know when he sleeps: but I find I am dozing, myself.

And then ... an awful shock! The raft seems to have struck some hidden rock. It is lifted right out of the water, and even seems to be thrown some distance. "Eh!" cries my uncle. "What's happening?" And Hans raises his hand and points to where, about two hundred yards away, a great black mass is heaving. Then I know my worst fears have been realized.

"It's some ... monster!" I cry.

"Yes," cries the Professor, "and over there is a huge sea lizard!"

"And beyond it ... a crocodile! But who ever saw such a crocodile! Such hideous jaws! Such terrible teeth!"

"And a whale!" the Professor shouts. "See those enormous fins! And see how it blows air and water!"

And indeed two columns of water rise from the surface of the

sea as he speaks, reaching an immense height before they fall back into the sea with an enormous crash. The whole cave in which this great sea is set, its walls and roof invisible to us, echoes with the sound of it. We are at the centre of the most tremendous uproar! And then we see – and how tiny we feel! – that we are in the middle of a great circle of these creatures. Here, a turtle, forty feet wide: here, a serpent even longer, its ghastly head peering out of the water. Wherever we look, there are more of them: great teeth, frightful eyes, great coiling bodies! They are everywhere! I snatch up my rife, and think at once how useless it is. What effect would a bullet have on the armour that encases the bodies of these monsters?

Chapter Two

There seems no hope for us. Though, suddenly, most of the creatures have plunged under the surface and are no longer to be seen, they leave behind a mighty crocodile and a prodigious sea serpent: and they are making towards us, and the end seems near. I think that, useless though it is, I will fire a shot. But Hans makes a sign for me to wait. For these monsters, having come so close to the raft, suddenly turn and make a rush at each other. In their fury they appear not to have seen us. And at that moment we realize how very small we are. To their great eyes, we must seem nothing bigger than an inch or so of floating scrap.

And so, in a thunder of broken water, the battle begins. At first I think all the other creatures have come to the surface and are taking part. There is a whale! – there a lizard! – a turtle! – and other monsters for which I can find no name. I point them out to Hans. But he shakes his head.

"*Tva!*" he cries.

"*Tva?* Two? Why does he say two? There are more than two!" I cry.

"No, Hans is right," says my uncle. "One of those monsters has the snout of a porpoise, the head of a lizard, the teeth of a crocodile ... It is the ichthyosaurus, or great fish lizard."

"And the other?"

"The other is a serpent, but it has a turtle's shell. It is the plesiosaurus, or sea crocodile."

He is right!

There seem to be half a dozen monsters, or more, but the truth is there are only two!

And ours are the first human eyes ever to look at these great primitive reptiles! I am amazed by the flaming red eyes of the ichthyosaurus, each bigger than a man's head. Those eyes, I know, are of enormous strength, since they have to resist the pressure of water at the very bottom of the ocean. The creature is a hundred feet long, at least, and when I see his tail rise out of the water, angrily flicked like the hugest whip you could imagine, I can guess at his width. His jaw is larger than I'd ever dreamed a jaw could be, and I remembered that naturalists have said the jaw of the ichthyosaurus must have contained at least one hundred and eighty-two teeth. They were making their calculations, of course, from the fossilized bones of creatures they imagined had been extinct for millions of years. Now I, and Hans, and the Professor, are gazing, from our tiny raft, at a *living* ichthyosaurus, rising from an ocean deep inside the Earth!

The other creature is the mighty plesiosaurus, a serpent with a trunk like an immensely long cylinder, with a short thick tail and fins like the banks of oars in a Roman galley. Its body is enclosed in a shell, and its neck, flexible as a swan's, rises thirty feet above the surface of the sea.

No other human being has ever seen such a combat! They raise mountains of water, and time and time again the raft seems about to be upset. Time and again we imagine we are drowned.

Term 2 | **Unit 8**

The creatures hiss at each other – and the hissing is worse than the sound of the wildest winds you can imagine, all blowing together. Then they seize each other in a terrible grip, giant wrestlers: and then, break away again. And again comes the great hissing, the furious disturbance of the water!

And in the middle of it all, how tiny we are! We crouch on the raft, expecting that any moment it will be overturned and we shall drown in that wildly disturbed sea, hundreds of miles below the surface of the Earth: far, far from the sky, trees, the blessed fresh air!

And then, suddenly, ichthyosaurus and plesiosaurus disappear together under the waves. Their going down, in one enormous plunge, draws the sea down with them, as if a great hole had been made in the water, and we are nearly dragged down with them. For a while there is silence. The water grows calmer. And then, not far from the raft, an enormous shape appears. It is the head of the plesiosaurus.

The monster is mortally wounded. All we can make out is its neck, a serpent's. It is twisted and coiled in the agonies of death. With it the creature strikes the water as if with some great whip. Then it wriggles, as some vast worm might do, cut in two. Every dreadful movement stirs the sea violently, and we are nearly blinded as the tormented water sweeps over the raft. But bit by bit the great writhings die down, and at last the plesiosaurus lies dead on the surface.

As for the ichthyosaurus, he was surely recovering from the struggle in some deep cave. He could not have been unhurt. He must need to lick his wounds.

Or was he on his way to the surface again, to destroy us?

Homecoming

by Stephen David

Part One

At the beginning and end of the typhoon season, when the winds were rising and falling, you could use the current to glide between the Cities in a flitter with its small motor turned off. The favoured game was to ignore the flight decks and glide straight in at one of the portals, swooping over the galleries and terrifying the people walking there. Naturally, this was extremely dangerous. If you missed the portal, the impact with the City's hull could kill you; if it didn't, the two-kilometre drop to the ground probably would. It was a very popular game, and though it wasn't illegal to turn your motor off, it was very illegal to fly in populated areas of the Cities.

Jann had never played the Game. The idea of hurtling through the air with nothing between him and the ground was terrifying. He sometimes had nightmares of falling, hurtling down, seeing the twin Cities towering above him, then turning over in the air to see the ground and the waving heads of the tall trees

Term 2 | Unit 8

spinning crazily beneath him. Each time, he would wake, sometimes shouting.

It was just such a dream that woke him one night. It was the middle of the season of Roaring Winds and as he lay, sweating, in his bunk, he could feel the swaying motion as the City strained against its massive mooring cables. In the bunk below him his sister Katya stirred and mumbled. Jann threw back his quilt, slipped to the ground and padded quietly into the tiny kitchen. His father was sitting quietly at the counter, watching a scientific programme on the small viewing screen. He looked up.

"Can't sleep?"

"I had the dream again," Jann said. He climbed on the stool next to his father's and sat, rubbing his eyes.

"The falling dream?" Jann nodded. This was the fifth time since the typhoons had started.

"Well," his father said, "you'd better stay up till the dream's gone. Look." He pointed at the viewing screen. "They're showing the lift-off simulations." On the screen a computer image showed the City slowly revolving. Down the side of the screen a scale showed that from base to top the City was just over two kilometres high. Narrow at the base, it broadened out to the kilometre-deep cylinder that housed the living and industrial areas, then tapered again towards the top where the command centres were. Coloured arrows showed the wind direction. At first the arrows moved slowly, then gradually got faster. The City was spinning, like a top, the speed of rotation increasing as the thrust motors augmented the wind's effect. Again, the speed increased, and again, until the lines of the City were a blur. Then it was moving forwards and upwards, its rotation forcing it out to break free of the planet's weak gravity. Instead of sailing majestically a kilometre or so above the surface, harvesting the fever trees where they could, the Cities would finally break free entirely and sail where those who had

158

built them had intended them to go: into space, into the galaxy – and home. The long exile would be over.

"When will we go?" Jann asked.

"Next typhoon season," his father said. "We need another half-year's good harvesting, then we'll have supplies to last us years in space."

Jann frowned. "Tomas didn't want us to go."

"I think Tomas was just repeating what his parents said."

"No," said Jann, irritated. "He thought a lot about it. He said we'd been here hundreds of years and no one on Earth would remember us, and even if we got back there we wouldn't be happy. He said we should just build small ships and send a few people back to make contact. There must be lots of inhabited planets by now, and we wouldn't have to go all the way back to Earth before finding one."

"No," said his father, with an air that Jann knew meant the discussion was over, "there would be no point. This planet will never be a good place to live. We don't want to spend our lives trapped in these floating Cities – and even if I have to, there's no reason for you to. In my lifetime or yours we've got to go Home, back where we belong. And it's a long journey. On a small ship, the crew might be dead of old age before they got anywhere."

"Well," said Jann, "Tomas is staying."

"Tomas is dead, Jann," his father said softly. "He played the Game and he fell. No one could survive that."

"No," said Jann. "I suppose not." He slid off the stool and went back to his bunk and a dreamless sleep.

Term 2　Unit 8

Part Two

The typhoon roared on. From the Cities to the horizon little could be seen through the clouds of reddish pollen blown by the shrieking gales. The preparations for the Return continued. In the great public halls people listened to lectures on why they were going, talks on Earth's history and culture. In the long corridors, the shopping plazas, and the cafés, they wondered: how long would it take, would any of them live to see the Homecoming? Might they roam space for decades, for hundreds of years, wandering the galaxy lost and hopeless? And if they found Earth, what would it be like? Would they be remembered – the descendants of the colonists who had disappeared hundreds of years before? Might Earth even be a dead planet, devastated by war or epidemic? On and on went the talk, round and round in circles. And in the tiny living quarters, families listened to the instructions blaring from the City's public address system and practised strapping themselves into their bunks as they would have to when the time of departure came.

Slowly the winds dropped. The quiet season came and the harvesting went on. People continued to talk. Every evening Jann would listen to his parents discussing the departure. He thought about Tomas, his friend, who would not be going.

There came a day when the winds began to rise again. Standing in the vast gallery that overlooked the space between his City, City One, and City Two, Jann could see the first flitters swoop through the early pollen clouds, wheeling and circling before dropping towards the flight decks or portals of the City. That was the way Tomas had gone. No one had seen it happen, but he had left City One and was never seen again. His name was added to the list of victims of the Game; his family and friends mourned him; and Jann wondered. He wondered, because when it happened he had not been surprised. While some of

Tomas's friends argued about whether he had smashed into the City's hull or lost control and plummeted to his death, Jann thought of the conversation he and Tomas had had only a few days before Tomas disappeared.

They had been walking along the main corridor on "D" level, on their way home from class. As so often, they were talking about departure. At times like these, Jann always felt that Tomas might be right: he was so passionate, but also so logical. It was only when he repeated Tomas's arguments to his parents that they seemed not to work so well.

"*We'll* be foreigners," Tomas had said. "We've all grown up in the Cities, we only know Earth from the material in the libraries – and all of that was recorded hundreds of years ago…"

"But we *came* from Earth," Jann protested. "They must remember that a shipful of colonists went missing. Maybe they've even been searching –" Tomas laughed, though not pleasantly.

"When someone goes down in the Game," he said harshly, "how

Term 2 | **Unit 8**

long do they look for them?" He did not wait for an answer. "These days, they don't. They assume the person's death. And they'd only have to search a few square miles to make sure, not half an interstellar space. C'mon, Jann: a ship travelling at near light speeds goes missing after passing through an asteroid belt? Who's gonna search? You assume the whole thing's dust and carry on looking for the next inhabitable planet. Shall I tell you what will happen if we turn up near a human-occupied planet?" Jann grunted, unwilling, but Tomas steamed on. "Two massive ships – *they* won't know they're cities – appear in your segment of space, so big you could fit an Earth-type city into each of them. If we're *lucky*, they surround us and escort us out of their bit of the galaxy. If we're unlucky, they just blast us out of the space. We don't *belong* there – we belong *here*." He gestured round. Although it looked as if he was pointing at the wide, crowded corridor, it seemed to Jann that he meant something else.

"But this planet is so hostile –" Jann began to say.

"It's not the planet," said Tomas fiercely, "it's *us*! We never tried. When the colony ship landed here, they took one look at the place, said 'Ugh!' and started planning ways of escaping. And ever since, every effort we're capable of, all our energy, have been put towards getting away. If we'd spent all that time and cleverness in figuring out ways of staying we wouldn't be cooped up in these rusty tin cans now ..." Jann looked around. True, parts of the City were looking a little dilapidated. The Council always said there was no time for "minor maintenance".

"But Tomas," Jann said, feeling as ever slow and witless in the face of Tomas's conviction, "everyone else seems to agree we've got to go. Surely people wouldn't go on believing something that's not true for so long?"

162

| Term 2 | Unit 9 |

From:

The Rime of the Ancient Mariner

The fair breeze blew, the white foam flew,
　The furrow followed free;
We were the first that ever burst
　Into that silent sea.

Down dropt the breeze, the sails dropt down,
　'Twas sad as sad could be;
And we did speak only to break
　The silence of the sea!

All in a hot and copper sky
　The bloody sun, at noon,
Right up above the mast did stand,
　No bigger than the moon.

Day after day, day after day,
　We stuck, nor breath nor motion;
As idle as a painted ship
　Upon a painted ocean.

Water, water, everywhere,
    And all the boards did shrink;
Water, water, everywhere,
    Nor any drop to drink.

The very deep did rot: O Christ!
    That ever this should be!
Yea, slimy things did crawl with legs
    Upon the slimy sea.

About, about, in reel and rout
    The death-fires danced at night;
The water, like a witch's oils,
    Burnt green, and blue, and white.

And some in dreams assurèd were
    Of the spirit that plagued us so;
Nine fathom deep he had followed us
    From the land of mist and snow.

And every tongue, through utter drought,
    Was withered at the root;
We could not speak, no more than if
    We had been choked with soot.

Ah! Well-a-day! what evil looks
    Had I from old and young!
Instead of the cross, the Albatross
    About my neck was hung.

Samuel Taylor Coleridge

The Jumblies

I

They went to sea in a Sieve, they did,
   In a Sieve they went to sea:
In spite of all their friends could say,
On a winter's morn, on a stormy day,
   In a Sieve they went to sea!
And when the Sieve turned round and round,
And everyone cried, "You'll all be drowned!"
They called aloud, "Our Sieve ain't big,
But we don't care a button! We don't care a fig!
   In a Sieve we'll go to sea!"
     Far and few, far and few,
       Are the lands where the Jumblies live;
      Their heads are green, and their hands are blue,
       And they went to sea in a Sieve.

II

They sailed away in a Sieve, they did,
   In a Sieve they sailed so fast,
With only a beautiful pea-green veil
Tied with a riband by way of a sail,
   To a small tobacco-pipe mast;
And everyone said, who saw them go,
"O won't they be soon upset, you know!
For the sky is dark, and the voyage is long,
And happen what may, it's extremely wrong
   In a Sieve to sail so fast!"
     Far and few, far and few,
       Are the lands where the Jumblies live;
      Their heads are green, and their hands are blue,
       And they went to sea in a Sieve.

III

The water it soon came in, it did,
    The water it soon came in;
So to keep them dry, they wrapped their feet
In a pinky paper all folded neat,
    And they fastened it down with a pin.
And they passed the night in a crockery-jar,
And each of them said, "How wise we are!
Though the sky be dark, and the voyage be long,
Yet we never can think we were rash or wrong,
    While round in our Sieve we spin!"
      Far and few, far and few,
        Are the lands where the Jumblies live;
      Their heads are green, and their hands are blue,
        And they went to sea in a Sieve.

IV

And all night long they sailed away;
    And when the sun went down,
They whistled and warbled a moony song
To the echoing sound of a coppery gong,
    In the shade of the mountains brown.
"O Timballoo! How happy we are,
When we live in a Sieve and a crockery-jar,
And all night long in the moonlight pale,
We sail away with a pea-green sail,
    In the shade of the mountains brown!"
      Far and few, far and few,
        Are the lands where the Jumblies live;
      Their heads are green, and their hands are blue,
        And they went to sea in a Sieve.

V

They sailed to the Western Sea, they did,
   To a land all covered with trees,
And they bought an Owl, and a useful Cart,
   And a pound of Rice, and a Cranberry Tart,
     And a hive of silvery Bees.
And they bought a Pig, and some green Jack-daws,
And a lovely Monkey with lollipop paws,
And forty bottles of Ring-Bo-Ree,
   And no end of Stilton Cheese.
     Far and few, far and few,
       Are the lands where the Jumblies live;
     Their heads are green, and their hands are blue,
     And they went to sea in a Sieve.

VI

And in twenty years they all came back,
   In twenty years or more,
And everyone said, "How tall they've grown!
For they've been to the Lakes, and the Torrible Zone,
   And the hills of the Chankly Bore";
And they drank their health, and gave them a feast
Of dumplings made of beautiful yeast;
And everyone said, "If we only live,
We too will go to sea in a Sieve, –
   To the hills of the Chankly Bore!"
     Far and few, far and few,
       Are the lands where the Jumblies live;
     Their heads are green, and their hands are blue,
     And they went to sea in a Sieve.

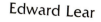

Edward Lear

Term 2 | **Unit 9**

The Black Pebble

There went three children down to the shore,
Down to the shore and back;
There was skipping Susan and bright-eyed Sam
And little scowling Jack.

Susan found a white cockle-shell,
The prettiest ever seen,
And Sam picked up a piece of glass
Rounded and smooth and green.

But Jack found only a plain black pebble
That lay by the rolling sea,
And that was all that ever he found;
So back they went all three.

The cockle-shell they put on the table,
The green glass on the shelf,
But the little black pebble that Jack had found,
He kept it for himself.

James Reeves

168

Term 2 | Unit 10

Seasons of Splendour

by Madhur Jaffrey

Holi – Festival of Spring

Holi is the Indian Spring Festival, a time when winter crops, such as wheat and mustard seeds, are harvested.

I cannot tell you how much I looked forward to this festival. In fact, I longed for it a good three hundred and sixty-four days of the year.

The reason was that our whole family did *such* unusual things to celebrate Holi.

First of all, on the day of the full moon, around late February or early March, we built a huge bonfire. This was called "burning Holi", because on this day, ages ago, a wicked princess, Holika, was consumed by flames that she had intended for her innocent nephew Prahlad.

Frankly, I cared less for Holika, who was burnt in ancient history, than I did for the stuff we actually threw into our own bonfire. We threw whole sheafs of green wheat, whole bundles of green chickpeas, still on their stalks, pinecones filled with strategically hidden pinenuts, and then watched them as their skins got charred.

Only the outside skins were allowed to burn. That was the trick. Each one of us then used a stick to pull out whatever we wanted to eat. My favourite was the chickpeas – tiny chickpeas still in their green skins. Of course, the skins would turn brownish-black but the peas themselves would be deliciously roasted. Everything would be hot – we would almost burn our fingers trying to peel the chickpeas and remove the shells from

169

the pinenuts. Their taste would have to last us for the rest of the year as we licked our lips and remembered. By the end of it all, our faces were black and our clothes and hands were sooty, but no one seemed to mind, not even our parents.

The funny thing about Holi was that we could "burn" it one night and "play" it the next morning. While the "burning" had to do, naturally, with fire, the "playing" had to do with water and colours.

It was said that Lord Krishna, the blue god, played Holi with the milkmaids, so who were we to do any less?

As the Spring Festival approached, an army of us young cousins would, in great secrecy and in competing groups, begin its preparation of colours.

At Holi, all Indians, of all ages, have the licence to rub or throw colours – water-based, oil-based or in powder form – on the victims of their choice. No one is considered worthy of exemption, dignified grandmothers included.

Holi is a leveller, and there was no one we wanted to level more than those against whom we held grudges. A special ugly colour was prepared for them.

First, we would go to the garage and call on one of the chauffeurs.

"Masoom Ali? Masoom Ali?" we would call.

Masoom Ali would poke his head out from the pit under the gleaming Ford. "I am busy. Why are you children always disturbing me? Always coming here to eat my head. Barrister Sa'ab, your grandfather, wants the car at noon and I still have much work to do."

"Just give us some of the dirtiest grease from under the car."

"So, Holi is upon us again? Why don't you children use the normal red, green and yellow colours?"

"If you give us the grease, we won't spray you with the awful magenta paint we have prepared in the garden watertank. It is a fast colour too."

"Threatening an old man, are you! All right, all right. Just don't eat my head."

The grease would be combined with the mud, slime and permanent purple dye. The concoction would be reserved for the lowliest enemies. Elderly relatives got a sampling of the more dignified, store-bought powders, yellow, red and green. For our best friends, we prepared a golden paint, carefully mixing real gilt and oil in a small jar. This expensive colour, would, as I grew older, be saved only for those members of the opposite sex on whom I had the severest crushes – transforming them, with one swift application, into golden gods.

The Wicked King and his Good Son
Part One

Hiranya Kashyap thought very highly of himself. He was good looking, rich – and he was the King. What more could anyone want? One day, a wise Sage, who could see into the past and the future, came to him and said, "Your majesty, according to what I see in the stars, you cannot be killed by man, beast or weapons, during the day or during the night, on earth or in water, inside a house or, indeed, outside it."

That, as far as King Hiranya Kashyap was concerned, made him immortal. If he was arrogant before, he now became unbearable and was very cruel to those subjects who did not flatter him endlessly. If he said, "This bread is stale," all his palace cooks would have to agree and throw it out, even if they had just cooked it. If he said, "The River Ganges flows up from the sea to the Himalaya Mountains," all the courtiers would have to nod their heads in agreement even though they knew that the

Ganges began as a series of cool, icy trickles from the cracks of the world's highest mountains and then flowed, slowly and gracefully, down to the sea.

The sad fact of the matter was that Hiranya Kashyap thought he was God. Not only did he make his subjects kneel and pray to him but he bullied and tortured those who did not.

He had a sister called Holika who had been told by the same wise Sage that she could never be burnt by fire. Hiranya Kashyap and Holika became so vain that they behaved as if they were owners of the entire universe.

Then, one day, all this changed.

Hiranya Kashyap's wife gave birth to a baby boy whom they named Prahlad.

Hiranya Kashyap found no need, or time, to rejoice.

When the courtiers came to him and said, "Congratulations, your majesty, on the birth of your heir," he only snarled, saying, "Bah, what do I need an heir for? I shall live for ever. I am God. Heirs mean nothing to me."

One day, when Prahlad was four, he was playing outside the potter's kiln and saw the potter praying.

"What are you doing?" he asked.

"I am praying to God to save my kittens," she replied. "They have got locked up in the kiln by accident."

"You should pray to my father." said Prahlad.

"Your father cannot save my kittens from that awful fire inside," she said, "only God can."

"My father will punish you if you use God's name," Prahlad advised her.

"I'll have to take my chances," the potter replied.

"Your God can do nothing to help," Prahlad said.

172

"Oh yes he can," the potter answered.

"Then I'll wait here and see," the young boy said. Prahlad waited. When it was time to open the kiln, he heard, "Meaow, meaow." It was the kittens. They were safe!

A year later, when Prahlad was five and playing in the garden, his father chanced to pass that way. The King paused long enough to ask his son, "Who is the greatest being in the whole Universe?" He expected the same answer he got from all his flatterers.

"God," said the child.

The King was taken aback for a second. Then he smirked. "See, see," he boasted to his courtiers, "even this small child recognizes that I am God."

"No," said the child, "you are not God. You are the King and that is all you will ever be."

Hiranya Kashyap's face turned purple with rage. "Take this child," he ordered, "and hurl him from the highest cliff in the Kingdom."

The courtiers were very fond of the gentle child but were terrified of his father. So they scooped little Prahlad up and carried him to the highest mountain in the Himalayas. There, they stood on a peak that touched the sky and dropped the boy.

Part Two

Prahlad fell ... fell ... fell. But to his surprise – and to that of the courtiers looking down from above – he landed in the midst of the warmest, sweetest softness that could be imagined. God had been watching from his heavenly window and had decided to catch the child in his lap.

When Hiranya Kashyap found out what had happened, he turned black with anger. He had the boy brought to the court and thrown at his feet.

"You were very lucky to be saved," he raged.

"It was God who saved me," Prahlad replied.

"As I was saying," the King continued angrily, "you were lucky to land in such a soft patch. The courtiers who threw you down there will have their heads chopped off and then I'm going to have a roaring fire made and have you burnt in it. Let us see what your God can do for you then!"

The King commanded that a huge bonfire be made the following day. Logs were collected and piled into a massive pyre. Then the pyre was lit.

Hiranya Kashyap called his sister, Holika, and said, "If we just toss this child into the fire, he will squirm and run out. Since you have been granted the boon of never being burnt by fire, why don't you take Prahlad in your arms, walk into the flames and sit down. Hold the child tightly. When he is quite dead, you can walk out."

Holika took Prahlad in her arms and walked into the middle of the fire. There, she put him in her lap and sat down.

The flames were leaping hundreds of feet into the sky. Hiranya Kashyap was quite pleased with himself. He was finally getting rid of this troublesome child.

The flames were very hot and made the King perspire. At first he contented himself with moving back a few yards. Then, when the heat and smoke became quite overwhelming, he said to his courtiers, "I'm going into my cool palace. Let me know when all this is over."

A strange thing happened amidst the flames. Holika had a change of heart. She looked up towards heaven and prayed, "God, please do not save me from the fire. I am ready to meet my Maker. But please save this innocent life. I give my boon to this young boy. Let him live."

The fire burnt for several hours. The King had just sat down to enjoy his dinner when one of his courtiers came running in.

"Your majesty," he said bowing, "your majesty."

"Yes, yes, what is it? You know I do not like being disturbed at dinner time."

"The fire has burnt itself out."

"And?" prompted the King.

"Holika has perished in the flames."

"What!" cried the King, "And the child?"

"Your majesty ... Well, your majesty ..."

"Well, what? Answer quickly or I'll have your tongue pulled out."

"Prahlad is still alive."

Hiranya Kashyap kicked his food away and stood on his feet, puffed up with fury like a balloon.

"Bring that brat to me. I'll kill him myself."

The courtiers dragged in little Prahlad and threw him in front of his father.

"So," said the father, "you managed to escape a second time."

"I did not escape," said Prahlad, "God saved me."

"God, God," cried the King. "I'm sick of your God. Where is he anyway?"

"He is everywhere – in fire, water – even in that pillar."

"Oh, he is in that pillar, is he?" the King yelled. "Well, I am going to tie you up to that same pillar and kill you. Let's see if your God will come out to save you."

Prahlad was tied up to the pillar and Hiranya Kashyap raised his sword to finish him off. Just then, there was a loud thunderclap and the pillar broke in two.

Out of the pillar came God.

Term 2 | **Unit 10**

He had assumed a strange shape.

The upper part of the body was that of a lion, the lower that of a man.

So he was neither man nor beast.

He lifted the King and carried him to the threshold of the palace and then placed him in his lap.

So the King was neither in a house nor outside it.

Then he killed Hiranya Kashyap with one swipe of his long lion's claws.

So no weapon was used.

The time of the day was dusk.

So it was neither morning nor night.

Pink and grey clouds puffed along in the sky. Hiranya Kashyap was finally dead, despite all his arrogant predictions.

The courtiers cried, "Long live the King," as they placed the young Prahlad on his father's throne, happy in the knowledge that they were now going to be ruled with justice.

The Old Man and the Magic Bowl

Part One

The old man's life had been hard, but somehow, he had always managed to earn enough to feed himself and his wife.

With the passing years, an awful stiffness had attacked his hands and feet – and then spread with well-aimed cruelty to his legs, arms and back. He could hardly move, let alone go out to work.

He could not pay his rent, so he lost his house and had to live in a hut. He could not work for a living, so he and his wife began to starve.

When the Nine Days' Festival arrived, the old man felt more depressed than ever.

He was standing listlessly by the roadside when a friend of his passed by.

"Well," said the friend, "and how are you today?"

"Not so good," replied the old man.

"Why, what is the matter?" asked his friend.

"My bones are stiff," said the old man. "I have no job and no house. My wife and I have not eaten for seven days."

"Well," said the friend, "if you take my advice …"

"Yes?" said the old man.

"My advice is that you go straight to Parvati's temple and throw yourself at her mercy. She is bound to help you. You had better hurry or the festival might end."

The old man could hardly hurry. With tiny, painful steps, he began the long journey towards Parvati's temple.

It was evening when he got there.

The temple was packed as were all the courtyards that surrounded it. People were spilling out into the streets.

The old man could hear the prayers and smell the far-off incense. But he could not get in.

Inside the temple, the goddess Parvati was beginning to feel uncomfortable. She turned to one of her many child-attendants

Term 2 | **Unit 10** ○ ○ ○ ○ ○ ○ ○ ○ ○ ○ ○

and said, "Someone's problems are weighing on me like a ton of bricks. Go and find out who is in trouble and bring that person to me."

Two of the child-attendants flew around the courtyards and into the street. There they spotted the old man standing stiffly under a tree. They circled him once and made a perfect landing at his feet.

"The goddess Parvati summons you," they chanted together. Each attendant took one of the old man's hands, lifted him off the ground, and then flew him into the temple's innermost chambers. Parvati was leaning casually against a door, her pale, beautiful face radiating as much light as her gold sari.

"Why are you so unhappy?" she asked gently.

"Praise be to you, goddess," the old man began as he kneeled and touched her feet, "I have not eaten for several days."

"Take this," said the goddess, handing the old man a simple wooden bowl made from the knot in a teak tree. "Whenever you are hungry, wash the bowl and pray. Then wish for any food that your heart desires."

"Any food I want and as *much* as I want?" asked the old man.

"Any food you want and as much as you want," answered the goddess.

The old man wrapped his precious bowl in rags and began the slow walk home to his wife where they hugged each other, marvelling at Parvati's generosity.

The old man said to his wife, "Now tell me what you want to eat."

"How about a sweet mango?"

The old man washed the bowl, prayed and then wished for a sweet mango. Before he could even finish his thought, there was the mango sitting in his bowl.

178

"What else do you want?" asked the old man.

"How about a rice pilaf made with the meat of a fat-tailed sheep?"

"Here it comes," said the husband. The bowl was soon brimming over with the fragrant pilaf.

"How about a creamy pudding, dotted with raisins?" ventured the wife.

The wooden bowl was now filled with the tastiest pudding the old couple had ever eaten.

"This is a meal fit for a king," declared the old man.

"It certainly is," agreed the wife.

The old man began to think. "You know," he started, "all our lives we have been poor. We have hardly had enough food for ourselves, let alone enough food to entertain guests with. Now that we can have all the finest, rarest delicacies of this world, why don't we invite the King for a meal."

"You must be mad," said the wife. "Why should the King come to eat with the likes of us?"

"And why not?" asked he old man. "He cannot get a better meal anywhere else. We will be offering the King the best food our heavens can provide."

So saying, the old man set off to invite the King.

When he arrived at the palace gate, the old man said, "I have come to invite the King to dinner."

The guards laughed. "So you want to invite the King? And why not? This might just make his day."

They led the old man into the King's chamber thinking that the King would enjoy the joke.

The old man joined his palms and bowed respectfully before the King. "Your majesty, I have come to invite you to my home for dinner."

Term 2 | Unit 10

The King and his courtiers began to laugh. Some of the courtiers laughed so hard, they practically doubled up from the effort.

"So," said the King, "you, ha-ha-ha-ha, want to invite me to, ha-ha-ha-ha, dinner. Do you want me to come alone or do you want my Queen and courtiers as well?"

"Oh, well," said the old man, "your Queen and the courtiers are all welcome."

"Ha-ha-ha-ha," laughed the whole court.

Now, the King had quite an evil Prime Minister who added his suggestion: "What about the army? Aren't you going to invite the whole army?"

"Certainly. The whole army is invited as well," said the old man.

The King and the courtiers laughed so hard, they did not even notice the old man leave.

Part Two

The day before the dinner, the evil Prime Minister said to the King, "Your majesty, would it not be a good idea to check on the old man? Perhaps we should send out some spies to see if dinner for hundreds of thousands is actually being prepared."

Spies were sent out to the old man's hut. They snooped around for several hours and came back to the palace with this information. "Your majesty," they said, "we saw a large, neat hut in which enough shiny leaf-plates and earthenware cups were laid out to feed an entire kingdom. But we did not see any signs of food being cooked. No grain was being ground, no rice was soaking and no vegetables were being stewed in pots."

"Strange. Very strange," said the King. "Now that we have accepted the invitation, we will just have to go and see what the old man has in store for us."

"And if the food is not adequate, we will cut off the old man's head," the Prime Minister said viciously.

The next day the King, Queen, courtiers and army set off for the old man's hut.

Carpets had been spread on the floor and all the places neatly laid out. There was no sign of food.

The Prime Minister sniffed. "I cannot smell any kitchen smells. Strange."

The old man joined his palms together and bowed before the King. "Please be seated, your majesties. It was kind of you to come." He then washed his wooden bowl and prayed. "Let the King, Queen, courtiers and army get whatever they desire to eat," the old man commanded the bowl.

Before anyone could move an eyelid, there appeared muskmelons from Central Asia, as sweet as sugar, Persian rice pilaf flavoured with saffron and oranges, pheasants and puddings and creams and stews and halvas. As each man and woman dreamt of a particular food, it appeared in the bowl.

The King and his people were amazed. When dinner was finished, the evil Prime Minister turned to the King and said, "Such an unusual wooden bowl doesn't really belong to this stupid old man. He can eat any old thing. Even scraps. It is you – and your court – who should own this treasure."

As the King's party was leaving, the evil Prime Minister stretched out his hand, saying, "The King thanks you for your meal and desires that you let him take care of the bowl."

What could the old man do? He handed over his bowl – and was left to starve again.

Meanwhile, the King put the old man's bowl into one of his many storerooms and forgot all about it.

181

When the Nine Days' Festival came around again, the old man returned to Parvati's temple and bowed his head in prayer.

"Oh, goddess Parvati, I made such a mistake. I tried to be so grand. I even invited the King for dinner. Now he has taken away the wooden bowl and we are starving."

Parvati handed the old man a wooden rod and said, "Take this and whenever you are hungry, wash it, pray and ask for whatever you desire. And do not forget to invite the King to dinner once again."

The old man did as he was told. He went to the King and asked him to return for another meal. "Your majesty, I do hope you will not forget your Queen, courtiers and army."

This time the King and his courtiers did not laugh. But they were curious. "I wonder what trick the old man has up his sleeve this time?" mused the evil Prime Minister.

Once again, the King sent spies to the old man's hut a day before the dinner. Once again, the spies returned saying, "Your majesty, we saw a large, neat hut in which enough shining leaf-plates and earthenware cups were laid out to feed an entire kingdom. But we didn't see any signs of food being cooked. No grain was being ground, no rice was soaking and no vegetables were being stirred in pots."

"Strange. Very strange," said the King, "but we have accepted the invitation and must find out what the old man has in store for us."

The next day the King, Queen, courtiers and army set out for the old man's hut.

The old man put his palms together and bowed before the King and Queen. "Please be seated, your majesties. It was so kind of you to come." He then washed his wooden rod and prayed. "Let the King, Queen, courtiers and army get whatever they desire," he commanded the rod.

But instead of producing food, the rod began flying through the air, beating everyone. It beat the King, it beat the courtiers, and most of all, it beat the evil Prime Minister.

"Ouch, ouch, ouch," they all cried.

"Ouch," cried the evil Prime Minister.

The King turned to the old man. "Did you call us to dine or did you call us so we could be beaten?" the King asked. "What is going on here?"

"I beg your forgiveness your majesty," the old man said. "I did, indeed, invite you for dinner. The fact of the matter is that this rod is the master and the bowl you have is his wife. The rod is in a bad temper because he wants his wife returned to him."

The King did not want to be beaten any more so he said to his Prime Minister, "Where on earth is that wooden bowl we took away from the old man?"

"It is probably lying in some storeroom or other," said the evil Prime Minister, still rubbing himself all over after his beating.

So the King sent off a servant to his storeroom to find the bowl.

It was only after the bowl was returned to the old man that the beatings stopped.

Then the old man washed both the bowl and the rod, prayed and said, "Let the King, Queen, courtiers and army be served whatever foods they desire."

The best food from heaven was served.

The old man was happy.

So was his wife.

And so was goddess Parvati.

Bible Stories

Sentence of Death   *retold by Pat Alexander*

The armed guard hurried Jesus through the sleeping streets. At the house of the High Priest lamps were burning and the Council had been summoned. Peter followed at a safe distance – all the others had run away. They took Jesus inside and Peter hung about in the courtyard. It was cold and he edged nearer to the fire. A servant-girl passed.

"Aren't you a friend of the man they've arrested?" she said.

Peter had never felt so frightened. He shrank back into the shadows. "No! No! You've made a mistake. I don't know the man."

Three times that night the same question was asked. Each time Peter made the same reply.

"I don't know the man. I don't know the man."

Then, as dawn broke, he heard a cock crow – and Peter remembered Jesus' words. He went away, sobbing as if his heart would break.

Inside the house the Council were having a hard time of it. The prisoner would not answer their questions. He just stood there, not saying a word. Even when they hit him he made no move to defend himself.

The witnesses they had dragged from their beds could not agree. The Council could not make their charges stick.

Almost in despair the High Priest turned to Jesus.

"In God's name, tell us: are you the promised King, the Son of God?"

"I am," Jesus said. "One day everyone will know, when you see me seated at God's right hand and coming with the clouds of heaven."

"Enough!" shouted the High Priest. "He is speaking against God. That is blasphemy."

"We find the prisoner guilty," said the Council. And they sentenced him to death.

But there was still one problem. They had to get the Roman Governor's consent. They took Jesus to Pilate.

"This man is guilty of treason," they said. "He has tried to make himself king." They knew the Roman Emperor wouldn't like that! Pilate would have to take the matter seriously.

"Are you the king of the Jews?" Pilate asked Jesus. But there was no reply.

Every Passover Pilate set one of his prisoners free. So he went outside and spoke to the crowd.

"Shall I free your king?"

"No!" they shouted back. "We want Barabbas." (He was a murderer.)

"Then what shall I do with Jesus?"

"Crucify him! Crucify him!"

185

Pilate washed his hands of the affair. If that was what they wanted ... He handed Jesus over to his soldiers and they took him away. Then they began to make fun of him. They dressed him up in a purple robe and gave him a crown of sharp thorns. Then he was whipped and made to carry the wooden beam of the cross to Skull Hill. There they crucified him, with two thieves, one on either side.

"Father, forgive them," Jesus prayed, as he hung there in great pain. Then, with a loud cry – "It is finished!" – he died.

Two secret friends of Jesus begged Pilate for the body. Hurriedly they buried him in a new tomb, cut out of the rock. They rolled a great stone across the entrance to seal it.

The Body that Wasn't There! *retold by Pat Alexander*

Jesus died on Friday afternoon. For three hours the sun was blotted out and the whole land was dark. The Roman soldiers, used to seeing prisoners die, had seen nothing like this before. "It must have been true," said the officer in charge. "This man really was the Son of God."

Saturday was the Sabbath, the day of the Festival and a day of rest. All was quiet.

But on Sunday morning the women got up early – as soon as it was light. Three of them hurried to the tomb, carrying sweet-smelling spices. (There had been so little time on Friday, when Jesus' body was buried.) The spices were to put on the body – if only they could roll away the stone.

To their surprise, when they got there, the stone was already rolled back – and there was someone sitting there, dressed all in white.

"Don't be afraid," he said. "I know you are looking for Jesus. But he's not here. He's alive! Go and tell all his friends – especially Peter."

Mary Magdalene took in only one thing. The body had gone. She ran to find Peter, arriving all out of breath.

"Peter! John! They've taken Jesus away!"

The two friends set off at a run. John got there first. He stopped and looked in. There were the strips of cloth they had wound round the body, and the cloth for his head. He waited for Peter to catch up. Then they both went inside. The wrappings were all in place – they hadn't been taken off the body. There was just no body inside them.

Then they knew! The body wasn't there – because Jesus was alive again. He'd come back as he had promised.

A little later, Mary returned; she had followed slowly. She stood outside the tomb, crying. Through her tears she saw two angels dressed in white where the body of Jesus had been.

"Why are you crying?" they asked.

"Because they've taken Jesus away."

She turned and caught a glimpse of someone. Perhaps it was the gardener. He would know.

"If you took him away, please tell me where he is."

"Mary!"

As soon as she heard his voice, she *knew*!

"Teacher!" she said – her heart so full of joy she thought it would burst.

Late that evening Jesus' friends were together behind locked doors. Suddenly Jesus was there

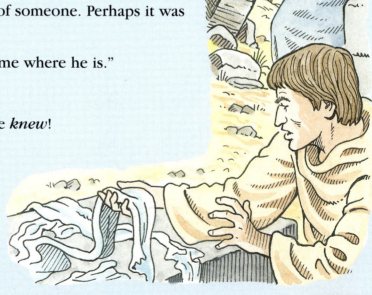

Term 2 | **Unit 11**

in the room with them. He showed them the marks on his hands and feet, where the nails had fastened him to the cross. Then they knew it was him. He was real! He was alive! They were too glad even to speak!

Thomas wasn't there that night.

"I don't believe it," he said when they told him what had happened. "Dead men don't come back to life. I *won't* believe unless I see the marks of the nails and touch the scars myself."

A week later, Jesus came again. He held out his hands for Thomas to see. But there was no need. Thomas was kneeling at Jesus' feet.

"My Lord and my God!" he said.

Easter *retold by Jan Pienkowski*
Part One

Jesus stood before the governor: and the governor asked him, Art thou the King of the Jews? And Jesus said, Thou sayest it. Pilate went out unto the Jews, and saith to them, I find in him no fault at all. But ye have a custom, that I should release unto you one at the passover: Will ye therefore that I release unto you the King of the Jews?

Then cried they all, Not this man but Barabbas.

Now Barabbas was a robber.

And Pilate said again to them, What will ye then that I shall do unto him whom ye call the King of the Jews? And they cried out, Crucify him. Then Pilate said, Why, what evil hath he done? And they cried out the more exceedingly, Crucify him.

When Pilate saw that he could prevail nothing, he took water,

188

and washed his hands before the multitude, saying, I am innocent of the blood of this just person. Then released he Barabbas unto them: and when he had scourged Jesus, he delivered him to be crucified.

The soldiers plaited a crown of thorns, and put it on his head, and they put on him a purple robe. And they bowed the knee before him saying, Hail, King of the Jews! And they smote him with their hands.

After they had mocked him they took the robe off from him and led him away to crucify him.

As they led him away, they laid hold upon one Simon, a Cyrenian, coming out of the country, and on him they laid the cross, that he might bear it after Jesus.

And there followed him a great company of people and of women, which bewailed and lamented him.

And when they were come to the place which is called Calvary, there they crucified him, and with him two thieves; the one on his right hand, and the other on his left.

Then said Jesus, Father, forgive them: for they know not what they do.

And it was the third hour.

Part Two

One of the thieves which were crucified with him railed on him, saying, If thou be Christ, save thyself and us. But the other rebuked him, saying, Dost not thou fear God? For we receive the due reward of our deeds: but this man hath done nothing amiss. And he said to Jesus, Lord, remember me when thou comest into thy kingdom.

And Jesus said to him, Today shalt thou be with me in paradise.

Now there stood by the cross of Jesus his mother, and his mother's sister, and Mary Magdalene. When Jesus saw his

Term 2 | Unit 11

mother and the disciple whom he loved, he saith to his mother, Woman, behold thy son! Then saith he to the disciple, Behold thy mother!

And from that hour that disciple took her unto his own home.

It was about the sixth hour, and there was a darkness over all the earth until the ninth hour. The sun was darkened, and the veil of the temple was rent in twain from the top to the bottom; and the earth did quake, and the rocks rent.

And when Jesus had cried with a loud voice, he said, Father, into thy hands I commend my spirit: and having said thus, he gave up the ghost.

Now when the centurion, and they that were with him, saw the earthquake, they feared greatly, saying, Truly this was the Son of God.

When the even was come, there came a rich man of Arimathaea, named Joseph, who also was Jesus' disciple.

He went boldly to Pilate, and begged the body of Jesus. Then Pilate commanded the body to be delivered.

And when Joseph had taken the body, he wrapped it in a clean linen cloth with spices, myrrh and aloes, and laid it in his own new tomb which he had hewn out in the rock.

And he rolled a great stone to the door of the sepulchre, and departed.

Term 2 | Unit 12

Tornadoes and Hurricanes

Trail of destruction as whistler whips through at height of storm bringing ... Isle of Wight

TORNADO TERROR

by Suzanne Pert

A tornado ripped a trail of destruction from Atherfield through to Shorwell at the height of the storm which lashed the Island on Sunday.

The sheer force of the wind tore off roofs, demolished historic barns and hurled into the air bricks, stones and domestic fowl and even an 18ft sailing boat complete with trailer.

During a week of storms and torrential rain which caused structural damage across the Island with winds gusting to hurricane force 80 mph and on-shore winds whipping up huge waves in Gurnard, and along the West Wight coastline, the freak tornado wreaked the most havoc.

Between 20 to 30 trees came down across roads and lanes elsewhere on the Island and the road between Gurnard and Cowes was closed for a time by police because of the danger as the sea breached the wall and waves broke spectacularly sending spray 30ft or more into the air.

In South Wight several witnesses saw the start of the tornado as a swirling tower of wind, topped by a large black cloud, rose from the sea off Atherfield Point.

It hit land at the Coastguard Cottages where one man caught outside in its path, a burly 16-stone policeman, crouched beside a car in fear for his life.

Term 2 | **Unit 12**

It left a trail of devastation towards Shorwell where it destroyed four barns at Kingston Farm, one brick-built and one built of stone, dating from the 1660s and 1700s.

The hugely powerful whirling wind sent a barrage of timbers and stones shooting into the adjacent Kingston Manor, the sheer force smashing more than a dozen windows and sending a chimney crashing to the ground at the newer 1818 end of the house.

Owners of the 17th century manor house, Professor Denis Picton and his wife, Jane, were thankful they were sitting in the sheltered end of the house.

"It could have been very dangerous if we had been in the kitchen where timbers from the barns whistled through the air and actually broke through the kitchen door," said Prof Picton, who is retired.

The tornado was then spotted over Chillerton Down and captured on video for 90 seconds by prison officer Mr Sidney Barton from his home at Camp Hill. He described it as a funnel with a big black cloud on top, really swirling and moving from west to east.

Most dramatic account came from PC Gareth Bloomfield, 28, who was visiting a house at Coastguard Cottages and had gone outside at about 11.45 am when there appeared to be a lull in the storm.

Suddenly there was a change in air pressure, together with a sucking sound.

"I looked up, the sky was dark with a swirling cloud above the houses coming from the sea.

"I realised that I was in imminent danger. I caught a glimpse of some heavy ridge stones being plucked from a neighbouring roof as I threw myself to the ground," said PC Bloomfield.

To protect himself, he tucked his shoulder into the underside of the car and sheltered his head.

"I was aware of violent rushing wind and the ground around me was a mass of swirling dirt.

"The car was lifting up to about ten centimetres from the ground and the Camper van in front of my car was lifting two feet off the ground.

"It took all my strength to keep myself, all 16 stone of me, on the ground with the car.

"But when I stood up and looked at what had happened that's when I got the real shock and I realised how lucky I'd been," said PC Bloomfield, who reckons the car saved him from serious injury, and possibly even saved his life.

Resident Annie Sefton, whose home escaped serious damage, said, "It was like a bomb site. We came down the path and saw Gareth standing next to his car.

"There was glass and debris everywhere because the wind had picked up an 18ft sailing dinghy and its trailer and thrown it onto Gareth's car.

"The boat came from one of the front yards a good 30ft away," said Ms Sefton.

Most badly damaged cottage was the most exposed, belonging to Mrs Mary Farquhar, whose two sons, Peter, 18 and James, 14, were in the house at the time.

193

| Term 2 | Unit 12 |

"It was like something out of the Wizard of Oz," said Mrs Farquhar, as she surveyed the pile of timbers in her back garden.

Her chicken shed had disappeared and was later found two gardens away, and a goat and sheep shed was lifted up and smashed to pieces across the field as the tornado left.

A chimney stack was destroyed, a sun lounge pulled from its foundations and almost all roof tiles removed.

Part of her kitchen and an upstairs bedroom were condemned as unsafe, pending repair of the chimney.

Her ducks were found in fields 500 metres away, some had been killed outright, tossed into the air as if they were pieces of paper.

Said Mrs Farquhar, "The RSPCA was wonderful. We had to have some ducks put down and others treated.

"I would also praise the fire brigade and my neighbours who were marvellous in helping us out," said Mrs Farquhar.

The Met Office HQ in Bracknell confirmed that a tornado was quite possible, given the weather conditions on Sunday.

Mr Andrew Yeatman said, "When there is an unstable area with a mixture of cold and warm air, these tornadoes are possible.

"They compound the wind speed. Damage is caused by the fact that the wind is coming from different directions," he said.

High Winds

Winds of Force 12 and above on the Beaufort Scale are called **hurricanes**. Great whirling storms build up around a central area of calm, called the **eye**. Hurricanes can devastate an area as much as 500 km (300 miles) across.

Trees are uprooted, buildings torn apart, and huge waves are driven against island shores and coastlines. Hurricanes are

194

frequent in the Caribbean and the Gulf of Mexico. In some parts of the world, hurricanes are called typhoons or cyclones. In Queensland, Australia, they are known locally as willy-willies.

The highest winds of all occur in **tornadoes**, whose wind speed can be anything from 150 to 450 kph (100 to 300 mph). Tornadoes are narrow whirlwinds of great violence which develop during thunderstorms. They can lift a railway truck weighing many tonnes high into the air, or smash a house to pieces. Tornadoes occur most often in the central USA and Australia.

Whirlwinds sometimes carry large amounts of sea or lake water, spinning it around and around to form a **water-spout**. In desert regions sand and dust are picked up by strong winds and carried for thousands of kilometres. Such whirlwinds can create sandstorms or form whirling columns called **dustdevils**.

The Wizard of Oz

by L Frank Baum

From the far north they heard a low wail of the wind, and Uncle Henry and Dorothy could see where the long grass bowed in waves before the coming storm. There now came a sharp whistling in the air from the south, and as they turned their eyes that way they saw ripples in the grass coming from that direction also.

Suddenly Uncle Henry stood up.

"There's a cyclone coming, Em," he called to his wife. "I'll go look after the stock." Then he ran towards the sheds where the cows and horses were kept.

Aunt Em dropped her work and came to the door. One glance told her of the danger close at hand.

"Quick, Dorothy!" she screamed. "Run for the cellar!"

Toto jumped out of Dorothy's arms and hid under the bed, and the girl started to get him. Aunt Em, badly frightened, threw open the trap door in the floor and climbed down the ladder into the small, dark hole. Dorothy caught Toto at last, and started to follow her aunt. When she was halfway across the room there came a great shriek from the wind, and the house shook so hard that she lost her footing and sat down suddenly upon the floor.

A strange thing then happened.

The house whirled around two or three times and rose slowly through the air. Dorothy felt as if she were up in a balloon.

The north and south winds met where the house stood, and made it the exact centre of the cyclone. In the middle of a cyclone the air is generally still, but the great pressure of the wind on every side of the house raised it up higher and higher, until it was at the very top of the cyclone; and there it remained and was carried miles and miles away as easily as you could carry a feather.

It was very dark, and the wind howled horribly around her, but Dorothy found she was riding quite easily. After the first few whirls around, and one other time when the house tipped badly, she felt as if she were being rocked gently, like a baby in a cradle.

Term 3	Unit 1

The Midnight Fox

By Betsy Byars

"In all my life I never saw anything like that fox standing there with her pale green golden eyes on me and this great black fur being blown by the wind."

Tom had hated the idea of going to his uncle's farm for a holiday, but in spite of his protests, off he went to stay on his uncle's farm, and it's on a day when he's just written to Petie that he suddenly sees the fox jumping into the wind-blown grass, and he goes out each day afterwards looking for her.

Fourteen times Tom sees the fox, and makes fourteen secret notches on the edge of his suitcase, but the fifteenth notch is on the dreadful day when Uncle Fred determines to shoot her for attacking a turkey – and Tom has to go along to see what he can do to help the animal he admires and loves.

Betsy Byars was born in North Carolina, USA, in 1928. Her early aspirations were to work with animals, but in 1950 she married an engineering lecturer and moved to Illinois. Housebound with young children, Betsy began to write articles for newspapers and magazines. As the children started to read, so she began to write stories for them. Using her own children's experiences and memories from her childhood, she produced many children's books. She now lives in South Carolina, preferring to write in winter, so as to spend the summer with her husband, gliding and learning to fly!

Part One

Chapter One: Bad News

Sometimes at night when the rain is beating against the windows of my room, I think about that summer on the farm. It has been five years, but when I close my eyes I am once again by the creek watching the black fox come leaping over the green, green grass. She is as light and free as the wind, exactly as she was the first time I saw her.

Or sometimes it is that last terrible night, and I am standing beneath the oak tree with the rain beating against me. The lightning flashes, the world is turned white for a moment, and I see everything as it was - the broken lock, the empty cage, the small tracks disappearing into the rain. Then it seems to me that I can hear, as plainly as I heard it that August night, above the rain, beyond the years, the high, clear bark of the midnight fox.

To begin with, I did not want to go to the farm. I was perfectly happy at home. I remember I was sitting at the desk in my room and I had a brand new $1.98 Cessna 180 model. I was just taking off the cellophane when my mom came in. I was feeling good because I had the model, and all evening to work on it, and then my mom told me in an excited way that I was going to Aunt Millie's farm for two whole months. I felt terrible.

"I don't want to go to any farm for two months," I said.

"But, Tommy, why not?"

"Because I just don't want to."

"Maybe you don't *now*," my mom said, "but after you think about it for a bit, you will. It's just that I've taken you by surprise. I probably shouldn't have come bursting in like –"

"I will never want to go."

She looked at me with a puzzled shrug. "I thought you would be so pleased."

"Well, I'm not."

"What's wrong?"

"There's nothing wrong. I would just hate to stay on a farm, that's all."

"How do you know? You can't even remember Aunt Millie's farm. You don't know whether you'd like it now or not."

"I know. I knew I wasn't going to like camp, and I didn't. I knew I wasn't going to like figs, and I don't. I knew I wasn't –"

"The trouble with you, Tommy, is that you don't *try* to like new things."

"You shouldn't have to *try* to like things. You should just very easily, without even thinking about it all, *like* them."

"All right," she said, and her upper lip was beginning to get tight. "When I first saw this farm, I very easily, without thinking about it at all, *loved* it. It is the prettiest farm I ever saw. It's in the hills and there are great big apple trees to climb and there are cows and horses and –"

"Animals hate me."

"Tom, I have never heard anything so silly in my life. Animals do not hate you."

"They do. How about that dog that came running up at about a hundred miles an hour and bit me for no reason? I suppose that dog loved me!"

"The lady explained that. The dog had a little ham bone and you stepped on it and the dog thought you were going to take it. Anyway," she continued quickly, "just wait till you see the baby lambs. There is nothing dearer in the world. They are –"

"I'll probably be the only kid in the world to be stampeded to death by a bunch of baby lambs."

"Tom!"

"I tell you, animals don't like me. Perfectly strange animals come charging at me all the time."

My mom ignored this and went on about the fun I would have in the garden, and especially gathering eggs. There was, according to her, no such fun in the world as going out to the henhouse, sticking your hand under some strange hen, grabbing an egg, and running back to the house with it for breakfast. I could picture that. I would be running to the house with my egg, see, having all this fun, and then there would be a noise like a freight train behind me. A terrible noise growing louder and louder, and I would look around and there would come about two hundred chickens running me down. CHAROOOOOOM! Me flattened on the ground while the lead hen snatches the egg from my crushed hand and returns in triumph to the coop.

My mom could see I wasn't listening to her, so she stopped talking about the fun and said, "I should think, Tom, that even if you do not particularly want to go to the farm –"

"I don't want to go at all."

"– even if you do not *particularly* want to go to the farm," she continued patiently, "you would realize how much this trip means to your father and me. It is the only chance we will ever have to go to Europe. The only chance."

Part Two

My mom and dad were going to Europe with about fifty other very athletic people, and they were going to bicycle through five countries and sleep in fields and barns. You can see that parents who would do that could never understand someone not wanting to go to the farm. I could not understand it myself completely. I just knew that I did not want to go, that I would never want to go, and that if I had to go, I would hate, loathe, and despise every minute of it.

"Don't you want your father and me to have this trip?"

"Yes."

"You're not acting like it."

"I *want* you to have the trip. I want you to have a hundred trips if you want them, just as long as I don't have to go to any crummy farm."

"You make it sound like a punishment."

"Why can't I stay here?"

"Because there's no one for you to stay with," she said.

"There's Mrs Albergotti." This shows how desperate I was. Mrs Albergotti was the kind of sitter who would come in the room where I was sleeping to see if I was still breathing.

"Mrs Albergotti cannot stay with you for two months."

"Why not?"

"Because she has a family of her own. Now, Tom, will you be reasonable? You are not a baby any more. You are almost ten years old."

"I am being reasonable."

My mother looked at me for a long time without saying anything. I lifted the lid off my model box. Usually this was a great moment for me. It was usually so great that trumpets should have blown - TA-DAAAAAAA! This time I looked down at the grey plastic pieces and they were just grey plastic pieces.

"Your father will talk to you when he gets home," she said, and left the room. I could hear her cross the hall into her room and shut the door. My mom cried easily. The week before we had been watching a TV show about an old elephant who couldn't do his circus routine any more, and suddenly I heard a terrible sob, and I looked over and it was my mom crying about the old elephant. Well, we all laughed, and she laughed too, only it was not so funny to hear my mom crying now, not because of an old elephant, but because of me.

That evening my father came in and talked to me. My dad is a high-school coach who likes to tell about things like the Lehigh-Central basketball game, when he won the game in the last two seconds with a free throw. If anything, I knew that he would be less understanding than my mom. He had not understood, for example, why I did not want to be in Little League even after he

had watched me strike out seventeen times straight.

"This is a wonderful opportunity," my dad said enthusiastically. "Wonderful! There's a pond here – did you know that? You can go swimming every day if you like."

"I'm not much of a swimmer," I reminded him. This was the understatement of the year. Having a body that would not float would be a great handicap to anybody.

"Well, you can learn! That is why this is such a wonderful opportunity." Then he said earnestly, "If you go to the farm with the right attitude, Tom, that's the main thing."

Part Three

Chapter Five: The Black Fox

The first three days on the farm were the longest, slowest days of my life. It seemed to me in those days that nothing was moving at all, not air, not time. Even the bees, the biggest fattest bees that I had ever seen, just seemed to hang in the air. The problem, or one of them, was that I was not an enormously adaptable person and I did not fit into new situations well.

I did a lot of just standing around those first days. I would be standing in the kitchen and Aunt Millie would turn around, stirring something, and bump into me and say, "Oh, my goodness! You gave me a scare. I didn't even hear you come in. When *did* you come in?"

"Just a minute ago."

"Well, I didn't hear you. You are so *quiet.*"

Or Uncle Fred would come out of the barn wiping his hands on a rag and there I'd be, just standing, and he'd say, "Well, boy, how's it going?"

"Fine, Uncle Fred."

"Good! Good! Don't get into any mischief now."

"I won't."

I spent a lot of time at the pond and walking down the road and back. I spent about an hour one afternoon hitting the end of an old rope swing that was hanging from a tree in the front yard. I made my two models, and then I took some of the spare plastic strips and rigged up a harness, so that the horse was pulling the car, and Aunt Millie got very excited over this bit of real nothing and said it was the cleverest thing she had ever seen.

I wrote a long letter to Petie. I went down to the stream and made boats of twigs and leaves and watched them float out of sight. I looked through about a hundred farm magazines. I weeded Aunt Millie's flowers while she stood over me saying, "Not that, not *that*, that's a zinnia. Get the chickweed – see? Right here." And she would snatch it up for me. I had none of the difficult chores that I had expected because the farm was so well run that everything was already planned without me. In all my life I have never spent longer, more miserable days, and I had to keep saying, "I'm fine, just fine," because people were asking how I was all the time.

The one highlight of my day was to go down to the mailbox for the mail. This was the only thing I did all day that was of any use. Then, too, the honking of the mail truck would give me the

feeling that there was a letter of great importance waiting for me in the box. I could hardly hurry down the road fast enough. Anyone watching me from behind would probably have seen only a cloud of dust, my feet would pound so fast. So far, the only mail I had received was a postcard from my mom with a picture of the statue of Liberty on it telling me how excited and happy she was.

This Thursday morning when I went to the mailbox there was a letter to me from Petie Burkis and I was never so glad to see anything in my life. I ripped it open and completely destroyed the envelope I was in such a hurry. And I thought that when I was a hundred years old, sitting in a chair with a rug over my knees, and my mail was brought in on a silver tray, if there was a letter from Petie Burkis on that tray, I would snatch it up and rip it open just like this. I could hardly get it unfolded – Petie folds his letter up small – I was so excited.

Dear Tom,

There is nothing much happening here. I went to the playground Saturday after you left, and you know that steep bank by the swings? Well, I fell all the way down that. Here's the story:

BOY FALLS DOWN BANK WHILE GIRL ONLOOKERS CHEER

Today Petie Burkis fell down the bank at Harley Playground. It is reported that some ill-mannered girls at the park for a picnic cheered and laughed at the sight of the young, demolished boy. The brave youngster left the park unaided.

Not much else happened. Do you get Chiller Theatre? There was a real good movie on Saturday night about mushroom men.

Write me a letter,

Petie Burkis

I went in and gave the rest of the mail to Aunt Millie who said, "Well, let's see what the government's sending us today," and then I got my box of stationery and went outside.

205

There was a very nice place over the hill by the creek. There were trees so big I couldn't get my arms around them, and soft grass and rocks to sit on. They were planning to let the cows into this field later on, and then it wouldn't be as nice, but now it was the best place on the farm.

Incidentally, anyone interested in butterflies would have gone crazy. There must have been a million in that one field. I had thought about there being a contest – a butterfly contest and hundreds of people would come from all over the country to catch butterflies. I had thought about it so much that I could almost see this real fat lady from Maine running all over the field with about a hundred butterfly nets and a fruit jar under her arm.

Anyway, I sat down and wrote Petie a letter.

Dear Petie,

I do not know whether we get Chiller Theatre or not. Since there is no TV set here, it is very difficult to know what we could get if we had one.

My farm chores are feeding the pigs, feeding the chickens, weeding the flowers, getting the mail, things like that. I have a lot of time to myself and I am planning a movie about a planet that collides with Earth, and this planet and Earth become fused together, and the people of Earth are terrified of the planet, because it is very weird-looking and they have heard these terrible moanlike cries coming from the depths of it. That's all so far.

       Write me a letter,

            Tom

I had just finished writing this letter and was waiting for a minute to see if I would think of anything to add when I looked up and saw the black fox.

Part Four

I did not believe it for a minute. It was like my eyes were playing a trick or something, because I was just sort of staring across this field, thinking about my letter, and then in the distance, where the grass was very green, I saw a fox leaping over the crest of the field. The grass moved and the fox sprang towards the movement, and then, seeing that it was just the wind that had caused the grass to move, she ran straight for the grove of trees where I was sitting.

It was so great that I wanted it to start over again, like you can turn movie film back and see yourself repeat some fine thing you have done, and I wanted to see the fox leaping over the grass again. In all my life I have never been so excited.

I did not move at all, but I could hear the paper in my hand shaking, and my heart seemed to have moved up in my body and got stuck in my throat.

The fox came straight towards the grove of trees. She wasn't afraid, and I knew she had not seen me against the tree. I stayed absolutely still even though I felt like jumping up and screaming, "Aunt Millie! Uncle Fred! Come see this. It's a fox, a *fox*!"

Her steps as she crossed the field were lighter and quicker than a cat's. As she came closer I could see that her black fur was tipped with white. It was as if it were midnight and the moon were shining on her fur, frosting it. The wind parted her fur as it changed directions. Suddenly she stopped. She was ten feet away now, and with the changing of the wind she got my scent. She looked right at me.

I did not move for a moment and neither did she. Her head was cocked to one side, her tail curled up, her front left foot raised. In all my life I never saw anything like that fox standing there with her pale green golden eyes on me and this great black fur being blown by the wind.

Suddenly her nose quivered. It was such a slight movement I almost didn't see it, and then her mouth opened and I could see the pink tip of her tongue. She turned. She still was not afraid, but with a bound that was lighter than the wind – it was as if she was being blown away over the field – she was gone.

Still I didn't move. I couldn't. I couldn't believe that I had really seen the fox.

I had seen foxes before in zoos, but I was always in such a great hurry to get on to the good stuff that I was saying stupid things like, "I want to see the go-rilllllas," and not once had I ever really looked at a fox. Still, I could never remember seeing a black fox, not even in a zoo.

Also, there was a great deal of difference between seeing an animal in the zoo in front of painted fake rocks and trees and seeing one natural and free in the woods. It was like seeing a kite on the floor and then, later, seeing one up in the sky where it was supposed to be, pulling at the wind.

I started to pick up my pencil and write as quickly as I could, "P.S. Today I saw a black fox." But I didn't. This was the most exciting thing that had happened to me, and "P.S. Today I saw a black fox" made it nothing. "So what else is happening?" Petie Burkis would probably write back. I folded my letter, put it in an envelope, and sat there.

Grandpa Chatterji

by Jamila Gavin

Part One

On the day of his arrival, Mum and Dad got up very early and drove off to the airport to meet Grandpa Chatterji. Neetu and Sanjay didn't go because there wouldn't be room in the car on the way back. Old Mrs Bennet from next door came in to look after them.

They waited and waited. Sanjay looked out of the window and Neetu looked out of the other. What would he be like? Would he wear a smart suit and shiny black shoes like Dad's dad? Would he smoke cigars and sit in the best easy chair and talk business with Dad in a big boomy voice? Would he have the best bed? Would he be served first at table? Would he always insist on using the bathroom first in the morning, even though he took the longest and made them late for school? And would he be critical and strict and insist on total obedience at all times?

They waited and waited. Suddenly, Sanjay shouted, "They're here!" The little red Mini had pulled up outside the house.

"Oh dear," cried Neetu, suddenly going all shy, "I'm going to hide."

They both hid behind the sofa. They heard the front door open. They heard Mum come in and say gently, "Welcome to our home!" They heard Dad say, "I'll take your luggage up to your room," and they heard a thin, quiet, soft voice say, "And where are my little grandchildren?"

Then there was silence. Crouched behind the sofa, Neetu and Sanjay hardly breathed. Then suddenly, although they didn't hear Grandpa Chatterji come into the room, they knew he was there because they saw a pair of bare, dark-brown, knobbly, long-toed, bony feet.

The feet came and stood right close by them. The feet emerged from beneath thin, white trousers, and as their eyes travelled all the way up, past a white tunic and brown waistcoat and past a red and blue woolly scarf round the neck, they found themselves looking into a round, shining, kind, wrinkly face, with deep-as-oceans large, brown eyes, and a mass of pure, white, fluffy hair which fell in a tangle over his brow.

"Ah!" exclaimed Grandpa Chatterji with a great, loving sigh, and he opened his arms to embrace them.

After they had all hugged each other, Mum said, "Children, take Grandpa up to his room, he will want to bath and change after his long journey. I'll go and make a nice cup of tea."

Sanjay began chattering as he clambered up the stairs, leading the way.

"Why aren't you wearing any shoes?" he asked.

"Because I took them off at the door, so as not to bring any dirt into the house. We always do that in India," answered Grandpa Chatterji.

"Did you come with lots of suitcases, Grandpa?" Sanjay went on, "and did you bring us lots of presents?"

"Ssh!" said Neetu, embarrassed. "That's rude, Sanjay."

"Just you wait and see," replied Grandpa, who didn't mind at all.

When they went into the guest room, they couldn't see any suitcases at all.

"Where is your luggage?" asked Neetu.

"Oh, I only ever travel with my bedroll," said Grandpa. "My needs are very simple," and he pointed to a roly-poly round khaki, canvas roll, all held together with leather straps, and covered in airline stickers and labels.

"Does that mean we don't have presents?" sighed Sanjay.

"Just you wait and see," replied Grandpa again.

"You've got the best room in the house," chattered Sanjay, bravely trying to ignore the mysterious roll which contained everything that Grandpa had brought.

"You've got the nicest sheets and duvet and curtains to match, you have the plumpiest pillows and the softest bed. It's the best bed in the house for bouncing on," and Sanjay flung himself on to the bed, which Mum had made all smooth and neat, and he rumpled it all up.

"Sanjay!" cried Neetu with horror, dragging him off. "Look what you've done," and she tried to straighten it out.

"If you like this bed so much, you'd better sleep in it," said Grandpa Chatterji. "I prefer something harder."

"Where will you sleep then, Grandpa?" asked Neetu looking worried.

"I'll sleep on the floor as I always do," he replied. "I am like a snail, my dear," murmured Grandpa. "All I need, wherever I go, is my bedroll. It carries all my belongings, and when I unroll it, it becomes my bed."

The children looked in awe at the khaki, canvas roll. It suddenly seemed to be the most important thing in the world. "Can we unroll it, Grandpa?" whispered Sanjay.

Term 3 | Unit 2

Part Two

Grandpa bent over the roll and undid the old leather straps, then he slowly unrolled it alongside the bed. At first it seemed that all it contained was one sheet and one blanket. Sanjay was sure there were no presents; but then Grandpa wriggled his hand into the large pocket at one end of the roll and pulled out a tooth mug and toothbrush all wrapped in a towel, a hair brush and comb and his shaving things. Sanjay stared expectantly. Were there any presents?

Then Grandpa went to a pocket at the other end and wriggled his hand inside. He pulled out a woolly jumper, a woolly hat, some socks, underwear, hankies, a shirt, a tunic and waistcoat, but still no presents.

At last, he folded back the sheet. Between the sheet and the blanket was a small, faded rug. He pulled back the rug to show lots of different packages.

"Presents!" breathed Sanjay, full of expectation.

"Why did you bring that old rug?" asked Neetu in a puzzled voice.

Grandpa Chatterji lifted it out as though it were the most precious thing in the world. "I never go anywhere without this," he murmured. "It is my meditation rug. I sit on it to do all my thinking and praying."

"Are those things presents?" asked Sanjay, pointing to the packages.

"Yes, yes, here you are," laughed Grandpa. He handed Sanjay two long thin packages.

"Thank you, thank you!" yelled Sanjay, ripping them open. "What are they?"

"One is a specially made, wooden wriggly snake, and the

other is an Indian flute. Later I will teach you some tunes, but for now, you can just blow. It makes a lovely sound. Snakes love the sound of the flute. It makes them sway and puts them into a good mood."

Sanjay flung his arms round his old grandfather. "Thank you, thank you, Grandpa Chatterji!" and he rushed off to show his mum and dad.

Neetu waited patiently. Which package was for her? He bent over and handed her one of the larger ones. "What a beauty you are, my dearest, little granddaughter! This is for you."

When Neetu opened up her package, she found a beautiful pink and green and gold sari. It was a special small-sized sari for little girls. In India they have to wait until they are nearly grown-up before they can wear a sari, but all little girls love to have a sari they can dress up in, and this is what her grandfather had brought for her.

It made Neetu feel very solemn and proud. "Oh thank you, Grandpa!" she declared in a grown-up voice, "I'll go and ask Mum to help me put it on."

Later, when Grandpa Chatterji had bathed and changed, Neetu, all dressed up in her sari, and Sanjay, with his snake and flute, went upstairs to find him. They knocked on his door.

"Come in!" he said in his soft, high voice.

They went in. Grandpa was sitting on the floor on his old rug. He was sitting very straight, his eyes staring in front and his arms stretched over his cross-legged knees.

"What are you doing, Grandpa?" asked Sanjay.

"I'm being a lotus flower floating quietly on a sea of milk."

"Why are you being a lotus flower?" asked Neetu. She was looking like such a beautiful grown-up lady in her new sari.

Grandpa looked at her and smiled with admiration. "Come, children. Come and sit next to me. There's room on the rug."

Neetu and Sanjay sat cross-legged one on each side of their grandfather. They stretched out their arms over their knees and straightened their backs.

"We are being lotus flowers because we are trying to be as calm and peaceful and perfect as lotus flowers are," explained Grandpa Chatterji, "and if you close your eyes, you can imagine you are floating on a sea of milk before the creation of the world."

The children closed their eyes and floated away.

Then Grandpa suddenly woke up with a shout and cried, "I feel rested now! Come on! Where's that cup of tea your mother promised me? And while I'm drinking my tea, Sanjay can play the flute, and Neetu can dance! Will you?" he begged, his dark eyes glittering.

Neetu and Sanjay nodded with excitement. "Oh, Grandpa Chatterji! We're so glad you came."

Part Three

Chapter Two: 'Õm...Õm...Õm...'

When Neetu awoke the next morning, the first thing she thought was, "Did Grandpa Chatterji really sleep on the floor?"

She sat up wide awake. It must be very early, because her room was still dark. Just a faint grey streak of light slipped between the curtains. Outside, the first blackbird had begun his dawn song.

She crept along to Grandpa Chatterji's room. His door was open. She peeped inside. At first she couldn't see anything. Then as her eyes adjusted, she saw that the spare bed, with its flowery duvet, was empty and hadn't been touched. On the floor, rolled out with a flat pillow and blanket was Grandpa Chatterji's bedroll; but there was no sign of Grandpa. Then she heard a sound. A slow, low repeating sound like the throbbing of a fridge, or the wind strumming the telephone wire. Or was it? Neetu listened carefully. Was it her own heart beating? No. Her heart was going boom, boom, boom, like a softly muffled drum. This sound was more like the waves beating against the shore; or a giant breathing ... or ...?

Õm...Õm...Õm... The sound seemed to be everywhere; inside and outside. Was it Sanjay playing his flute? She tiptoed out of her bedroom and looked into her brother's room. He lay fast asleep, sprawled across his bed with his feet sticking out, and an arm flung over his best teddy. His wooden flute lay waiting patiently upon his pillow. Sanjay wasn't making the sound. Was it Dad snoring? She crept into her parents' bedroom. She saw their two humps side by side like bookends under the double duvet. She went closer and stood listening. But no, Mum and Dad were still so deeply asleep that you could hardly hear them breathing at all.

215

So she went downstairs, past the ticking clock in the hall, past the puff of the boiler as it fired the central heating, past the low throbbing of the fridge and up to the back door. Here, the sound seemed louder. It was coming from the garden. Õm...Õm...Õm... Was it the tree moaning in the wind?

She went outside. It wasn't a very big garden. Just a patch of lawn with two long flower beds running the length of the fence on each side. The best thing was the tree at the bottom. It wasn't the sort of tree anyone would plant. Its seed had been blown there by the wind long before Neetu was even born. It had grown quietly and secretly without anybody noticing. It had grown and grown till it was taller than their house. Its branches stretched out like lots of arms, and sometimes the wind blew around it making it creak and swish. It was where the blackbird sang his songs and where the sparrows caused kerfuffles among the clumps of ivy which clung to the trunk. But as Neetu stood outside the back door, she realised that it was a perfectly still morning, with not one breath of wind to even rustle the leaves. Õm...Õm...Õm...

Then she saw him. Grandpa Chatterji was standing at the base of the tree. He wasn't wearing stripy pyjamas as Grandpa Leicester always did. He was bare-footed and was only wearing a thin white cloth wrapped round his waist and a white thread across his bare chest. He had spread out his precious rug, and he stood on one leg with his arms upstretched to the sky, as if he too were part of the tree.

Part Four

Õm...Õm...Õm... Neetu moved softly. She had nearly called out to her grandfather, but something told her not to. Silently, she walked across the grass and stood at his side. She looked up into his face. It was completely calm. His eyes were open, but he didn't look at her. He didn't even seem to know she was there. He breathed in a long, long breath which expanded his chest, and then he breathed out very very slowly. As he did, the deep, throbbing sound of Õm soared through the air.

There was just room on the rug for Neetu. Without asking, she stood by his side. She tried to stand on one leg, but wobbled. She tried again, and managed to stand for a little longer. She raised her arms and looked up at the sky. Dawn was breaking through the grey branches, creating islands of pink clouds. Õm...Õm... She copied.

After a while, Grandpa Chatterji looked down at his granddaughter and smiled.

"What are we doing, Grandpa?" she whispered.

"We're praying to God and welcoming a new day. When you make a round shape with your lips and say 'O' you are making the shape of the sun, the shape of the world and the shape of the universe. When you make the sound 'Õm...' you are talking to the Creator of Everything."

Then suddenly, Grandpa stopped being holy.

"I'm starving!" he cried. "Let's make *pooris*!"

He seemed to fly down the garden and into the kitchen. Neetu had to run to keep up.

"Where's the flour?" he asked.

Neetu found the flour.

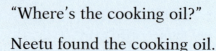

"Where's the cooking oil?"

Neetu found the cooking oil.

"Where's the mixing bowl?"

Neetu found the mixing bowl.

Then Grandpa Chatterji put down his rug on the floor in a corner of the kitchen and began to mix the dough.

Sanjay came in playing his flute. He was still in his pyjamas and his eyes were sticky with sleep.

"Where have you been? I was looking everywhere for you," he grumbled.

"Grandpa and I were saying hello to the sun," explained Neetu. "Look! We stood like this."

"Come and help me with the *pooris*, you two!" interrupted Grandpa. "Look! I've kneaded the dough. Now you take a handful and work it round into a ball. Then flatten it out on this wooden board and roll it into a circle with the rolling pin. I'll heat up the cooking oil."

When the oil was smoking hot, one by one, Grandpa dropped the rolled out circles of dough into the sizzling pan.

"Look!" cried Neetu excitedly. "Look how they puff up!"

"They're just like little footballs!" yelled Sanjay.

"They're round like Õm," said Neetu.

Soon they had a plate piled high with *pooris*.

Part Five

When they went home and told Grandpa Chatterji about the fair, his eyes gleamed with pleasure. "I love fairs," he beamed. "I love watching all the elephants and camels and horses and bullock carts, and all the women in their glittering skirts and saris, and all the men wearing their most colourful turbans. Oh good, oh good!" And he rubbed his hands together in anticipation.

"But, Grandpa," exclaimed Sanjay in a puzzled voice, "fairs here aren't like that."

"You're thinking of an Indian fair," laughed Mum. "This will be quite different."

"Oh!" said Grandpa, looking rather downcast. "What will this fair be like?"

"It will have dodgem cars and merry-go-rounds and waltzers and a ghost train. It will have lots of stalls with games and competitions. I won a fluffy cat last year. I guessed the right number when I tossed in a coin," Neetu told him.

"Grandpa, will you go on the rockets with me?" begged Sanjay. "Everyone else is too scared."

"I'll go on anything," boasted Grandpa, looking excited again.

"You'll remember your age, Pa, that's what you'll do," said Mum firmly.

But Grandpa Chatterji couldn't remember his age. He was ageless. Sometimes he seemed as old and as wise as the universe, and other times, it was as though he had only just been born and had come into the world full of wonder. Now, he looked forward to the fair with all the excitement of a child. He rushed about saying, "Come on, then. Let's go, let's go! What are we waiting for?"

"We'll go when its dark, Grandpa. It's much more fun," they told him.

The Love Letters of Ragie Patel

By Lee Hall

Characters
RAGIE PATEL A boy
JIMMY SPUD His friend
NANDINI Ragie's Auntie
GRANDDAD Ragie's Granddad
GRANDMA Ragie's Grandma
PAUL Nandini's boyfriend
RAMESH Her intended fiancé

Letter

Ragie: *(Reading out loud)* Dear Dad, I'm sitting in my chair now. It's quite good only the legs are wobbly – so that's why the pen squiggles like that. First I was downstairs for a while, but then I came up here to write you a letter. You'll probably be in India by now, because of the time change. Any rate it is quite boring on account of everyone being on their holidays like you.

By the way, I don't hate you and Mum any more for making me stay here. I think it is because I am very mature now. When I'm old I will go on holiday as well and leave my children with you. Anyway, I hope you have a safe landing and I'll write to you everyday, or sometimes twice if I can get some extra paper.

Yours sincerely, Ragie Patel. (Your Son)

PS. Don't forget to look for some of them pointy shoes I was telling you about. I think you can get them at the market.

Scene 1 Ragie's Bedroom

Granddad:	Ragie?
Ragie:	Granddad.
Granddad:	What are you doing up here?
Ragie:	I'm writing a letter.
Granddad:	He's only been gone forty minutes.
Ragie:	Oh.
Granddad:	Get yourself outside, it's a lovely day.
Ragie:	I thought I'd stay here.
Granddad:	I'm not having you moping around the house. I've got to go back down to the shop.
Ragie:	Do I have to?
Granddad:	You're just like your father. I hope you're not going to be insolent for the next six weeks.
Ragie:	But I haven't been insolent. I'm only trying to be good.
Granddad:	Well, get yourself some fresh air.
Ragie:	OK.
Granddad:	You might make yourself some new friends.
Ragie:	What friends will I make round here?
Granddad:	I don't know. Just get yourself out and see.

Ragie:	But Granddad, I'm not very forthcoming in public situations.
Granddad:	Look, just make sure you're back here sharpish for your tea.

Scene 2 The Back Lane

Jimmy:	Excuse me. Do you believe in God?
Ragie:	What do you mean?
Jimmy:	Well, do you think he exists and that?
Ragie:	God?
Jimmy:	Yeah.
Ragie:	I suppose so. Who are you?
Jimmy:	So, what do you think he looks like?
Ragie:	Well, there's different ones.
Jimmy:	No there's not.
Ragie:	There is in India.
Jimmy:	Are you from India?
Ragie:	No I'm from Durham.
Jimmy:	Oh.
Ragie:	But me Dad's from India. He's a doctor.
Jimmy:	Straight.
Ragie:	He went back though.
Jimmy:	Has he left you, like?
Ragie:	Just for the summer.
Jimmy:	That must mean you're like an orphan.
Ragie:	Not really. Maybes a temporary one.

Jimmy:	I'm Jimmy Spud.
Ragie:	Hello.
Jimmy:	So in India they have different Gods to what we have?
Ragie:	They've got loads of them.
Jimmy:	What for?
Ragie:	I don't know. One of them's got the head of an elephant and the body of a man.
Jimmy:	With a trunk?
Ragie:	And ears – the lot.
Jimmy:	That's a bit weird.
Ragie:	That's nowt. One of them's a monkey.
Jimmy:	Is your Granddad Mr Patel that lives above the shop?
Ragie:	Why, like?
Jimmy:	He's a right nutter, him.
Ragie:	Is he?
Jimmy:	He's got an axe under the counter you know. I seen him chase these lads with it.
Ragie:	My Granddad?
Jimmy:	He was running down the street with an axe. He's never chased you has he?
Ragie:	Not yet. I've only been here since this morning. I hardly ever come because Dad and Granddad have these arguments.
Jimmy:	He probably chased your Dad inall.
Ragie:	It's quite hot isn't it?

Jimmy: So there isn't just one God but loads of them?

Ragie: I think there's hundreds but some of them are the same one twice.

Jimmy: How do you mean?

Ragie: Like in different shapes and stuff.

Jimmy: They change shape.

Ragie: More like change lives. They keep coming back. Everybody does. That's what Granddad reckons.

Jimmy: What? You come back after you're dead?

Ragie: That's reincarnation. Like after you die, then you come back as someone else.

Jimmy: Will I come back?

Ragie: Probably. You're probably someone else already.

Jimmy: Christ. Who do you think I am?

Ragie: I don't know. Will you stop asking me questions?

Jimmy: Why?

Ragie: I don't really know very much about this, you know.

Jimmy: But how will I find out who I really am?

Ragie: I don't know. You can get books on it.

Jimmy: Maybes I'll go to the library then.

Ragie: Look, I think I'd better go in now. It's nearly time for me tea.

Jimmy: Oh.

224

Ragie:	Will you be my new friend while I'm here?
Jimmy:	I suppose. What do Indians have for their tea?
Ragie:	I don't know. Fish fingers or something.
Jimmy:	I thought you'd have curry.
Ragie:	I do sometimes. But I'm not really Indian you know.
Jimmy:	What do you mean?
Ragie:	I'm British.
Jimmy:	But you look like an Indian.
Ragie:	I know.
Jimmy:	OK then. See you around.
MUSIC:	"Dites-Moi" from *South Pacific*

Scene 3 Ragie's Bedroom

(A knock at the door)

Nandini:	It's only me.
Ragie:	I was just getting ready for bed.
Nandini:	Can I come in?
Ragie:	Yeah.

(Nandini comes in and closes the door.)

Nandini:	I brought you some sweets.
Ragie:	Aren't they Grandma's?
Nandini:	She gets enough.
Ragie:	Do you not like Grandma?

225

Nandini:	She's not the problem.
Ragie:	Are you really going to get married?
Nandini:	Supposedly.
Ragie:	You must be quite old.
Nandini:	Ranjiv, I'm only seventeen.
Ragie:	Well, that's quite old. *(Pause)* Do you not want to marry him?
Nandini:	I don't want to stay here. I mean, I asked them and everything.
Ragie:	Asked them?
Nandini:	To arrange it. But now it seems so sudden. I mean he's coming up at the weekend. We'll be married in a few weeks. I just didn't think things would turn out as they have.
Ragie:	But aren't you pleased he got you a husband?
Nandini:	I suppose.
Ragie:	I thought you'd be glad. Most people want to get married, don't they?
Nandini:	It's quite complicated.
Ragie:	Is it...?
Nandini:	I mean, what if I don't fall in love?
Ragie:	But you have to love your husband, don't you?
Nandini:	Not necessarily. You can't really help who you fall in love with.
Ragie:	Can you fall in love with anybody?
Nandini:	I suppose so.

Ragie:	Even if they weren't your husband?
Nandini:	Theoretically you could fall in love with anyone.
Ragie:	What does it mean exactly – falling in love?
Nandini:	You know, it's special. When someone makes you feel really nice.
Ragie:	You mean when they're friendly?
Nandini:	More than friendly. When you look at them, they should seem beautiful.
Ragie:	Like you?
Nandini:	Me?
Ragie:	You're beautiful.
Nandini:	Don't you think I'm fat?
Ragie:	I think you're perfect.
Nandini:	You're so sweet, Ragie Patel. *(She kisses him.)* Anyway, beauty's not just looks. It's the person inside that you fall in love with, don't you think? Their soul. I mean they could be anyone, but you see things that other people don't. I'm keeping you up.
Ragie:	It's alright – I like being kept up.
Nandini:	Ragie, if I give you this letter to deliver, will you promise not to tell anyone?
Ragie:	A letter?
Nandini:	Ssh.
Ragie:	What's in it?
Nandini:	It's personal.
Ragie:	What's personal about it?

Term 3 | **Unit 3**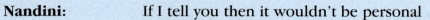

Nandini: If I tell you then it wouldn't be personal would it? Look, I'm asking you because this is very important.

Ragie: Who's it to?

Nandini: The man in the garage.

Ragie: The mechanic?

Nandini: Paul.

Ragie: You want me to give him a letter?

Nandini: Ssh. Yes.

Ragie: Why?

Nandini: Look, its just to get some information.

Ragie: What for?

Nandini: A project.

Ragie: A project?

Nandini: At school.

Ragie: About what?

Nandini: What does it matter what it's about? Engines.

Ragie: Oh.

Nandini: For science.

Ragie: Oh.

Nandini: Look, just don't tell anyone.

Ragie: Why? Are you cheating?

Nandini: No.

Ragie: What if I get caught?

Nandini: You won't get caught.

Ragie: You might get expelled.

Nandini: I won't be expelled. Stop fussing.

Ragie: I don't want to do anything bad.

Nandini: You're not doing anything bad. You're doing something very important.

Ragie: Are you sure it will help your project?

Nandini: Positive.

Ragie: OK.

Nandini: Oh thank you. *(She kisses him.)*

Ragie: Nandini.

Nandini: Yes?

Ragie: I hope you do fall in love.

Nandini: Thank you, Ragie, thank you. Night, night.

MUSIC: "There is Nothin' like a Dame" from *South Pacific*

Letter

Ragie: Dear Dad, Today has been great success. First off I met a new friend, then I talked to Auntie Nandini. She is very beautiful and quite brainy. She is doing a project on pistons for sociology or something then she's going to get married to some bloke from Manchester who is very handsome, except she doesn't know if she is in love. I took Grandma some sweets and we had a good chat. Sometimes she thought I was Granddad, but never mind. Don't forget I am a size four and a half.

        Yours sincerely,

                Ragie Patel.

Bottersnikes and Gumbles

by S.A. Wakefield

Chapter One

Bottersnikes are the laziest creatures, probably, in the whole world.

They are too lazy to dig burrows, like rabbits, or to find hollow trees to live in as the small animals do, and would be horrified at the work of building nests, like birds. Bottersnikes find their homes readymade, in rubbish heaps. When they find a pile of tins, pots, pans and junk, they think it is lovely, and crawl in. And live there, sleeping mostly. Best of all they like the rubbish heaps along dusty roadsides in the lonely Australian bush, where they can sleep for weeks, undisturbed.

Once, in a rubbish heap like this, two long black ears poked out of a watering can. The ears came first because they were twice as long as the head they belonged to. Between the ears appeared an ugly green face with slanted eyes, a nose like a cheese grater and a mean mouth with pointed teeth sticking out. The skin was wrinkly all over and little toadstools grew where the eyebrows should have been.

This was the King of the Bottersnikes. He squeezed out of the watering can.

The King's ears turned bright red because he was angry – this always happens to Bottersnikes when they get angry – and the cause of his temper was a thistle growing through the bottom of his bed. But he was too lazy to pull it out and just stood there looking, with his ears growing redder. Near him he saw an old rusting car, propped against a gum tree.

What a palace that would make for a Bottersnike King! "If someone would open the door," he thought, "I would get in."

So the King yelled at the top of his voice for help – and very loud that is; but the other Bottersnikes, all twenty or so of the King's band, snored loudly from their beds in the rubbish to show they had not heard.

Chapter Two

This meant that the King would have to pull someone out of bed, kick him and twist his tail till he woke up, and make him open the car door, so that the King could get in. Bottersnikes go to no end of trouble to do things the easiest way. "There is no one, no one at all," the King growled, "who will help." His ears glowed in a royal rage that was quite terrible to see.

As the King was yelling for help the Gumbles happened to be passing, which was just their bad luck. They were on their way down the hill to a little stream they knew of, called Earlyfruit Creek, where the water flowed into quiet pools and banks of sand made tiny beaches just right for Gumble paddling.

"Hey, you!" bawled the King to the Gumbles, "Come and open this door and help me in."

The Gumbles were a bit astonished, as all their friends in the Bush were much politer than this, but being cheerful little creatures and always ready to lend a hand, like good Brownies, they said: "Well, all right, if it won't take too long, because we're in a hurry to get to the creek, you see."

"Don't argue," the King said. "Just do as you're told."

By climbing up each other's backs the Gumbles managed to open the car door, and with a one-two-three altogether *shove*

they heaved the King into his new palace. Hearing the strange voices, the other Bottersnikes decided to wake up. They peered at these funny little creatures they'd not seen before and asked: "What are these?"

"Useful," the King said, clambering on to the steering wheel, "That's what they are. Grab 'em."

"Here, just a minute – you can't do that," the Gumbles cried, all speaking at once, "We only stopped to lend a hand. We're just running down to the beach. For a paddle in the cool water."

"Got you!" shouted the Bottersnikes, and they grabbed those little Gumbles – this was quite easy, for though they are so lazy Bottersnikes can move faster than Gumbles when they have to because their legs are longer. And when they grabbed them they discovered a peculiar thing about Gumbles.

Chapter Three

They discovered that you can squeeze Gumbles to any shape you like without hurting them, and that if you press them very hard they flatten out like pancakes and cannot pop back to their proper shapes unless helped.

"This," said the King, watching, "Is more useful than ever."

The Bottersnikes blinked. They couldn't see why it was useful at all – silly, squashy things, they thought.

"Because," the King growled, "We can pop 'em into something and squash 'em down hard so's they can't get away, and when I want some more work done they'll be ready and waiting to do it".

Now the Bottersnikes began to get the idea. They would have servants for ever, to tidy up and keep them comfortable. "Hoo, hoo!" they yelled, "What'll we pop 'em into?"

"Jam tins," roared the King. Another good idea! Naturally there were hundreds of them lying in the rubbish. "The proper thing is to shout, 'Got you!' and grab 'em, and pop 'em into jam tins."

"What a rotten thing to think of," cried the Gumbles, "When we only stopped to –"

"Got you!" shouted the Bottersnikes, and they grabbed the Gumbles and popped them into jam tins. And squashed them down hard, with horny fists. There were more than enough Gumbles for each Bottersnike to grab one. Some of the fattest, in fact, grabbed two.

How they snuffled through their noses – which meant that they were laughing – how they rorted and snorted and hooed with glee at what they had done. "We done ourselves a good turn," the King announced, "We done a good day's work."

Exhausted at the thought of this, they fell asleep at once, and the tinned Gumbles were left in the hot sun all afternoon, thinking of the cool creek where they had meant to paddle. Now, it seemed, they would never go there again.

Chapter Four

Towards evening some of the Bottersnikes woke up, disturbed by snores from the King's palace – most royal ones, like trombones blaring. "All very well for 'im," the Bottersnikes thought, their ears going red, "But we ain't got palaces to sleep in, and we ain't comfy, and what's to be done?" Then they remembered the Gumbles. "Stop being lazy in them tins," they ordered, "And come and put our places comfy."

So the Gumbles were hauled out of the tins and put to work building bigger and better rubbish heaps for the Bottersnikes to crawl into; a nastier job for Gumbles would be impossible

to find. "Harder, harder," the Bottersnikes bawled, "And don't try and run away, 'cos we're watching you!"

But they did not see one little Gumble under the King's car, where he was puzzling over a tin-opener he had found. This Gumble was the one who had Tinks – every Tink was a good idea – and as soon as he discovered how the tin-opener worked a real beauty came to him: *Tink!* Clear as if you had tapped the edge of a glass with a spoon.

Up jumped Tinkingumble with his bright idea and peered cautiously from behind the wheel. "Pssst! Bring me the jam tins one by one," he whispered to Happigumble and Merrigumble nearby. "Mind they don't see you!"

While the Bottersnikes were trying the new heaps to see if they were comfy, and squabbling over who should have the comfiest, they rolled the jam tins under the car where Tinkingumble cut the bottoms out of every one, working fast and secretly; then Happigumble and Merrigumble rolled them back again taking care to keep the parts together so that they looked all right from the top. The job was done just in time.

"It ain't good," the Bottersnikes growled, "Not a bit good, but it'll have to do for tonight 'cos we're tired, and you'll have to work harder tomorrow." They shouted "Got you!" and grabbed the Gumbles and popped them into the jam tins, and snuffled their noses about it because they knew they'd have servants tomorrow and forever. Then they went to sleep.

When they were snoring safely Tinkingumble called "Now!" and the Gumbles tried to stand up. The cut-out bottoms of the tins fell away nicely, just as planned, but they were still stuck in the round parts – absolutely wodged in.

"How are we going to get away?" said Happigumble. "My legs are so squashed up I can hardly move!"

"I hadn't thought of that," Tinkingumble said unhappily. A

Tink came to the rescue as he spoke – only a small one, but quite clear. Following Tinkingumble's, the jam tins blundered towards the road banging into each other as they went – it nearly made them giggly – and there they rocked themselves until the tins fell over on the sides, and the slope of the hill did the rest. The Gumbles ran down to the beach in their jam tins much, much faster than any Bottersnike could have chased them.

An Owl, who saw all the tins rolling down the hill in the moonlight, was so surprised that he flew straight into a moult, and declared he'd never seen such a sight in all his years of hooting.

At the bottom of the hill the Gumbles shot off the road into the Bush, where a friendly bandicoot poked them out of the tins with his long nose. They put the jam tins in a bin marked Please Be Tidy and spent the rest of the night paddling at their favourite beach, for Gumbles are too busy having fun to waste time sleeping and there is no one to tell them when to go to bed.

235

Look Forward to a Better Future

Join Friends of the Earth

Look forward to a better future

For thousand upon thousands of years, the Earth has sustained a wonderfully rich and interconnected **web of life.**

Now one single species – humankind – is putting it all at risk.

The world's forests are **disappearing** ... our air and water are no longer clean and pure ... species are dying out at a terrifying rate ... **toxic waste** is piling up ... people everywhere **suffer** from pollution and environmental damage.

It needn't be like this. For twenty-six years Friends of the Earth has led the way in putting forward **positive solutions** to these and many other environmental problems.

Thanks to the support of people like you who share our conviction that the natural world and all living things should be treated with wisdom and respect, we've won some tremendous **victories**.

Our successes are your successes

With the support of people like you, and backed by careful research, Friends of the Earth has: **persuaded** Parliament to pass five major environmental Acts that we helped to draft and promote ... **forced** UK aerosol makers to stop using ozone-destroying CFCs ... **pressured** the Government to speed up the removal of pesticides and nitrates from drinking water using the European and High Courts ... **pioneered** practical renewable energy and waste-recycling schemes ... **stopped** the hunting of otters in Britain ... **persuaded** the EC to ban the sale of all whale products ... **stopped** plans to build an unsafe nuclear waste dump at Sellafield ... **saved** wildlife reserves from development ... **forced** major corporations to abandon destructive projects in tropical rainforests ... **exposed** health-threatening traffic pollution levels ... **uncovered** the location of thousands of secret toxic waste dumps ... **persuaded** the largest DIY stores to stop selling peat from nature reserves and mahogany from tropical rainforests.

Join Friends of the Earth and become part of this **powerful force** for environmental protection.

Become a Friend of the Earth

Our supporters are to thank for every success we score on behalf of the natural world.

They finance almost all of our work. When you consider what we are up against – government, powerful industrial interests and the huge resources at their disposal – you can appreciate how important this funding is and how much it achieves.

We use all our supporters' contributions wisely. Less than 10% of our income is spent on administration.

As the pace of environmental destruction accelerates, it's all too easy to get downhearted. Even to give up on it all! But we are making progress, and a better future is possible.

And that's where Friends of the Earth comes in. Its track record in developing positive solutions to all those problems – internationally, nationally and locally – is second to none. It's a real force for change in a world that's stuck in a dangerous rut.

It's your support that make this work possible – and it's needed now more than ever before.

Jonathon Porritt

Special Adviser to Friends of the Earth

As a Friends of the Earth member you will receive...

- A welcome pack with information on all aspects of Friends of the Earth's work
- Regular updates on urgent campaigns
- A free subscription to our magazine Earth Matters.

Each issue is packed with news, regular contributions from experts and public figures and information and advice on what you can do to support our campaigns. It features a special Children's page, a prize green crossword, beautiful photography and much, much more.

237

SPECIAL OFFER: If you can pay your membership with a monthly standing order of £3 or more, we will send you a pack of 100 illustrated gummed labels to re-seal and re-use your envelopes, and spread the message "Save Trees – Re-use Envelopes."

For more information, or to join over the phone using your credit card, please call us on 01582 482 297

Five good reasons to support Friends of the Earth

We are effective: our campaigns get politicians and industry to take action – through persuasive argument, lobbying and use of the law when necessary.

We are authoritative: our pioneering research is widely used by governments, commerce, the media and other environmental organisations.

We inform: we publish a broad range of information to help everyone find out about and take action on environmental problems that affect them.

We are independent: we work with all political parties but are aligned to none.

We work at all levels: from our participation in Friends of the Earth International to the work carried out by over 250 local groups, we are uniquely placed to mobilise public opinion and campaign successfully – locally, nationally and internationally.

"Technical dialogue is often better from Friends of the Earth than from industry."

Dr David Slater, Chief Inspector, Her Majesty's Inspectorate of Pollution.

"About 15 years ago, someone told me that Friends of the Earth's campaigners were likely to know more about their subjects than the relevant Minister. I didn't believe it. Since then I have found that this has usually been the case. Friends of the Earth has maintained its reputation as a reliable and indispensable source of information."

Geoffrey Lean, Environment Correspondent, The Independent on Sunday.

Our National Campaigns

Friends of the Earth was the first environmental pressure group in the UK to start campaigns for whales, endangered species and tropical rainforests, and against acid rain, ozone depletion and climate change.
Today we campaign on more issues than any other environmental group in the country.

Make your voice heard – join us in fighting for:

- better protection for wildlife and the countryside
- organic farming and safer food
- the protection of the world's forests
- better air quality
- reducing waste and over-consumption
- cleaner rivers and drinking water
- controls on dangerous chemicals, including pesticides
- less traffic and better public transport
- a halt to dangerous climate change
- safer and cleaner energy sources

Friends of the Earth for the planet for people

My stamp album

My stamp album
is a window
to the world.
Little squares
of blues
and blacks
and reds
and whites
and yellows
and greens
and pinks too.

Well, then, suppose
I say to you my stamp album
is a window
full of windows.

Which one do you want
to look through?

But first, let's pretend
your eyes
are curtains.

John Agard

Gramma's biscuit tin

Gramma's biscuit tin
beside her bed
has odds and ends
like covers
that once belonged to pens
and letters from old-old friends.
Gramma's biscuit tin
beside her bed
has bits and pieces
like keys
that once belonged to locks
and screws
from broken clocks.
Gramma's biscuit tin
beside her bed
has all sorts of things
like rings
that once belonged to curtains
and fuses
from forgotten plugs.

And Gramma uses
that biscuit tin
beside her bed
for keeping her bingo card.
She prays to the Lord
that one day she'll win.
But win or lose
her dreams are in
that biscuit tin.

John Agard

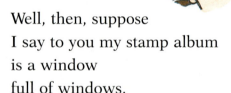

My ball

My ball is a bouncing sun
that lights up in the park.

When I take my ball to bed
it's my shining moon in the dark.

No one believes me when I tell them
that my ball catches me instead.

John Agard

Nine-o'Clock Bell!

On the way to school, suddenly there comes a sound, a loud insistent sound, breaking the morning:

        Nine-o'Clock Bell!
        Nine-o'Clock Bell!
All the small children and big ones as well,
Pulling their socks up, snatching their hats,
Cheeking and grumbling and giving back-chats,
Laughing and quarrelling, dropping their things,
These at a snail's pace, and those upon wings,
  Lagging behind a bit, running ahead,
  Waiting at corners for lights to turn red,
     Some of them scurrying,
     Others not worrying,
  Carelessly trudging or anxiously hurrying,
All through the streets they are coming pell-mell
      At the Nine-o'Clock
        Nine-o'Clock
        Nine-o'Clock
          Bell!

Eleanor Farjeon

Term 3 | Unit 7

Moonfleet

J. Meade Falkner

Part One

Chapter One: In Moonfleet Village

"So sleeps the pride of former days." – *Moore*

The village of Moonfleet itself lies half a mile from the sea on the right or west bank of the Fleet stream. This rivulet, which is so narrow as it passes the houses that I have known a good jumper clear it without a pole, broadens out into salt marshes below the village, and loses itself at last in a lake of brackish water. The lake is good for nothing except sea-fowl, herons, and oysters, and forms such a place as they call in the Indies a lagoon; being shut off from the open Channel by a monstrous great beach or dyke of pebbles, of which I shall speak more hereafter. When I was a child I thought that this place was called Moonfleet, because on a still night, whether in summer, or in the winter frosts, the moon shone very brightly on the lagoon; but learned afterwards that 'twas but short for "Mohune-fleet", from the Mohunes, a great family who were once lords of all these parts.

My name is John Trenchard, and I was fifteen years of age when this story begins. My father and mother had both been dead for years, and I boarded with my aunt, Miss Arnold, who was kind to me in her own fashion, but too strict and precise ever to make me love her.

I shall first speak of one evening in the fall of the year 1757. It must have been late in October, though I have forgotten the exact date, and I sat in the little front parlour reading after tea. My aunt had few books; a Bible, a Common Prayer, and some volumes of sermons are all that I can recollect now; but the Reverend Mr. Glennie, who taught us village children, had lent me a story-book, full of interest and adventure, called *The Arabian Nights Entertainment*. At last the light began to fail, and I was nothing loth to leave off reading for several reasons; as, first, the parlour was a chilly room with horse-hair chairs and sofa, and only a coloured-paper screen in the grate, for my aunt did not allow a fire till the first of November; second, there was a rank smell of molten tallow in the house, for my aunt was dipping winter candles on frames in the back kitchen; third, I had reached a part in the *Arabian Nights* which tightened my breath and made me wish to leave off reading for very anxiousness of expectation. It was that point in the story of the "Wonderful Lamp", where the false uncle lets fall a stone that seals the mouth of the underground chamber; and immures the boy, Aladdin, in the darkness, because he would not give up the lamp till he stood safe on the surface again. This scene reminded me of one of those dreadful nightmares, where we dream we are shut in a little room, the walls of which are closing in upon us, and so impressed me that the memory of it served as a warning in an adventure that befell me later on.

Part Two

Eagerness would not let me wait long, and I was off across the meadows towards the church, though not without sad misgivings as soon as the last house was left well behind me. At the churchyard wall my courage had waned somewhat: it seemed a shameless thing to come to rifle Blackbeard's treasure just in the very place and hour that Blackbeard loved; and as I passed the turnstile I half-expected that a tall figure, hairy and evil-eyed, would spring out from the shadow on the north side of the church. But nothing stirred, and the frosty grass sounded crisp under my feet as I made across the churchyard, stepping over the graves and keeping always out of the shadows, towards the black clump of yew-trees on the far side.

When I got round the yews, there was the tomb standing out white against them, and at the foot of the tomb was the hole like a patch of black velvet spread upon the ground, it was so dark. Then, for a moment, I thought that Blackbeard might be lying in wait in the bottom of the hole, and I stood uncertain whether to go on or back. I could catch the rustle of the water on the beach – not of any waves, for the bay was smooth as glass, but just a lipper at the fringe; and wishing to put off with any excuse the descent into the passage, though I had quite resolved to make it, I settled with myself that I would count the water wash twenty times, and at the twentieth would let myself down into the hole.

Only seven wavelets had come in when I forgot to count, for there, right in the middle of the moon's path across the water, lay a lugger moored broadside to the beach. She was about half a mile out, but there was no mistake, for though her sails were lowered her masts and hull stood out black against the moonlight. Here was a fresh reason for delay, for surely one must consider what this craft could be, and what had brought her here. She was too small for a privateer, too large for a fishing smack, and could not be a revenue boat by her low freeboard in the waist; and 'twas a strange thing for a boat to cast anchor in the midst of Moonfleet Bay even on a night so fine as this. Then while I watched I saw a blue flare in the bows, only for a moment, as if a man had lit a squib and flung it overboard, but I knew from it she was a contrabandier, and signalling either to the shore or to a mate in the offing. With that, courage came back, and I resolved to make this flare my signal for getting down into the hole, screwing my heart up with the thought that if Blackbeard was really waiting for me there, 'twould be little good to turn tail now, for he would be after me and could certainly run much faster than I. Then I took one last look round, and down into the hole forthwith, the same way as I had got down earlier in the day. So on that February night John Trenchard found himself standing in the heap of loose fallen mould at the bottom of the hole, with a mixture of courage and cowardice in his heart, but over-ruling all a great desire to get at Blackbeard's diamond.

Part Three

Out came tinder-box and candle, and I was glad indeed when the light burned up bright enough to show that no one, at any rate, was standing by my side. But then there was the passage, and who could say what might be lurking there? Yet I did not falter, but set out on this adventurous journey, walking very slowly indeed – but that was from fear of pitfalls – and nerving myself with the thought of the great diamond which surely would be found at the end of the passage. What should I not be able to do with such wealth? I would buy a nag for Mr. Glennie, a new boat for

| Term 3 | Unit 7 |

Ratsey, and a silk gown for Aunt Jane, in spite of her being so hard with me as on this night. And thus I would make myself the greatest man in Moonfleet, richer even than Mr. Maskew, and build a stone house in the sea-meadows with a good prospect of the sea, and marry Grace Maskew and live happily, and fish. I walked on down the passage, reaching out the candle as far as might be in front of me, and whistling to keep myself company, yet saw neither Blackbeard nor anyone else. All the way there were footprints on the floor, and the roof was black as with smoke of torches, and this made me fear lest some of those who had been there before might have made away with the diamond. Now, though I have spoken of this journey down the passage as though it were a mile long, and though it verily seemed so to me that night, yet I afterwards found it was not more than twenty yards or thereabouts; and then I came upon a stone wall which had once blocked the road, but was now broken through so as to make a ragged doorway into a chamber beyond. There I stood on the rough sill of the door, holding my breath and reaching out my candle arm's-length into the darkness, to see what sort of a place this was before I put foot into it. And before the light had well time to fall on things, I knew that I was underneath the church, and that this chamber was none other than the Mohune Vault.

Part Four

Here's John, remembering the time he was trapped in the vault.

They must have found glasses, though I could not remember to have seen any in the vault, for a minute later fugleman Ratsey spoke again –

"Now, lads, glasses full and bumpers for a toast. And here's to Blackbeard, to Father Blackbeard, who watches over our treasure better than he did over his own; for were it not the fear of him that keeps off idle feet and prying eyes, we should have the gaugers in, and our store ransacked twenty times."

So he spoke, and it seemed there was a little halting at first, as of men not liking to take Blackbeard's name in Blackbeard's place, or raise the Devil by mocking at him. But then some of the bolder shouted "Blackbeard", and so the more timid chimed in, and in a minute there were a score of voices calling "Blackbeard, Blackbeard", till the place rang again.

Then Elzevir cried out angrily, "Silence. Are you mad, or had the liquor mastered you? Are you Revenue-men that you dare shout and roister? or contrabandiers with the lugger in the offing, and your life in your hand? You make noise enough to wake folk in Moonfleet from their beds."

"Tut, man," retorted Ratsey testily, "and if they waked, they would but pull the blankets tight about their ears, and say 'twas Blackbeard piping his crew of lost Mohunes to help him dig for treasure."

Yet for all that 'twas plain that Block ruled the roost, for there was silence for a minute, and then one said, "Ay, Master Elzevir is right; let us away, the night is far spent, and we have nothing but the sweeps to take the lugger out of sight by dawn."

So the meeting broke up, and the torchlight grew dimmer, and died away as it had come in a red flicker on the roof, and the footsteps sounded fainter as they went up the passage, until the vault was left to the dead men and me. Yet for a very long time – it seemed hours – after all had gone I could hear a murmur of distant voices, and knew that some were talking at the end of the passage, and perhaps considering how the landslip might best be restored. So while I heard them thus conversing I dared not descend from my perch, lest someone might turn back to the vault, though I was glad enough to sit up, and ease my aching back and limbs. Yet in the awful blackness of the place even the echo of these human voices seemed a kindly and blessed thing, and a certain shrinking loneliness fell on me when they ceased at last and all was silent. Then I resolved I would be off at once, and get back to the moonlight bed that I had left hours ago, having no stomach for more treasure-hunting, and being glad indeed to be still left with the treasure of life.

Part Five

Thus, sitting where I was, I lit my candle once more, and then clambered across that great coffin which, for two hours or more, had been a mid-wall of partition between me and danger. But to get out of the niche was harder than to get in; for now that I had a candle to light me, I saw that the coffin, though sound enough to outer view, was wormed through and through, and little better than a rotten shell. So it was that I had some ado to get over it, not daring either to kneel upon it or to bring much weight to bear with my hand, lest it should go through. And now having got safely across, I sat for an instant on that narrow ledge of the stone shelf which projected beyond the coffin on the vault side, and made ready to jump forward on to the floor below. And how it happened I know not, but there I lost my balance, and as I slipped the candle flew out of my grasp. Then I clutched at the coffin to save myself, but my hand went clean through it, and so I came to the ground in a cloud of dust and splinters; having only got hold of a wisp of seaweed, or a handful of those draggled funeral trappings which were strewn about this place. The floor of the vault was sandy; and so, though I fell crookedly, I took but little harm beyond the shaking; and soon, pulling myself together, set to strike my flint and blow the match into a flame to search for the fallen candle. Yet all the time I kept in my fingers this handful of light stuff; and when the flame burnt up again I held the thing against the light, and saw that it was no wisp of seaweed, but something black and wiry. For a moment, I could not gather what I had hold of, but then gave a start that nearly sent the candle out, and perhaps a cry, and let it drop as if it were red-hot iron, for I knew that it was a man's beard.

Now when I saw that, I felt a sort of throttling fright, as though one had caught hold of my heartstrings; and so many and such strange thoughts rose in me, that the blood went pounding round and round in my head, as it did once afterwards when I was fighting with the sea and near drowned. Surely to have in hand the beard of any dead man in any place was bad enough, but worse a thousand times in such a place as this, and to know on whose face it had grown. For, almost before I fully saw what it was, I knew it was that black beard which had given Colonel John Mohune his nickname, and this was his great coffin I had hid behind.

Term 3 | Unit 8

Tom's Midnight Garden
by Philippa Pearce

I've chosen this as one of my favourite books because, as well as telling a wonderful story, it explores the mysteries of time travel in a serious and thoughtful way. For Tom – staying with relatives, lonely and bored – doesn't just accept the fact that the dreary back-yard of the house can be transformed into a magical garden at the midnight hour, he keeps trying to work out just how and when *he is able to move in and out of this fascinating Victorian world. He is also worried in case he gets suddenly trapped and will have to stay there for ever.*

Here is Tom on the verge of his first fantastic discovery, when he decides to investigate the grandfather clock which has just struck thirteen!

Kaye Webb

Part One

Tom put on his bedroom slippers, but decided against his dressing-gown: after all, it was summer. He closed his bedroom door carefully behind him, so that it should not bang in his absence. Outside the front door of the flat he took off one of his slippers; he laid it on the floor against the door jamb and then closed the door on to it, as on to a wedge. That would keep the door open for his return.

The lights on the first-floor landing and in the hall were turned out, for the tenants were all in bed and asleep, and Mrs Bartholomew was asleep and dreaming. The only illumination was a sideways shaft of moonlight through the long window part way up the stairs. Tom felt his way downstairs and into the hall.

250

Here he was checked. He could find the grandfather clock – a tall and ancient figure of black in the lesser blackness – but he was unable to read its face. If he opened its dial-door and felt until he found the position of the clock-hands, then his sense of touch would tell him the time. He fumbled first at one side of the door, then at the other, but there seemed no catch – no way in. He remembered how the pendulum-case door had not yielded to him either, on that first day. Both must be kept locked.

Hurry! hurry! the house seemed to whisper round him. The hour is passing ... passing ...

Tom turned from the clock to feel for the electric-light switch. Where had it been? His fingers swept the wall in vain: nowhere.

Light – light: that was what he needed! And the only light was the moonbeam that glanced sideways through the stairway window and spent itself at once and uselessly on the wall by the window-sill.

Tom studied the moonbeam, with an idea growing in his mind. From the direction in which the beam came, he saw that the moon must be shining at the back of the house. Very well, then, if he opened the door at the far end of the hall – at the back of the house, that is – he would let that moonlight in. With luck there might be enough light for him to read the clock-face.

Term 3 | Unit 8

Part Two

He moved down the hall to the door at its far end. It was a door he had never seen opened – the Kitsons used the door at the front. They said that the door at the back was only a less convenient way to the street, through a backyard – a strip of paving where dustbins were kept and where the tenants of the ground-floor back flat garaged their car under a tarpaulin.

Never having had occasion to use the door, Tom had no idea how it might be secured at night. If it were locked, and the key kept elsewhere ... But it was not locked, he found; only bolted. He drew the bolt, and, very slowly, to make no sound, turned the door-knob.

Hurry! whispered the house and the grandfather clock at the heart of it beat an anxious tick, tick.

Tom opened the door wide and let in the moonlight. It flooded in, as bright as daylight – the white daylight that comes before the full rising of the sun. The illumination was perfect, but Tom did not at once turn to see what it showed him on the clock-face. Instead he took a step forward on to the doorstep. He was staring, at first in surprise, then with indignation, at what he saw outside. That they should have deceived him – lied to him – like this! They had said, "It's not worth your while going out the back, Tom." So carelessly they had described it. "A sort of backyard, very poky, with rubbish bins. Really, there's nothing to see."

Nothing ... Only this: a great lawn where flower-beds bloomed; a towering fir tree, and thick, beetle-browed yews that humped their shapes down two sides of the lawn; on the third side, to the right, a greenhouse almost the size of a real house; from each corner of the lawn, a path that twisted away to some other depths of garden, with other trees.

Tom had stepped forward instinctively, catching his breath in surprise; now he let his breath out in a deep sigh. He would steal out here tomorrow, by daylight. They had tried to keep this from him, but they could not stop him now – not his aunt, nor his uncle, nor the back flat tenants, nor even particular Mrs Bartholomew. He would run full tilt over the grass, leaping the flower-beds; he would peer through the glittering panes of the greenhouse – perhaps open the door and go in; he would visit each alcove and archway clipped in the yew-trees – he would climb the trees and make his way from one to another through thickly interlacing branches. When they came calling him, he would hide, silent and safe as a bird, among this richness of leaf and bough and tree-trunk.

Part Three

The scene tempted him even now: it lay so inviting and clear before him – clear-cut from the stubby leaf-pins of the nearer yew trees to the curled-back petals of the hyacinths in the crescent-shaped corner beds. Yet Tom remembered his ten hours and his honour. Regretfully he turned from the garden, back indoors to read the grandfather clock.

He re-crossed the threshold, still absorbed in the thought of what he had seen outside. For that reason, perhaps, he could not at once make out how the hall had become different: his eyes informed him of some shadowy change; his bare foot was trying to tell him something...

The grandfather clock was still there, anyway, and must tell him the true time. It must be either twelve or one: there was no hour between. There is no thirteenth hour.

Term 3 | **Unit 8**

Tom never reached the clock with his inquiry, and may be excused for forgetting, on this occasion, to check its truthfulness. His attention was distracted by the opening of a door down the hall – the door of the ground-floor front flat. A maid trotted out.

Tom had seen housemaids only in pictures, but he recognized the white apron, cap and cuffs, and the black stockings. (He was not expert in fashions, but the dress seemed to him to be rather long for her.) She was carrying paper, kindling wood and a box of matches.

He had only a second in which to observe these things. Then he realized that he ought to take cover at once; and there was no cover to take. Since he must be seen, Tom determined to be the first to speak – to explain himself.

He did not feel afraid of the maid: as she came nearer, he saw that she was only a girl. To warn her of his presence without startling her, Tom gave a cough; but she did not seem to hear it. She came on. Tom moved forward into her line of vision; she looked at him, but looked through him, too, as thought he were not there. Tom's heart jumped in a way he did not understand. She was passing him.

"I say!" he protested loudly; but she paid not the slightest attention. She passed him, reached the front door of the ground-floor back flat, turned the door handle and went in. There was no bell-ringing or unlocking of the door.

Part Four

Tom was left gaping; and, meanwhile, his senses began to insist upon telling him of experiences even stranger than this encounter. His one bare foot was on cold flagstone, he knew; yet there was a contradictory softness and warmth to this flagstone. He looked down and saw that he was standing on a rug – a tiger-skin rug. There were other rugs down the hall. His eyes now took in the whole of the hall – a hall that was different. No laundry box, no milk bottles, no travel posters on the walls. The walls were decorated with a rich variety of other objects instead: a tall Gothic barometer, a fan of peacock feathers, a huge engraving of a battle (hussars and horses and shot-riddled banners) and many other pictures. There was a big dinner gong, with its wash-leathered gong-stick hanging beside it. There was a large umbrella stand holding umbrellas and walking-sticks and a parasol and an air-gun and what looked like the parts of a fishing-rod. Along the wall projected a series of bracket-shelves, each table-high. They were of oak, except for one towards the middle of the hall, by the grandfather clock. That was of white marble, and it was piled high with glass cases of stuffed birds and animals. Enacted on its chilly surface were scenes of hot-bloodshed: an owl clutched a mouse in its claws; a ferret looked up from the killing of its rabbit; in a case in the middle a red fox slunk along with a gamefowl hanging from its jaws.

In all that crowded hall, the only object that Tom recognized was the grandfather clock. He moved towards it, not to read its face, but simply to touch it – to reassure himself that this at least was as he knew it.

His hand was nearly upon it, when he heard a little breath

behind him that was the maid passing back the way she had come. For some reason, she did not seem to make as much sound as before. He heard her call only faintly: "I've lit the fire in the parlour."

She was making for the door through which she had first come, and, as Tom followed her with his eyes, he received a curious impression: she reached the door, her hand was upon the knob, and then she seemed to go. That was it exactly: she went, but not through the door. She simply thinned out, and went.

Even as he stared at where she had been, Tom became aware of something going on furtively and silently about him. He looked round sharply, and caught the hall in the act of emptying itself of furniture and rugs and pictures. They were not positively going, perhaps, but rather beginning to fail to be there. The Gothic barometer, for instance, was there, before he turned to look at the red fox; when he turned back, the barometer was still there, but it had the appearance of something only sketched against the wall, and the wall was visible through it; meanwhile the fox had slunk into nothingness, and all the other creatures were going with him; and, turning back again swiftly to the barometer, Tom found that gone already.

In a matter of seconds the whole hall was as he had seen it on his first arrival. He stood dumbfounded. He was roused from his stupefaction by the chill of a draught at his back: it reminded him that the garden door was left open. Whatever else had happened, he had really opened that door; and he must shut it. He must go back to bed.

He closed the door after a long look: "I shall come back," he promised silently to the trees and the lawn and the greenhouse.

Term 3 | Unit 9

Naturally Wight

Welcome – Welkom – Willkommen
to the island of landscape diversity and infinite beauty

Islands have a complex ecological significance which set them apart from large land masses. They are special and the Isle of Wight, that diamond off England's southern coast, is very special indeed.

For an island so small, it has a remarkable diversity of landscapes and habitats with a healthy complement of unique species of plants and animals. Some are rare: the difficult to discover dormice of Parkhurst Forest require special attention and protection to ensure their survival. Some are isolated: the extraordinary glanville fritillary butterfly occurs naturally nowhere else in Britain and has long been the focus of naturalists' forays to the Island. Some are simply charming: red squirrels, those nut-cracking, tufty eared arborealists, could not fail to excite anyone, naturalist or other, and the Isle of Wight is one of England's finest sanctuaries for this attractive animal.

Tourist Information

67 High Street,
Shanklin,
Isle of Wight,
PO37 6JJ
Tel: (01983) 862942

8 High Street,
Sandown,
Isle of Wight,
PO36 0DG
Tel: (01983) 403886

Western Esplanade,
Ryde,
Isle of Wight,
PO33 2LW
Tel: (01983) 562905

The Quay,
Yarmouth,
Isle of Wight,
PO41 4PQ
Tel: (01983) 760015

South Street,
Newport,
Isle of Wight,
PO30 1JU
Tel: (01983) 525450

The Arcade,
Fountain Quay,
Cowes,
Isle of Wight,
PO31 3AR
Tel: (01983) 291914

34 High Street,
Ventnor,
Isle of Wight,
PO38 1RZ
Tel: (01983) 853625

The mild and relatively dry south coast setting boosts the Island as a great refuge for all sorts of exciting other wildlife too. Better still though it is also accessible. There are more than 500 miles of well maintained and well marked footpaths and bridleways which can lead you to glades, downs, beautiful beaches, nature reserves and picturesque villages.

Whatever route you take, you will enjoy outstanding views of what is certainly one of the most attractive rural areas to explore anywhere in England. Frankly, this rural resource has until now been under used but, by using this handbook, you can redress that situation and enjoy some marvellous rambles and walks.

So here is a warm welcome to the Isle of Wight's wild spots. If you take the time to tread that way, you will, I am sure, find it very worthwhile.

Chris Packham
TV presenter, naturalist, wildlife photographer and author.

Exploring the Island
Extensive rights of way and panoramic bus routes

Footpaths, bridleways and byways give free public access to almost every part of the Isle of Wight's diverse countryside and coast.

Walking

Within an area of just 147 square miles (38,000 hectares) can be found over 500 miles of carefully maintained and well signposted rights of way. On your travels, you will chance upon secluded villages of thatch and stone, ancient churches and manor houses. Leafy lanes wind their way from coast to coast through green valleys, meadows, forest and over downland. Choose from the extensive range of maps, guides and leaflets available from Tourist Information Centres or join one of the many guided walks held throughout the year.

Cycling

The Isle of Wight Council has produced a series of leaflets highlighting some of the best routes for mountain bikers. These show off-road circular routes of all kinds; easy to tackle as well as the more demanding rides; those ideal for a leisurely outing on a summer's evening or satisfying all-day rides for the enthusiast and the family. All-weather level cycleways follow the routes of old railway tracks between Newport and Cowes, Shide and Blackwater, and Yarmouth and Freshwater. All are ideal for observing river and estuary wildlife. You can also explore the intricate network of country lanes that hold surprises around every corner.

Horse riding

There are wonderful opportunities to explore the Island's vast network of bridleways, some of which have been in use since the Stone Age, when early man travelled along the central chalk

Walkers on Nitton Down

ridge. Enjoy the panoramic views from these high tracks used by drovers, horsemen and carters, long before our present roads were built or a leisurely ride through ancient woodlands and sweet-scented meadows.

Public transport

If you can leave your car at home, you will help reduce traffic congestion and pollution and protect the environment. Buses and coaches reach all corners of the island – you often get an interesting perspective of the countryside from the top deck of a bus. Trains connect passenger ferries at Ryde with Sandown and Shanklin. Stops along the way include a connection with the Isle of Wight Steam Railway. Other options include tours by vintage coach and horse-drawn carriage.

FACT file

Travel on the Isle of Wight

Southern Vectis, the Island's bus company, operates an Islandwide service all year and a variety of coach tours and open top bus routes are available in summer. Timetables are published twice annually for summer and winter seasons.

Island Line

Operates a regular train service which connects with passenger ferries at Ryde Pier Head and runs as far as Shanklin. Bus and Train Rover Tickets for 1, 2 or 7 days are available.

Off the beaten track

Tour the country lanes and picturesque villages by vintage coaches of the 1930s–40s era.

Explore the Island's wild places with a llama trek or mini-bus guided tours (day or half-day) with refreshments.

Enjoy country or woodland rides on horseback or by horse-drawn carriage or cycle. Ask for a list of cycle hire companies or stables.

Experience special interest holidays, e.g. walking, painting, field studies, etc.

Further reading

Walks and Trails ranging from the 60 mile Coastal Path to short circular strolls and town trails are available.

Maps for walkers:

Ordnance Survey Outdoor Leisure 29 Isle of Wight 2.5 inch : 1 mile/4cm : 1km

Ordnance Survey Landranger 196 Solent and Isle of Wight 1.25 inch : 1 mile/2 cm : 1km

Byways and Bridleways by Mountain Bike (4 leaflets): Isle of Wight Council South East Wight (grassland and wetland) South Central Wight (lane, farm and village) West Wight (forest, down and creek) North East Wight (wood, field and marsh)

A Cyclist's Guide to the Isle of Wight – R. Crick.

Dinosaur Island
One of Europe's finest sites for dinosaur remains

120 million years ago, there was no Isle of Wight, it was landlocked, part of a large continent. In the muds and silts of ancient marshy environments, animals and plants were trapped and preserved as fossils. These can now be found in the cliffs and on the beaches around the Island's coast.

The oldest rocks are the wealdon clays formed when dinosaurs roamed the earth. The yellow, brown and grey rocks exposed in the bays of Compton, Brook and Brighstone contain fossilised trees and dinosaur bones! Giant casts of dinosaur footprints in stone are a famous feature at Hanover Point. Dinosaur fanatics will be fascinated by the exhibits on show at the Isle of Wight Museum of Geology in Sandown and the Dinosaur Farm along the Military Road, where you can watch geologists working on the Island's biggest ever dinosaur find, a giant Sauropod!

Term 3 Unit 9

Later, these ancient marshy environments were covered by deep tropical seas. In these oceans lived millions of minute plankton, shellfish and plants. When they died, their shell cases fell to the seabed and built up over millions of years to form chalk. When you walk on top of St Boniface Down (the Island's highest point), would you believe that you were treading the floor of an ancient sea over 70 million years old?

All these ancient layers were buried, compacted and then uplifted to be exposed in the rocks. The importance of the Island's strata was recognised in Victorian days when famous scientists, including the evolutionist, Charles Darwin, examined the cliffs to study the fossil remains. Today, geologists continue to examine the rocks to understand the complex processes which formed the present Isle of Wight. To help you enjoy and interpret this scenery, the Isle of Wight Museum of Geology leads field trips for all ages. It provides an up to date interpretation of rocks, fossils and landscape. Fossils found by visitors and specialist collectors can be brought to the museum for identification. Sometimes, a "find" proves very exciting, especially if it is unknown in the fossil record. Such fossils contribute to our knowledge of these ancient environments.

FACT file
Places to visit

Isle of Wight Museum of Geology, Sandown. See the little dinosaur excavated at Yaverland and many other fossils. The Curator will also arrange fossil hunts for school parties. Open all year. No entry charge. Tel: (01983) 404344

Dinosaur Farm, Military Road, Near Brighstone. View the giant Sauropod excavated from the adjacent cliffs in 1993 where it had been buried for 120 million years. Opening hours and admission charges on application. Tel: (01983) 740401

Other exhibitions and fossil hunts are organised from time to time. Details from Tourist Information Centres.

Warning – When exploring the base of certain cliffs to hunt for fossils, do not be tempted to climb them or venture around headlands where you may be cut off by the tide. If in doubt, check with Tourist Information Centres and purchase a tide table.

Areas of Outstanding Natural Beauty
Quality countryside being conserved for the future

Areas of Outstanding Natural Beauty are precious landscapes identified as having a distinctive character and natural beauty of such quality that it is in the nation's interest to protect them.

Almost half the island has been designated by the Countryside Commission as an Area of Outstanding Natural Beauty (189 sq km). Chalk cliffs, downland, tidal estuary, wooded coastline and the two Heritage Coasts are all recognised as being of special importance.

The Countryside Commission works to conserve and enhance the beauty of the English Countryside and to help people enjoy it. This is achieved by planning controls, practical countryside management through the AONB Project and by raising public awareness.

A walk in an Isle of Wight AONB.

Areas of Outstanding Natural Beauty are largely privately owned and continue to be "working landscapes", usually farmed. The Countryside Commission carries out its aims with regard to those who live and work in these areas and to those who visit them.

Our countryside is under great pressure but it is often the case that we only miss something when it has gone. AONB designation is a recognition that these areas are too precious to lose and aims to conserve the natural beauty of the landscape for its own sake and for future generations, as well as our own to enjoy.

Term 3 | **Unit 9**

Please follow the Country Code
- Enjoy the countryside and respect its life and work
- Guard against all risk of fire
- Fasten all gates
- Keep your dog under close control
- Keep to public paths across farmland
- Use gates and stiles to cross fences, hedges and walls
- Leave livestock, crops and machinery alone
- Take your litter home
- Help to keep all water clean
- Protect wildlife, plants and trees
- Take special care on country roads
- Make no unnecessary noise

Enjoy yourself!

FACT file
For more information
Contact the AONB Officer at Seaclose, Fairlee Road, Newport, Isle of Wight, PO30 2QS Tel: (01983) 822119

Factfile – whilst every care has been taken in compiling this information, no responsibility can be accepted for any changes which may subsequently occur. January 1996 © Isle of Wight Council copyrights reserved. This information may not be reproduced or photocopied whole or in part, unless written permission has been given beforehand.

Accessible Isle
Total journey times (approximate) between the island and ...
Portsmouth/Southsea (Hovercraft) – 9 mins
Portsmouth (fast passenger ferry) – 15 mins
Southampton (fast passenger ferry) – 23 mins
Lymington (vehicle ferry) – 30 mins
Portsmouth (vehicle ferry) – 35 mins
Southampton International Airport (fast ferry/rail) – 50 mins
Southampton (vehicle ferry) – 55 mins
London Waterloo (fast ferry/rail) – 1 hr 55 mins
Amsterdam to London (ferry/rail) – 8 hrs
Bonn to London (ferry/rail) – 13 hours

The Silver Sword

Ian Serraillier

This is a true story about almost unbearable hardship and suffering, but it is also hopeful, because all the characters in it are so courageous and determined.

It is the time of the last war, in Poland. Four children are left destitute when their parents are arrested by the Gestapo and their house is blown up. At first they live like rats in bombed cellars, scratching food from dustbins, hiding in daytime for fear of being taken by soldiers. Then Edek, the eldest brother, is caught and taken off to a slave-labour camp. After the Russians arrive the children decide to make the impossible journey to Switzerland, where they hope their parents may eventually return.

Here they are on their way to Berlin, after they have managed to find Edek, ill in hospital, and persuaded the authorities to let them continue their daunting journey.

Kaye Webb

Term 3 | **Unit 10** ○ ○ ○ ○ ○ ○ ○ ○ ○ ○ ○

Part One

There was still something left of the railway station at Posen, and the track had been mended. Of course there was no such thing as a timetable, but some trains – though much delayed – were getting through to Berlin, 250 miles to the west. In one of these trains, Ruth, Edek, Jan and Bronia were travelling. It was crowded with refugees. They leaned from the windows, stood on the footboards, lay on the carriage roofs. Ruth's family was in one of the open trucks, which was cold but not quite so crowded.

"I don't like this truck," said Bronia. "It jolts too much."

"Every jolt takes us nearer to Switzerland," said Ruth. "Think of it like that, and it's not so bad."

"There's no room to stretch."

"Rest your head against me and try and go to sleep. There, that's better."

"It's a better truck than the other ones," said Jan. "It's got a stove in it. And we can scrape the coal dust off the floor. That's why I chose it. When it gets dark they'll light a fire and we shall keep warm.

"The stove's right in the far corner. We shan't feel it from here," said Bronia.

"Stop grumbling, Bronia," said Ruth. "We're lucky to be here at all. Hundreds of people were left behind at Posen – they may have to wait for weeks."

"Edek was lucky to come at all," said Jan. "The doctor wanted to send him back to the Warthe camp, didn't he?"

"He said you wanted fattening up, as if you were a goose being fattened for Christmas," laughed Bronia.

"The doctor wouldn't have let him come at all, if I hadn't argued with him," said Jan.

"They wanted to keep us all, didn't they, Ruth?" said Bronia.

"It was because they wanted to look after us," said Ruth. And she thought with satisfaction how they had stuck to their point and persuaded the authorities to let them go.

266

Ruth looked at her brother. Bunched up against the side of the truck, he was staring out at the fields as they swept by. It was over two and a half years since she had last seen him. He was sixteen now, but did not look two and a half years older. So different from the Edek she remembered. His cheeks were pinched and hollow, his eyes as unnaturally bright as Jan's had once been, and he kept coughing. He looked as if he could go on lying there for ever, without stirring. Yet at the Warthe camp they had described him as wild.

She looked at Jan. She was surprised how helpful and good-tempered he had been since Jimpy's death in the scrum by the field kitchen. He had kept his sorrow to himself and not once referred to Jimpy since. Ruth could see that he was not entirely at ease with Edek yet. Did he resent his presence? There might be trouble here, for Edek must to some extent usurp the position that Jan had held, and Jan had a jealous nature.

She looked at Bronia. The child was asleep, her head in Ruth's lap, a smile on her face. Was she dreaming about the fairy-story that Ruth had been telling her, the one about the Princess of the Brazen Mountains?

Ruth sighed. She leaned back, her head against the side of the truck, and dozed.

And the train, with its long stream of trucks and carriages all crammed to bursting-point with refugees, rattled and jolted on towards Berlin.

In the evening the train stopped and was shunted into a siding. Everyone got out to stretch his legs, but no one went far away in case it started again. As the night came on and it grew colder, they drifted back to their carriages and trucks. Coal dust was scraped from the floorboards and wood collected from outside, and the fire in Ruth's truck kindled. The refugees crowded round, stretching out their hands to the warmth.

Part Two

It was the hour of the singer and the story-teller. While they all shared what little food they had, a young man sang and his wife accompanied him on the guitar. Another told of a long journey on the roof of a train.

"I can beat that for a yarn," said Edek.

Everyone turned round to look at the boy slumped down at the back of the truck. It was the first time he had spoken.

"I'll tell you if you'll give me a peep at the fire," he said. "And my sisters, too. And Jan. We're freezing out here."

Ungrudgingly they made a way for the family – the only children in the truck – to squeeze through to the stove. Ruth carried Bronia, who did not wake, and she snuggled down beside it. Jan sat on the other side, with his chin on his knees and his arms clasping them. Edek stood up, with his back to the side of the truck. When someone opened the stove to throw in a log, a shower of sparks leapt up, and for a few moments the flames lit up his pale features.

"I was caught smuggling cheese into Warsaw, and the sent me back to Germany to slave on the land," he said.

"In spring we did the sowing – cabbage crop, mostly. At harvest time we packed the plump white cabbage heads in crates and sent them into town. We lived on the outer leaves – they tasted bitter. I tried to run away, but they always fetched me back. Last winter, when the war turned against the Nazis and the muddles began, I succeeded. I hid under a train, under a cattle wagon, and lay on top of the axle with my arms and legs stretched out."

"When the train started, you fell off," said Jan.

"Afterwards I sometimes wished I had," said Edek, "that is, until I found Ruth and Bronia again. Somehow I managed to cling on and I got a free ride back to Poland."

Jan laughed scornfully. "Why don't you travel that way here? It would leave the rest of us more room."

"I could never do that again," said Edek.

"No," said Jan, and he looked with contempt at Edek's thin

arms and bony wrists. "You're making it all up. There's no room to lie under a truck. Nothing to hold on to."

Edek seized him by the ear and pulled him to his feet. "Have you ever looked under a truck?" he said, and he described the underside in such convincing detail that nobody but Jan would have questioned his accuracy. The boys were coming to blows, when the printer pulled Jan to the floor and there were cries of, "Let him get on with his story!"

"You would have been shaken off," Jan shouted above the din, "like a rotten plum!"

"That's what anyone would expect," Edek shouted back. "But if you'll shut up and listen, I'll tell you why I wasn't." When the noise had died down, he went on. "Lying on my stomach, I found the view rather monotonous. It made me dizzy too. I had to shut my eyes. And the bumping! Compared with that, the boards of this truck are like a feather bed. Then the train ran through a puddle. More than a puddle – it must have been a flood, for I was splashed and soaked right through. But that water saved me. After that I couldn't let go, even if I'd wanted to."

"Why not?" said Jan, impressed.

"The water froze on me. It made an icicle of me. When at last the train drew into a station, I was encased in ice from head to foot. I could hear Polish voices on the platform. I knew we must have crossed the frontier. My voice was the only part of me that wasn't frozen, so I shouted. The station-master came and chopped me down with an axe. He wrapped me in blankets and carried me to the boiler-house to thaw out. Took me hours to thaw out."

"You don't look properly thawed out yet," said the printer, and he threw him a crust of bread.

"Nothing like that must ever happen to you again," said Ruth.

She reached for his hand – it was cold, although he was close to the stove – and she clasped it tight, as if she meant never to let go of it again.

Little House in the Big Woods

Laura Ingalls Wilder

There are nine books about Laura and her pioneering family, with her restless father, always moving on to new places. The Big Woods, in Wisconsin, U.S.A., is where her life begins, but after that she has stories to tell about life on the Prairie, Plum Creek and the Silver Lake, while all the time she is growing up and learning how to cope with new ways of living.

The delight of these stories is that everything Laura Ingalls Wilder writes about really happened, including falling in love and getting married. Here is a very young Laura facing a serious danger...

Kaye Webb

Part One

Laura and Mary had never seen a town. They had never seen a store. They have never seen even two houses standing together. But they knew that in a town there were many houses, and a store full of candy and calico and other wonderful things – powder, and shot, and salt, and store sugar.

They knew that Pa would trade his furs to the storekeeper for beautiful things from town, and all day they were expecting the presents he would bring them. When the sun sank low above the treetops and no more drops fell from the tips of the icicles they began to watch eagerly for Pa.

The sun sank out of sight, the woods grew dark, and he did not come. Ma started supper and set the table, but he did not come. It was time to do the chores, and still he had not come.

Ma said Laura might come with her while she milked the cow. Laura could carry the lantern.

So Laura put on her coat and Ma buttoned it up. And Laura put her hands into her red mittens that hung by a red yarn string round her neck, while Ma lighted the candle in the lantern.

Laura was proud to be helping Ma with the milking, and she carried the lantern very carefully. Its sides were of tin, with places cut in them for the candle-light to shine through.

When Laura walked behind Ma on the path to the barn, the little bits of candle-light from the lantern leaped all around her on the snow. The night was not yet quite dark. The woods were dark, but there was a grey light on the snowy path, and in the sky there were a few faint stars. The stars did not look as warm and bright as the little lights that came from the lantern.

Laura was surprised to see the dark shape of Sukey, the brown cow, standing at the barnyard gate. Ma was surprised too.

It was too early in the spring for Sukey to be let out in the Big Woods to eat grass. She lived in the barn. But sometimes on warm days Pa left the door of her stall open so she could come

Term 3 | **Unit 10** ○ ○ ○ ○ ○ ○ ○ ○ ○ ○ ○

into the barnyard. Now Ma and Laura saw her behind the bars, waiting for them.

Ma went up to the gate, and pushed against it to open it. But it did not open very far, because there was Sukey, standing against it. Ma said:

"Sukey, get over!" She reached across the gate and slapped Sukey's shoulder.

Just then one of the dancing bits of light from the lantern jumped between the bars of the gate, and Laura saw long, shaggy, black fur, and two little, glittering eyes. Sukey had thin, short, brown fur. Sukey had large, gentle eyes.

Ma said, "Laura, walk back to the house."

So Laura turned around and began to walk towards the house. Ma came behind her. When they had gone part way, Ma snatched her up, lantern and all, and ran. Ma ran with her into the house, and slammed the door.

Then Laura said, "Ma, was it a bear?"

"Yes, Laura," Ma said. "It was a bear."

Laura began to cry. She hung on to Ma and sobbed, "Oh, will he eat Sukey?"

"No," Ma said, hugging her. "Sukey is safe in the barn. Think, Laura – all those big, heavy logs in the barn walls. And the door is heavy and solid, made to keep bears out. No, the bear cannot get in and eat Sukey."

Laura felt better then. "But he could have hurt us, couldn't he?" she asked.

"He didn't hurt us," Ma said. "You were a good girl, Laura, to do exactly as I told you, and to do it quickly, without asking why."

Ma was trembling, and she began to laugh a little. "To think," she said, "I've slapped a bear!"

272

Part Two

In the morning Pa was there. He had brought candy for Laura and Mary, and two pieces of pretty calico to make them each a dress. Mary's was a china-blue pattern on a white ground, and Laura's was dark red with little golden-brown dots on it. Ma had calico for a dress, too; it was brown, with a big, feathery-white pattern all over it.

They were all happy because Pa had got such good prices for his furs that he could afford to get them such beautiful presents.

The tracks of the big bear were all around the barn, and there were marks of his claws on the walls. But Sukey and the horses were safe inside.

All that day the sun shone, the snow melted, and little streams of water ran from the icicles, which all the time grew thinner. Before the sun set that night, the bear tracks were only shapeless marks in the wet, soft snow.

After supper Pa took Laura and Mary on his knees and said he had a new story to tell them.

"It was nearly sundown before I could start home.

"I tried to hurry, but the walking was hard and I was tired, so I had not gone far before night came. And I was alone in the Big Woods without my gun.

"There were still six miles to walk, and I came along as fast as I could. The night grew darker and darker, and I wished for my gun, because I knew that some of the bears had come out of their winter dens. I had seen their tracks when I went to town in the morning.

"Bears are hungry and cross at this time of year; you know they have been sleeping in their dens all winter long with nothing to eat, and that makes them thin and angry when they wake up. I did not want to meet one.

"I hurried along as quick as I could in the

dark. By and by the stars gave a little light. It was still black as pitch where the woods were thick, but in the open places I could see, dimly. I could see the snowy road ahead a little way, and I could see the dark woods standing all around me. I was glad when I came into an open place where the stars gave me this faint light.

"All the time I was watching, as well as I could, for bears. I was listening for the sounds they make when they go carelessly through the bushes.

"Then I came again into an open place, and there, right in the middle of my road, I saw a big black bear.

"He was standing up on his hind legs, looking at me. I could see his eyes shine. I could see his pig-snout. I could even see one of his claws, in the starlight.

"My scalp prickled, and my hair stood straight up. I stopped in my tracks, and stood still. The bear did not move. There he stood, looking at me.

"I knew it would do no good to try to go around him. He would follow me into the dark woods, where he could see better than I could. I did not want to fight a winter-starved bear in the dark. Oh, how I wished for my gun!

"I had to pass that bear, to get home. I thought that if I could scare him, he might get out of the road and let me go by. So I took a deep breath, and suddenly shouted with all my might and ran at him, waving my arms.

"He didn't move.

"I did not run very far towards him, I tell you! I stopped and looked at him, and he stood looking at me. Then I shouted again. There he stood. I kept on shouting and waving my arms, but he did not budge.

"Well, it would do me no good to run away. There were other bears in the woods. I might meet one any time. I might as well deal with this one as with another. Besides, I was coming home to Ma and you girls. I would never get here, if I ran away from everything in the woods that scared me.

"So at last I looked round, and I got a good big club, a solid, heavy branch that had been broken from a tree by the weight of snow in the winter.

"I lifted it up in my hands, and I ran straight at that bear. I swung my club as hard as I could and brought it down, bang! on his head.

"And there he still stood, for he was nothing but a big, black, burned stump!

"I had passed it on my way to town that morning. It wasn't a bear at all. I only thought it was a bear, because I had been thinking all the time about bears and being afraid I'd meet one."

"It really wasn't a bear at all?" Mary asked.

"No, Mary, it wasn't a bear at all. There I had been yelling, and dancing, and waving my arms, all by myself in the Big Woods, trying to scare a stump!"

Let's Kick Racism out of Football

▲ Arthur Wharton – the first black professional, played in goal for Preston North End at the start of the professional era in the 1880s. He was also a national sprint champion, a top cyclist, a pro cricketer and a boxer.

Kick it out

Many people think racism has all but disappeared from professional football – they remember the monkey chanting and banana throwing of the 1970s and '80s and assume that it's not a problem anymore. But every season incidents of racist abuse on the pitch and in the crowd get reported in the press, while dozens more go unseen and unheard.

What's more, while almost every professional club now has at least one black player, ethnic minorities are still under-represented in many areas of football: there has only ever been a handful of Asian-origin professional players, and none in the Premier League; only about 1% of fans who go to matches are from black communities; there are still very few black managers or coaches, referees, directors, administrators or officials. Ethnic minorities are still excluded from football by discrimination, and racist abuse still blights the lives and careers of many black and Asian players and spectators.

Kick It Out is working to eliminate racism from all aspects and all levels of football, so people from all backgrounds can enjoy the game without fear of racist abuse, discrimination or harassment.

▲ Laurie Cunningham – one of the best players of his generation who, together with Brendon Batson and Cyrille Regis, made West Bromwich Albion a European force and showed what black players could do in the '70s.

A Proud History...

Nearly a quarter of professional footballers in England and Wales today are black. But this wasn't always the case. The history of black footballers stretches back 100 years, as long as football has been a professional sport, and today's black pros owe a debt to those who came before them, those who forged their careers in the face of racism and prejudice.

Kicking it out...

Football fans led the fight against racism in football in the 1970s and 1980s. At Leeds United, for example, a group of supporters formed "Leeds fans against racism and fascism" and, through their fanzine, "Marching Altogether", helped to change the atmosphere at Elland Road. Similar campaigns were, and still are, being run at Everton, Leicester, Sheffield, Charlton Athletic and elsewhere. In Sheffield, Blades' supporters formed "Football Unites – Racism Divides" an anti-racist organisation that works with the local community. In 1994, the national Football Supporters' Association produced its own anti-racist fanzine, "United Colours of Football". Fans in other countries, such as Germany, have campaigned in similar ways.

Asians can't play football...

It's often assumed that Britain's Asian communities aren't interested in football. This is rubbish. Asians love to play and watch the game, as much as any other group in this country, but Asian players have found their path to the professional game blocked by prejudice and stereotyping. There are no Asian pros in professional football and merely a handful have ever made the grade throughout the history of the British game.

However, things are slowly changing. A new generation of young Asians are currently showing their skills on youth schemes and in the centres of excellence run by professional clubs up and down the country.

▲ Jack Leslie – front row, centre, played for Plymouth Argyle in the 1920s.

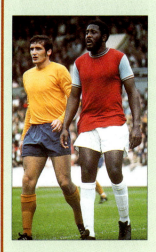

▲ Clyde Best – a striker for West Ham United in the 1960s and 1970s, Best became a role model for many up and coming black pros.

▲ Amrit Sidhu – Derby County apprentice.

▲ Chris Kamara – one of the few black managers to be given an opportunity.

▲ Hope Powell – after an established career with the England's women's team, now the national women's coach.

60% of Bengali boys play football

43.2% of Pakistanis play football

36.5% of Indians play football

Only 47% of lads of English-origin play football

A recent report into the lack of Asian footballers in the British game by Jas Bains and Raj Patel called "Asians Can't Play Football", revealed that levels of participation in Asian groups are among the highest of any ethnic group.

Behind the scenes...

The sight of a black professional footballer has long since ceased to be a novelty. But only in recent years have black players been able to find positions as coaches and managers.

Few black faces are to be found in the boardrooms and among the administrative staff behind the scenes of professional clubs, or involved with any of the governing bodies such as the Football Association; fewer still are in influential or senior positions. Similarly, precious few of the people who run football at local level, members of regional and County FAs, are from black groups.

Parklife...

In 1996, Bari FC, an Asian football team from east London who played in an amateur league in Essex, complained of persistent racist intimidation and abuse from the players and supporters of opposing teams. In October 1997, a mainly black amateur team in

◀ Ruud Gullit – esteemed Dutch international became the first black manager in the Premier League when he took over from Glenn Hoddle at Chelsea.

◀ Uriah Rennie, first black referee in the Premier League.

Leeds were chased and assaulted by a racist mob wielding knives, bats, bottles, a sword and a hammer. For each of the high profile racist incidents in professional football that create outrage in the media each season, there are dozens of unheard and unreported cases of racism that occur in the thousands of non-league and amateur football games which take place on our parks and playing fields week in, week out throughout the year.

Kick it out

Kick it out is the independent organisation running the *"Let's Kick Racism Out of Football"* campaign with the support of football's governing bodies, supporters' groups and local authorities.

Building on the achievements of the campaign since its launch by the Commission for Racial Equality and the Professional Footballers' Association in the season 1993/94, we are working to actively challenge and eradicate racism within the game at all levels.

We are currently working in the following areas:

Professional clubs – To ensure a continuing high profile amongst professional clubs, particularly in the lower leagues and Conference.

Young people – Developing educational resources for use by young people within schools, colleges and youth organisations.

Amateur football – Working within grassroots and amateur football to develop initiatives to eradicate the problem in "parks football".

Asians – Finding solutions to the problem of the exclusion of Asians from many areas of the game.

Black communities – Increasing participation of local ethnic minority communities within professional football clubs.

European football – Highlighting the problem of racism within European football.

▼ Highfield Rangers – from Leicester, one of the first amateur teams for people from black communities.

▼ Clint Eastman – attacked whilst playing in the Olympian League in Watford.

▼ Bari FC – victims of persistent racist abuse while playing in their local league.

279

Term 3 | **Unit 12**

From:
The Prelude, Book 1

by William Wordsworth

One summer evening (led by her) I found
A little boat tied to a willow tree
Within a rocky cave, its usual home.
Straight I unloosed her chain, and stepping in
Pushed from the shore. It was an act of stealth
And troubled pleasure, nor without the voice
Of mountain-echoes did my boat move on;
Leaving behind her still, on either side,
Small circles glittering idly in the moon,
Until they melted all into one track
Of sparkling light. But now, like one who rows,
Proud of his skill, to reach a chosen point
With an unswerving line, I fixed my view
Upon the summit of a craggy ridge,
The horizon's utmost boundary; for above
Was nothing but the stars and the grey sky.
She was an elfin pinnace; lustily
I dipped my oars into the silent lake,
And, as I rose upon the stroke, my boat
Went heaving through the water like a swan;

280

When, from behind that craggy steep till then
The horizon's bound, a huge peak, black and huge,
As if with voluntary power instinct
Upreared its head. I struck and struck again,
And growing still in stature the grim shape
Towered up between me and the stars, and still,
For so it seemed, with purpose of its own
And measured motion like a living thing,
Strode after me. With trembling oars I turned,
And through the silent water stole my way
Back to the covert of the willow tree;
There in her mooring-place I left my bark, –
And through the meadows homeward went, in grave
And serious mood; but after I had seen
That spectacle, for many days, my brain
Worked with a dim and undetermined sense
Of unknown modes of being; o'er my thoughts
There hung a darkness, call it solitude
Or bland desertion. No familiar shapes
Remained, no pleasant images of trees,
Of sea or sky, no colours of green fields;
But huge and mighty forms, that do not live
Like living men, moved slowly through the mind
By day, and were a trouble to my dreams.

Stopping by Woods on a Snowy Evening

by Robert Frost

Whose woods these are I think I know.
His house is in the village though;
He will not see me stopping here
To watch his woods fill up with snow.

My little horse must think it queer
To stop without a farmhouse near
Between the woods and frozen lake
The darkest evening of the year.

He gives his harness bells a shake
To ask if there is some mistake.
The only other sound's the sweep
Of easy wind and downy flake.

The woods are lovely, dark and deep,
But I have promises to keep,
And miles to go before I sleep,
And miles to go before I sleep.

Author Index

Agard, John *Gramma's biscuit tin* 240
Agard, John *My ball* 241
Agard, John *My stamp album* 240
Alexander, Pat *Sentence of Death* 184
Anon *Somebody said that it Couldn't be Done* 65
Apollinaire, Guillaume *Bird Whistle* 65
Apollinaire, Guillaume *The Cathedral* 65
Apollinaire, Guillaume *The Evening Star* 65
Baum, L Frank *The Wizard of Oz* 195
Bosley, Keith *Snake Glides* 63
Byars, Betsy *The Midnight Fox* 197
Clegg, Gillian *Homes, Villages and Towns* 122
Clegg, Gillian *Landmarks from the Past* 120
Coleridge, Samuel Taylor *The Rime of the Ancient Mariner* 163
Corrin, Stephen *Bedd Gelert* 92
Corrin, Stephen *Odysseus and Circe* 95
Corrin, Stephen *Scheherezade* 88
David, Stephen *Homecoming* 157
Farjeon, Eleanor *Nine-o'clock Bell!* 241
Fatchen, Max *Clumsy* 63
Field, Rachel *Something told the Wild Geese* 140
Fines, Anne *Bill's New Frock* 40
Friends of the Earth *Look Forward to a Better Future* 236
Frost, Robert *Stopping by Woods on a Snowy Evening* 282
Garfield, Leon *Sabre-tooth Sandwich* 29
Gavin, Jamila *Grandpa Chatterji* 209
Grimm Brothers *Red Riding Hood* 110
Hall, Lee *The Love Letters of Ragie Patel* 220
Harris, Valentina *Classic Italian* 104
Hawthorne, Nathaniel *alternative ending to Theseus and the Minotaur* 103
Hopkins, Gerard Manley *Spring* 139
Hughes, Shirley *Here Comes Charlie Moon* 8
Hughes, Ted *The Iron Woman* 80
Ingalls Wilder, Laura *Little House in the Big Woods* 270
Jaffrey, Madhur *Seasons of Splendour* 169
Kay, Jackie *Down at the very bottom* 27

Kay, Jackie *Duncan Gets Expelled* 28
Kay, Jackie *Waves* 27
Kick it Out Project *Let's Kick Racism out of Football* 276
Killeen, Richard *Nelson Mandela* 68
Lear, Edward *The Jumblies* 165
Lesley *A Boa-Constrictor* 66
Mahy, Margaret *The Good Fortunes Gang* 142
Mark, Jan *The Dead Letter Box* 52
Masters, Anthony *The Haunted Lighthouse* 6
Meade Falkner, J *Moonfleet* 242
Morley, Jacqueline *Theseus and the Minotaur* 100
Morris, Hayley *Muffin, my Dog* 134
Nicholls, Judith *The Dare* 133
Nicholls, Judith *Amazonian Timbers, Inc* 135
Nicholls, Judith *Dusk* 136
Nicholls, Judith *Partners* 141
Nicholls, Judith *Shadows* 137
Nicholls, Judith *Song of the Forest* 137
Nicholls, Judith *Song of the Xingu Indian* 135
Nicholls, Judith *The Coming of Night* 136
Nicholls, Judith *The Experiment* 141
Nicholls, Judith *Tiger* 137
Nicholls, Judith *Wolf* 137
Noyes, Alfred *Daddy Fell into the Pond* 62
Peake, Mervyn *My Uncle Paul of Pimlico* 139
Pearce, Phillipa *Tom's Midnight Garden* 250
Pert, Suzanne *Tornadoes and Hurricanes* 191
Pienkowski, Jan *Easter* 188
Place, Robin *Wood* 36
Powell, Mark *Excited* 67
Reeves, James *The Black Pebble* 168
Roden, Claudia *The Food of Italy* 108
Saunders, Pete *Be Safe Outdoors* 22
Serraillier, Ian *The Silver Sword* 265
Simon *Clock Spring* 66
Te, Cam Phung *Haircuts* 67
Tourist Information *Naturally Wight* 257
Verne, Jules *A Fight Between Lizards at the Centre of the Earth* 151
Wakefield, S.A. *Bottersnikes and Gumbles* 230
West, Colin *Geraldine Giraffe* 64

Westall, Robert *Blitz* 73
Wolfe, Humbert *The Blackbird* 64
Wordsworth, William *The Prelude* 280
Zephaniah, Benjamin *I love me mudder* 138

Acknowledgements

The editors and publishers wish to thank the following for permission to use copyright material:

Aladdin Books Ltd for extracts from *Be Safe Outdoors* by Pete Sanders;

Anness Publishing Ltd. for extracts from *Classic Italian* published by Anness Publishing Ltd;

BBC Worldwide Limited for "The Love Letters of Ragie Patel" and "Ragie's Bedroom" from *Spoonface Steinberg and Other Plays* by Lee Hall © Lee Hall;

Keith Bosley for "Snake Glides";

Cadbury Ltd for "Haircuts" by Cam Phung Te, "Excited" by Mark Powell and "Muffin – my dog" by Hayley Morris, from *Cadbury's Seventh Book of Children's Poetry* (Beaver Books);

Laura Cecil Literacy Agency for the extract from *Blitz* by Robert Westall, © the Estate of Robert Westall 1994 and "The Black Pebble" © James Reeves from *Complete Poems for Children* (Heinemann) reprinted by permission of the James Reeves Estate;

HarperCollins Publishers Australia for the extract from *Bottersnikes and Gumbles* by S A Wakefield;

Gallery 5 for *Easter* retold by Jan Pienkowski from extracts of the Authorized King James Version of the Bible;

David Higham Associates for "My Uncle Paul from Pimlico" by Mervyn Peake, from *Rhymes without Reason*, "Nine-o'Clock Bell" by Eleanor Farjeon, extracts from *Bill's New Frock* by Anne Fine (Longman), *The Food of Italy* by Claudia Roden and *Grandpa Chatterji* by Jamila Gavin;

Egmont Children's Books Ltd for the extract from *Little House in the Big Woods*, by Laura Ingalls Wilder, published by Methuen Children's Books;

Faber & Faber for an extract from *The Midnight Fox* by Betsy Byars; "The Experiment", "Partners", "The Dare", "Song of the Xingu Indian", "Amazonian Timbers Inc.", "Dusk", "Shadows", "The Coming of Night", "Song of the Forest", "Tiger" and "Wolf" all from *Midnight Forest* by Judith Nicholls; "Scheherezade", "Bedd Gelert" and "Odysseus and

Circe" all from *Stories for Nine-Year-Olds* by Stephen Corrin; and extracts from *The Iron Woman* by Ted Hughes all published by Faber and Faber;

Friends of the Earth for material from their flagship leaflet "Look forward to a better future";

Isle of Wight Tourism for material from their brochure "Naturally Wight";

Isle of Wight County Press for "IW Tornado Terror" by Suzanne Pert;

John Johnson Ltd for "Clumsy" by Max Fatchen;

Kick it Out Project for *Let's Kick Racism out of Football* © Kick it Out;

Kingfisher Publications for "A Fight between Lizards at the Centre of the Earth" from *Voyage to the Centre of the Earth* by Jules Verne, and for the extract from *Homecoming* by Stephen David, both from *Science Fiction Stories* chosen by Edward Blishen © 1988;

Lion Publishing and Pat Alexander for "Sentence of Death" and "The body that wasn't there!" from *The Lion Children's Bible*, retold by Pat Alexander, published by Lion Publishing plc, and reproduced with permission;

Macdonald Publishers for *The Haunted Lighthouse* by Anthony Masters, *Theseus and the Minotaur* by Jacqueline Morley and *Sabre-tooth Sandwich* by Leon Garfield;

Hugh Noyes for "Daddy fell into the Pond" by Alfred Noyes;

Oxford University Press for the extract from *Tom's Midnight Garden*, by Philippa Pearce, and for "Clock Spring" and "A boa-constrictor" from *Wordscapes* compiled by Barry Maybury;

Pavilion Books for the extracts from *Seasons of Splendour* by Madhur Jaffrey;

Penguin UK Ltd for the extract from *The Dead Letter Box* by Jan Mark (Hamish Hamilton, 1982) © Jan Mark 1982, "Down at the very bottom", "Waves" and "Duncan gets Expelled" from *Two's Company* by Jackie Kay (Blackie, 1992) © Jackie Kay 1992, back cover blurb from Penguin Popular

285

Classics Grimm's Fairy Tales (Penguin/Godfrey Cave, 1995) copyright © Penguin Books Ltd 1995, and for three introductions to – *Tom's Midnight Garden* by Philippa Pearce, *The Silver Sword* by Ian Serraillier and *Little House in the Big Woods* by Laura Ingalls Wilder – by Kaye Webb from *I Like this Story*, chosen by Kaye Webb (Puffin, 1986). Reprinted by permission of Penguin Books Ltd. "Calligram (15 May 1915)" and "Letter to Andre Billy. 9 April 1915" from *Selected Poems; Apollinaire* translated by Oliver Bernard (Penguin Books, 1965) translation © Oliver Bernard 1965. Reproduced by permission of Penguin Books Ltd.,

Random House UK Ltd for extracts from *Here Comes Charlie Moon* by Shirley Hughes, published by Bodley Head and *The Silver Sword* by Ian Serraillier, published by Jonathan Cape; Random House UK Ltd, John Agard and Bodley Head for "My Stamp Album", "Gramma's Biscuit Tin" and "My Ball" from *Grandfather's old bruk-a-down car* by John Agard, published by Bodley Head; Random House UK Ltd, the Estate of Robert Frost and the editor Edward Connery Lathem for "Stopping by woods on a snowy evening" from *The Poetry of Robert Frost* published by Jonathan Cape;

The Society of Authors as the literary representative of the Estate of J.Meade Falkner for the extract from *Moonfleet*;

Transworld Publishers Ltd for the extracts and blurb from *The Good Fortunes Gang* by Margaret Mahy, published by Doubleday, a division of Transworld Publishers Ltd © Margaret Mahy 1993. All rights reserved;

Wayland Publishers for *Landmarks from the Past* and *Clues from the Past* by Gillian Clegg and *Nelson Mandela* by Richard Killeen;

Colin West for "Geraldine Giraffe";

Anne Wolfe for "The Blackbird" by Humbert Wolfe;

Benjamin Zephaniah for "I love me mudder";

Illustrations © STP by Dick Barton, Louise Barton, Claire Boyce, Harry Bell, Joan Corlass, Beverly Curl, Debbie Clark, Anna Cattermole, Jackie East, Serena Feneziani, Jane Gerwitz, Dianna Gold, Michelle Ives, Karen Kett, Jean de Lemos, Mandy Lillywhite, Tony O'Donnell, Mike Pell, Zara Slattery, Margaret Theakston, Kirsty Wilson.

Photographs ©
Laurie Cunningham, Hope Powell, Chris Kamara, Ruud Gullit and Uriah Rennie © Mark Leech Sports Photography; Clyde Best and Jack Leslie © Colorsport; Arthur Wharton © P. Vasili; Amrit Sidhu © Raymonds Press Agency; Highfield Rangers © Highfield Rangers Football Club; Clint Eastman, Bari FC © Kick it out; Carloway Broch © Collections/Fay Godwin; Packhorse Bridge, Wycoller and Pontcysyllte Aqueduct © Collections/Brian Shuel; A set of wooden panpipes © York Archaeological Trust; Mosaic floor © Corinium Museum; Various pictures on pages 257-264 © Isle of Wight Council; Johannesburg © South African Tourism Board; Crop marks © F.M.Radcliffe.

Details on p121 reproduced from the 1997 Landranger 87, Hexham & Haltwhistle, Ordnance Survey map by permission of Ordnance Survey on behalf of the Controller of Her Majesty's Stationery Office © Crown Copyright MC 88814M0001.